ST. IRENAEUS OF LYONS

Against the Heresies

Ancient Christian Writers

THE WORKS OF THE FATHERS IN TRANSLATION

No. 65

ST. IRENAEUS OF LYONS: AGAINST THE HERESIES

TRANSLATED AND ANNOTATED

BY

DOMINIC J. UNGER, OFM CAP.

Late of St. Patrick Friary

St. Louis, Missouri

WITH FURTHER REVISIONS

BY

JOHN J. DILLON

INTRODUCTION

BY

MICHAEL SLUSSER

Book 2

THE NEWMAN PRESS
New York/Mahwah, NJ

Library of Congress Cataloging-in-Publication Data

Irenaeus, Saint, Bishop of Lyons.
    [Adversus haereses. English]
    Against the heresies/St. Irenaeus of Lyons; translated and annotated by Dominic J. Unger with further revisions by John J. Dillon.
        p. cm.—(Ancient Chiristan writers; no. 55-)
    Translation of: Adversus haereses.
    Includes bibliographaical references and index.
    ISBN 0-8091-0454-7 (v. 1)
    ISBN 978-0-8091-0599-1 (v. 2)
    ISBN 978-0-8091-0589-2 (v. 3)
    1. Gnosticism—Controversial literature—Early works to 1800. 2. Theology, Doctrinal—Early works to 1800. I. Unger, Dominic J. II. Dillon, John J. III. Title. IV. Series: Ancient Christian writers; no. 55, etc.
    BR60.A35 no. 55, etc.
    [BR65.I63]
    270 s—dc20
    [239′.3]
                                                                91-40838
                                                                CIP

Published by The Newman Press
an imprint of Paulist Press
997 Macarthur Boulevard
Mahwah, New Jersey 07430

www.paulistpress.com

CONTENTS

LIST OF ABBREVIATIONS

ACW	Ancient Christian Writers. Westminster, MD, et al.: Newman Press, 1946–.
ANF	The Ante-Nicene Fathers. Buffalo, NY: Christian Literature Co., 1885–96; repr., Peabody, MA: Hendrickson, 1994.
Aristophanes, *Av.*	Aristophanes, *Aves*
Aristotle, *Metaph.*	Aristotle, *Metaphysica*
Aristotle, *Ph.*	Aristotle, *Physica*
Athanasius, *Ar.* 1–3	Athanasius, *Orationes tres adversus Arianos*
Augustine, *C. Jul.*	Augustine, *Contra Julianum libri 6*
Augustine, *Catech. rud.*	Augustine, *De catechizandis rudibus*
Augustine, *Civ.*	Augustine, *De civitate Dei*
Augustine, *Doct. christ.*	Augustine, *De doctrina christiana*
Augustine, *Haer.*	Augustine, *De haeresibus ad Quodvultdeum*
Basil, *Spirit.*	Basil, *Liber de Spiritu sancto*
Benoît	André Benoît. *Saint Irénée: Introduction à l'étude de sa théologie.* Paris: Presses universitaires de France, 1960.
Bibl. Stud.	*Biblische Studien*
2d ed. BKV	Bibliothek der Kirchenväter. Kempten and Munich: J. Kösel, 1911–30.
BLE	*Bulletin de littérature ecclésiastique*
Caesar, *Gall.*	Caesar, *De bello Gallico*
CBQ	*Catholic Biblical Quarterly*
CCL	Corpus Christianorum. Series Latina. Turnhout: Brepols, 1953–.
CE	*Catholic Encyclopedia.* New York: Robert Appleton, 1907–12.
Cicero, *De nat. deor.*	Cicero, *De natura deorum*
Cicero, *De orat.*	Cicero, *De oratore*

Cicero, *Rab. Post.*	Cicero, *Pro C. Rabiro Postumo oratio*
Cicero, *Tusc.*	Cicero, *Tusculanarum disputationum liber*
Clement of Alexandria, *Ecl.*	Clement of Alexandria, *Eclogae ex scripturis propheticis*
Clement of Alexandria, *Exc. Thdot.*	Clement of Alexandria, *Excerpta Theodoti*
Clement of Alexandria, *Paed.*	Clement of Alexandria, *Paedagogus*
Clement of Alexandria, *Strom.*	Clement of Alexandria, *Stromateis*
Clement of Rome, *1 Clem.*	Clement of Rome, *Epistula Clementis ad Corinthios*
2 Clem.	*Homilia sive epistula secunda Clementis ad Corinthios* (spurious)
Coll. Messina	*The Origins of Gnosticism: Colloquium of Messina 13–18 April 1966.* Edited by Ugo Bianchi. Leiden: E. J. Brill, 1967.
CPG 1	*Clavis Patrum Graecorum*, vol. 1: *Patres Antenicaeni.* Edited by Maurice Geerard. Turnhout: Brepols, 1983.
CPh	*Classical Philology*
CSCO	Corpus Scriptorum Christianorum Orientalium. Louvain, 1903–.
CSEL	Corpus Scriptorum Ecclesiasticorum Latinorum. Vienna: C. Geroldi Sons, 1866–.
CW	*The Classical World*
Cyril of Jerusalem, *Procatech.*	Cyril of Jerusalem, *Procatechesis*
DACL	*Dictionnaire d'archéologie chrétienne et de liturgie.* Paris, 1907–53.
DBS	*Dictionnaire de la Bible.* Supplément. Paris: Letouzey et Ané, 1926–.
DCB	*A Dictionary of Christian Biography, Literature, Sects, and Doctrines.* Edited by William Smith and Henry Wace. London: J. Murray, 1877–87; repr., New York: AMS, 1984.
DHGE	*Dictionnaire d'histoire et de géographie ecclésiastiques.* Paris: Letouzey et Ané, 1912–.

Diogenes Laertius	Diogenes Laertius, *De clarorum philosophorum vitis...libri decem*
DSp	*Dictionnaire de Spiritualité.* Paris: Beauchesne, 1932–.
DTC	*Dictionnarie de théologie catholique.* Paris: Letouzey et Ané, 1903–50.
Dufourcq *Irénée*	Albert Dufourcq. *Saint Irénée. Les Saints.* Paris: Librairie Victor Lecoffre, 1904.
EEC	*Encyclopedia of the Early Church.* Edited by Angelo Di Berardino. Translated from the Italian by Adrian Walford. With a Foreword and Bibliographic Amendments by W. H. C. Frend. 2 volumes. Cambridge: James Clarke, 1992.
Epiphanius, *Haer.*	Epiphanius, *Panarion* seu *Adversus lxxx haereses*
Eusebius, *H.e.*	Eusebius, *Historia ecclesiastica*
Eusebius, *P.e.*	Eusebius, *Praeparatio evangelica*
Eusebius, *Theoph. fr.*	Eusebius, *Fragmenta ex opere de theophania*
Filaster, *Haer.*	Filaster, *Diversarum haereseon liber*
GCS	Die griechischen christlichen Schriftsteller der ersten drei Jahrhunderte. Leipzig: Hinrichs; Berlin: Akademie-Verlag, 1897–.
Gk. Epiph.	The Greek text of Irenaeus's *Adversus haereses* contained in Epiphanius and edited by Karl Holl in GCS 25 (1915), 31 (1922), 37 (1933).
Goodspeed	*Die ältesten Apologeten: Texte mit kurzen Einleitungen.* Edited by Edgar. J. Goodspeed. 1914. Repr., Göttingen: Vandenhoeck & Ruprecht, 1984.
Grabe	The edition of the *Adversus haereses* by Joannes Ernestus Grabe. Oxford, 1702.
Harvey	The edition of the *Adversus haereses* by W[illiam] Wigan Harvey. Cambridge: Typis Academicis, 1857.
HERE	*Encyclopedia of Religion and Ethics.* Edited by James Hastings. With the Assistance of John A. Selbie and Other Scholars. New

	York and Edinburgh: T. & T. Clark, 1908–26.
Hermas, *Mand.*	Hermas, *Mandata pastoris*
Hesiod, *Op.*	Hesiod, *Opera et Dies*
Hippolytus, *Haer.*	Hippolytus, *Refutatio omnium haeresium sive philosophoumena*
Hippolytus, *Trad. ap.*	Hippolytus, *Traditio apostolica*
Homer, *Il.*	Homer, *Ilias*
Homer, *Od.*	Homer, *Odyssea*
HTR	*Harvard Theological Review*
Ignatius of Antioch, *Smyrn.*	Ignatius of Antioch, *Epistula ad Smyrnaeos*
JEH	*Journal of Ecclesiastical History*
Jerome, *Ad Jovin.*	Jerome, *Adversus Jovinianum libri 2*
Jerome, *Epist.*	Jerome, *Epistula*
Jerome, *In Tit.*	Jerome, *Commentarius in epistulam Pauli ad Titum*
Jerome, *Vir. ill.*	Jerome, *De viris illustribus*
JThS	*Journal of Theological Studies*
Justin, *Dial.*	Justin, *Dialogus cum Tryphone Judaeo*
Justin, *1, 2 Apol.*	Justin, *Apologiae*
Klebba, BKV	*Des heiligen Irenäus Fünf Bücher Gegen die Häresin.* Translated by E. Klebba. BKV 3–4. Kempten and Munich: J. Kösel, 1912.
Lactantius, *Inst.*	Lactantius, *Divinarum Institutionum Libri*
Lampe, PGL	*A Patristic Greek Lexicon.* Edited by G. W. H. Lampe. Oxford: Clarendon Press, 1961.
Lat. Iren.	The Latin version of Irenaeus's *Adversus haereses*
Lebreton-Zeiller	Jules Lebreton and Jacques Zeiller. *History of the Primitive Church.* Translated by Ernest C. Messenger. 2 volumes. New York: Macmillan, 1949.
LSJ	*A Greek-English Lexicon,* compiled by Henry George Liddell and Robert Scott, revised and augmented by Henry Stuart Jones and Roderick McKenzie et al. Oxford: Clarendon Press, 1940.

LSJ Suppl.   H. G. Liddell, R. Scott, H. Stuart Jones, *Greek-English Lexicon: A Supplement.* Edited by E. A. Barber with the assistance of P. Maas, M. Scheller, and M. L. West. Oxford: Clarendon Press, 1968.

LTK   *Lexikon für Theologie und Kirche.* Edited by Michael Buchberger. Freiburg: Herder, 1930–38.

LTK²   *Lexikon für Theologie und Kirche.* 2nd ed. Edited by Josef Höfer and Karl Rahner. Freiburg: Herder, 1957–67.

Lundström, *Studien*   Sven Lundström. *Studien zur lateinische Irenäusübersetzung.* Lund: Håkan Ohlssons Boktryckeri, 1943.

Marius Victorinus, *Adv. Arrium*   Marius Victorinus, *Adversus Arrium libri 4*

Marius Victorinus, *Gen. div. verb.*   Marius Victorinus, *De generatione divini verbi*

Maximus Confessor, *Schol. e.h.*   Maximus Confessor, *Scholia* in Pseudo-Dionysius Areopagita, *De ecclesiastica hierarchia*

MG   *Patrologia Graeca.* Edited by Jacques-Paul Migne. 162 volumes. Paris, 1857–66.

ML   *Patrologia Latina.* Edited by Jacques-Paul Migne. 221 volumes. Paris, 1844–64.

M. Polyc.   *Martyrium Polycarpi*

NCE   *New Catholic Encyclopedia.* New York, 1967.

Nilus the Ascetic, *Ep.*   Nilus the Ascetic, *Epistula*

NJBC   *The New Jerome Biblical Commentary.* Edited by Raymond E. Brown, Joseph A. Fitzmyer, and Roland E. Murphy. Englewood Cliffs, NJ: Prentice-Hall, 1990.

NRT   *Nouvelle revue théologique*

NTAbhand.   Neutestamentliche Abhandlungen

OCD   *The Oxford Classical Dictionary.* Edited by M. Cary [and others] with the assistance of H. J. Rose, H. P. Harvey, and A. Souter. Oxford: Clarendon Press, 1949.

OCD[2]	*The Oxford Classical Dictionary*. 2nd ed. Edited by N. G. L. Hammond and H. H. Scullard. Oxford: Clarendon Press, 1970.
ODCC[2]	*The Oxford Dictionary of the Christian Church*. 2nd ed. Edited by F. L. Cross and E. A. Livingstone. London and New York: Oxford University Press, 1974.
Origen, *Cels.*	Origen, *Contra Celsum*
Photius, *Cod.*	Photius, *Bibliothecae codices*
Plato, *Ti.*	Plato, *Timaeus*
Plautus, *Most.*	Plautus, *Mostellaria*
Pliny, *Nat.*	Pliny, *Naturalis historia libri 37*
PO	*Patrologia Orientalis*. Edited by R. Graffin and F. Nau. Paris, 1904–.
Proof	*Saint Irenaeus: Proof of the Apostolic Preaching*. Translated by Joseph P. Smith. ACW 16. Westminster, MD: Newman Press, 1952.
Ps.-Justin, *Coh. Gr.*	Pseudo-Justin, *Cohortatio ad Graecos*
Ps.-Plutarch, *De placit. philos.*	Pseudo-Plutarch, *De placitis philosophorum*
Ps.-Tertullian, *Haer.*	Ps.-Tertullian, *Liber adversus omnes haereses*
Quasten, *Patr.*	Johannes Quasten, *Patrology*. 3 volumes. Westminster, MD, Utrecht, and Antwerp: Newman Press, 1950–60. Repr., Westminster, MD, 1983.
RAC	*Reallexikon für Antike und Christentum*. Edited by T. Klauser, E. Dassmann, and others. Stuttgart:Hiersemann, 1950–.
RB	*Revue bénédictine*
RBibl	*Revue biblique*
RE	A. Pauly. *Real-Encyclopädie der classischen Altertumswissenschaft*. Edited by G. Wissowa and others. Stuttgart: J. B. Metzler, 1893–.
RGG	*Die Religion in Geschichte und Gegenwart*, 3rd ed. Edited by K. Galling. Tübingen: Mohr Siebeck, 1957–65.
RHE	*Revue d'histoire ecclésiastique*

RPT	*Realencyklopädie für protestantische Theologie und Kirche.* Leipzig, 1896–1913.
RSPT	*Revue des sciences philosophiques et théologiques*
RecSR	*Recherches de science religieuse*
RSR	*Revue des sciences religieuses*
RTAM	*Recherches de théologie ancienne et médiévale*
Rudolph, *Gnosis*	Kurt Rudolph. *Gnosis: The Nature and History of Gnosticism.* Translation edited by Robert McLachlan Wilson. San Francisco: Harper & Row, 1983; also in paperback edition, San Francisco: Harper-SanFrancisco, 1987.
Sagnard, *Gnose*	François Sagnard. *La gnose valentinienne et le témoignage de saint Irénée.* Études de philosophie médiévale 36. Paris: J. Vrin, 1947.
SC	Sources chrétiennes. Paris: Cerf, 1942–.
SCent	*The Second Century*
Seneca, *Prov.*	Seneca, *De providentia*
Stieren	The edition of the *Adversus haereses* by A. Stieren. Leipzig: T. O. Weigel, 1848–53.
Tacitus, *Ann.*	Tacitus, *Annales (ab excessu divi Augusti) libri 16*
TDNT	*Theological Dictionary of the New Testament.* Edited by Gerhard Kittel. Translated and edited by Geoffrey Bromiley. 10 volumes. Grand Rapids: Eerdmans, 1964–76.
Tertullian, *Adv. Marc.*	Tertullian, *Adversus Marcionem*
Tertullian, *Adv. Prax.*	Tertullian, *Adversus Praxean*
Tertullian, *Adv. Val.*	Tertullian, *Adversus Valentinianos*
Tertullian, *Anim.*	Tertullian, *De anima*
Tertullian, *Apol.*	Tertullian, *Apologeticum*
Tertullian, *Carn.*	Tertullian, *De carne Christi*
Tertullian, *Cult. fem.*	Tertullian, *De cultu feminarum*
Tertullian, *Or.*	Tertullian, *De oratione*
Tertullian, *Praescr.*	Tertullian, *De praescriptione haereticorum*
Tertullian, *Spec.*	Tertullian, *De spectaculis*

Theodoret, *Ep.*	Theodoret, *Epistula*
Theodoret, *Haer.*	Theodoret, *Haereticarum fabularum compendium*
Theophilus of Antioch, *Auto.*	Theophilus of Antioch, *Ad Autolycum*
ThRdschau	*Theologische Rundschau*
ThS	*Theological Studies*
TLL	*Thesaurus Linguae Latinae.* Leipzig, 1900–.
TRE	*Theologische Realenzyklopädie.* Edited by G, Krause, G. Müller, and others. Berlin: de Gruyter, 1976–.
TU	Texte und Untersuchungen zur Geschichte der altchristlichen Literatur. Leipzig: Hinrichs, 1882–1943; Berlin: Akademie-Verlag, 1951–.
VC	*Vigiliae Christianae*
VD	*Verbum Domini*
Vernet	F. Vernet, "Irénée (Saint)," in DTC 7.2.2394–2533.
ZKT	*Zeitschrift für katholische Theologie*
ZNTW	*Zeitschrift für die Neutestamentliche Wissenschaft und die Kunde des Urchristentums*
ZRGG	*Zeitschrift für Religions- und Geistesgeschichte*
ZTK	*Zeitschrift für Theologie und Kirche*

INTRODUCTION

In 1992, Book 1 of Irenaeus's *Adversus haereses* (*Against the Heresies*) was published in the "Ancient Christian Writers" series in the modern English translation by Fr. Dominic J. Unger, OFM Cap, as revised by Dr. John J. Dillon after Fr. Unger's death. When Fr. Unger died in 1982, he left behind a typescript of his translation of the complete *Adversus haereses*, with accompanying notes. The present volume is a step toward completing the publication of Fr. Unger's work and providing the first complete English translation with full scholarly notes in over a century. The principal reason for the delay has been the need to revise Unger's translation and notes to bring them up to date, in terms not only of the style of the series but more particularly of the extensive scholarly work on Irenaeus that has been done during the last twenty-five years. That scholarly work affects the translation itself as well as the notes. The Rev. Dr. Dillon has carried out the work of revision on the translation of Book 2 while serving the Catholic Archdiocese of Washington as a parish priest. Books 3–5 have been entrusted to other scholars.

Transmission of the Text

From the point of view of the modern scholar and reader, Book 2 stands out by comparison with Book 1 not only for its content but also for the way in which it has been transmitted. While the Greek text of Book 1 has been preserved to a large extent through its use by Hippolytus and Epiphanius in their catalogues of heresies, Book 2 has been transmitted to us almost exclusively in the early Latin translation. E. P. Meijering proposes a possible reason why Book 2 was so seldom cited by later Greek theologians: Irenaeus was a preeminent theological authority, but the rational arguments that he uses in this

1

book did not make a great impression, because he said only what
many others also were saying.[1] Nonetheless, the Greek text apparently
did circulate, since quoted fragments survive in Greek, Armenian,
Arabic, and Syriac. In volume 1 of the "Sources chrétiennes" edition,
Adelin Rousseau has presented the twelve Greek fragments, which
represent eleven different passages of the book, since one text is represented in two different fragments.[2] Rousseau also gives the six
Armenian and the single Arabic fragment;[3] the two Syriac quotations
are presented by Louis Doutreleau.[4] Since it is hardly imaginable that
the oriental traditions would have been translated from the Latin
translation, and since several parts of Book 2 are represented in the
quotations, our book must have continued to circulate in Greek for a
considerable time, presumably along with the other four books.

PURPOSE OF THE BOOK

Book 1 of Irenaeus's *Against the Heresies* exposed a range of
Gnostic and Marcionite doctrines, and Book 2 can be seen as the refutation of those heresies. That picture is supported by the double title
of the entire work, *elenchos kai anatropētēs pseudōnumou gnōseōs*, that is,
"exposition and refutation of the falsely so-called knowledge." In
reading Book 1, however, one finds that Irenaeus cannot restrain himself from offering some immediate refutation of the teachings that he
is describing, sometimes by his heavy sarcasm in the exposition itself.
Similarly, Book 2 is more than merely refutation. While Irenaeus gen-
erally works from within the worldview of his opponents, bringing to
light the problems and contradictions internal to their systems, there
are many places where he presents his own convictions and argues for
them. For example, when Irenaeus professes that "the God of All
established and made everything by his word" (2.2.4), he proceeds
directly to a creedal formula and appeals to Moses, the prophets, and
the apostles (2.2.5-6).[5] Likewise, in 2.6.1 he speaks in his own person
about God, contrasting *eminentiam* with *providentiam*—the one beyond
our sight, the other knowable. In the later books, this contrast will
appear as one between greatness (*magnitudo*) and love (*dilectio*).[6] The
reader will notice other instances.

It seems clear that Book 2 was part of Irenaeus's original project
to provide material that his contemporaries could use against

Gnostics. There is less agreement among modern scholars about whether Books 3–5 were part of the plan from the beginning. The late Richard A. Norris, Jr., thinks that they were: "It is scarcely possible, then, to picture the contents of Books 3–5 as 'appendices' or afterthoughts. Their business is of the essence of Irenaeus's project from the start."[7] Denis Minns, on the other hand, sees in the preface to Book 3 a clear sign "that the first two books were originally intended to meet the title of the whole as 'The Detection and Overthrow of Knowledge Falsely So-Called.'…The first two books had already been sent to the friend who requested them when Irenaeus was writing Book III."[8] It is probably not necessary to resolve that question in order to read Book 2 with appreciation.[9] Later in this introduction this issue will be treated in greater detail.

A recent article suggests that Book 1 did not originally address the doctrines of Marcion of Sinope at all, but that Irenaeus, "early on in the process of writing book two," went back and inserted material on Marcion into Book 1 and arranged the argument in Book 2 to be directed as forcefully against Marcion as against the Valentinians.[10] I think it more likely that Irenaeus's correspondent had asked only for a book against the disciples of Ptolemaeus,[11] but Irenaeus, student of Justin and admirer of Polycarp of Smyrna, both of whom were fierce opponents of Marcion, found it appropriate from the first to include Marcion in his "exposition and refutation."

At the end of the preface to Book 2, Irenaeus declares his intention, on the one hand, to instruct (*instruemus*) within the limits of his ability and the time available and, on the other, to overturn (*euertemus*) his opponents' "every rule" (*omnem ipsorum regulam*). Irenaeus sees that the "rule of faith," to which he has made detailed reference in Book 1,[12] faces competition from alternative "rules," the Gnostic doctrines. The secrecy in which many of those doctrines have been shrouded requires from Irenaeus a particular strategy. By "pointing out and overturning their open and manifest syzygies"[13] (that is, the parts of their account of their beliefs that they have allowed to come to light), he will "wipe out their hidden ones" (that is, whatever other doctrines they may claim as revealed only to the most deeply initiated). Norris expresses this strategy in different terms, as an attack by Irenaeus on the fundamental Valentinian "hypothesis." Thus Norris describes the challenge that faced Irenaeus in Book 2: "It had to be shown not only that the content of the Valentinian *hypothesis* did not square with the subject-matter of the Scriptures, but also—and without reference to the Scriptures—that the Gnostic *hypothesis* was false."[14]

STRUCTURE

Many scholars have attempted to delineate a structure for Book 2, and in general these attempts resemble the outline proposed by Adelin Rousseau in the "Sources chrétiennes" edition:

I. (Chapters 1–30) refutation of the main theses of the Valentinian school
    1. (1–11) the absurdity of the Valentinian thesis that there is a Pleroma higher than God the Creator
    2. (12–19) the many contradictions and improbabilities in the Valentinian doctrine about how the Aeons are produced, about the passion of the Aeon Sophia, and the manifestations of her seed
    3. (20–28) the Valentinians' speculations about numbers...the heretics' use of Scripture...the fantastic nature of gnostic exegeses...their pride, their refusal to let themselves be taught by God
    4. (29–30) a sort of appendix...about two particular theses of the Valentinian system: that concerning the final destiny of the three natures or substances, and that which does not recognize in the Creator-Demiurge any nature above the psychic or animal.
II. (Chapters 31–35) refutation of some theses that reflect doctrine that is not Valentinian in the proper sense[15]

While this outline may serve as a guide to the contents of Book 2, it falls short of presenting a structure that helps the reader to understand the movement of Irenaeus's thought. Rowan Greer has pointed out with considerable justification, "Although it is true that all the evidence points in the direction of the divisions that have been suggested, it seems impossible to locate them in the text." Even the outline that he himself offers does not, he admits, help "us to understand and describe the unity of Book 2."[16] That unity must be found, claims Greer, in the contrast that Irenaeus draws between the Gnostic doctrines and the orthodox understanding of God: "It will be my contention...that the formula 'God contains all things, but is uncontained' supplies a simple and concise definition of Irenaeus's theological premise. The details of his doctrinal position may all be derived from the one formula."[17]

THE ARGUMENT OF BOOK TWO

Greer's analysis, although it does not cover the full range of the issues dealt with in Book 2, does seem to me to be very helpful to the reader of the book. The formula that Greer cites, "God contains all things, but is uncontained," appears in 2.1.2.[18] The force of the axiom is most damaging to the Valentinian cosmological speculations, because they posit a divine world or Pleroma that is supposedly above the creator and beyond his ken, but Irenaeus does not hesitate to adapt it for use against Marcion also (2.1.2, 4). By comparison with the Creator God evoked by that formula, the Valentinians' God and that of Marcion are "unstable," argues Irenaeus (2.3.1); that is, they lack real substance, being qualified and limited, both externally and internally. Irenaeus also calls on the corollary principle that God does not have needs (2.2.1–4), and that therefore to suggest that the world could not have been made without preexisting matter or the assistance of inferior beings is unworthy of a true concept of God. This conviction has biblical roots[19] as well as being entailed by the conviction that there is nothing outside of God and therefore nothing for God conceivably to need.

Irenaeus finds another way to state the clear line between orthodox belief and Gnostic doctrine when, in 2.9–10, he says that everyone (even his opponents!) agrees that God created the world; where the Gnostics go wrong is in fabricating another "Father" superior to the Creator. Irenaeus here is pursuing a double strategy: on the one hand, he denounces the Gnostic "Father" above the Creator as a pure invention. On the other hand, he shows the Creator, whom the Gnostics belittle, to be far more transcendent than their fictitious "Father." The Gnostics charge that orthodox Christians, since they are merely animal (*psychikoi*), are by nature incapable of attaining the knowledge of the higher mysteries, which are accessible to themselves, the spirituals (*pneumatikoi*). Rather, Irenaeus charges, it is the Gnostics who prefer their human fable to the divine mystery; like the dog in Aesop's fable chasing its own shadow, they lose the bread of true life that they already had (2.11.1).[20] Irenaeus calls them either to return to the truth or to come up with much better arguments (2.11.2).

In a second section of the anti-Valentinian polemic, chapters 12–19, Irenaeus attacks the details of the alleged emissions of spiritual Aeons within the Pleroma. Being spiritual and impassible, they ought impassibly to produce beings that are of the same substance and perfection as the ones who produce them, but somehow that went wrong with the thirtieth Aeon, Sophia. In this section, Irenaeus first addresses the scheme of thirty emissions, bringing in other philosophers to assist in his argumentation: the pre-Socratic Xenophanes (2.13.3–4, 9)[21] and Antiphanes, whose Theogony is proposed as a source of the Valentinians' terminology for their Aeons. Then he returns to the larger question of how they claim to deal with creation by making it the fruit of ignorance, an ignorance that ought not to have arisen in the perfection of the Pleroma. Finally, Irenaeus shows the illogicality of the theory that the "seed" of Sophia constitutes the essential inner being of Gnostics and differentiates them from the Demiurge and other classes of human beings (2.19).[22]

Chapters 20–28—section 3 in Adelin Rousseau's outline given above—falls into two distinct sections. In 2.20–24, Irenaeus takes up several examples of the Gnostic use of numerology to find hidden meanings in the Scriptures. Most of this section is devoted to Valentinian interpretations of the numbers in Scripture, but 2.24 addresses Marcosian[23] speculations about letters of the alphabet and their numerical value.[24] Section 2.25 seems to bring this argument to a conclusion. William R. Schoedel's acute observation about the similarity between Irenaeus's arguments in this section and the approach of the Empiric school of ancient medicine applies to 2.26–28.[25] That school shared with the philosophical Skeptics a reluctance to theorize on the causes behind things and events, when those causes were hidden. For Empiric medicine, exact observation of phenomena has priority over any attempt to categorize those phenomena according to a theory of elements or humors or disease. When Irenaeus adopts a similar approach, he makes some adjustments to the demands of the controversy in which he is involved: he introduces charity (*agapē*) as a means of knowing God (1.26.1) that is superior to knowledge (*scientia*); he brings in two Gospel passages important to the Gnostics, the adjuration "Seek and you shall find," and the parable of the wise and foolish virgins.[26] One who tries to follow the Gnostic rule will seek and never find, and by forsaking the clear preaching that admits anyone to the nuptial chamber for free, he goes off instead to buy interpretations of the parables from those who are themselves in the dark (2.27.2). Those who follow the clear public preaching may not know the reasons for everything, but they at least know the reality and can try humbly to discern how God has arranged things (2.28.1). Even then there are innumerable matters that we shall not understand— Schoedel points out that most of these natural mysteries were regularly cited by classical authors before Irenaeus[27]—but there is no reason to take the desperate step of conjecturing another creator God (2.28.2). Even in Scripture there are some things that God allows us to know and others that we leave to God, who is always the teacher, we the learners.

Irenaeus returns in 2.29–30 to deal with another aspect of Valentinian teaching, the three natures of human beings and the respective fates of spiritual, "psychic," and material people, which he laid out in 1.7.1–5.[28] The very notion that the spirituals, that is, the Gnostics, ascend above the Demiurge, above the heavens, strikes Irenaeus as full of problems. The Demiurge has accomplished far greater and better things than they or their alleged Mother have or will, as Scripture shows (2.30.1). They have done nothing themselves and have not even been instruments in any achievements (2.30.4–5). As for their claim not to have been created but to have been produced spiritually (2.30.6), Scripture says that even all the spiritual beings are also created by God the Creator. Irenaeus concludes with a peroration in which he restates the orthodox belief about God the Father and his Word and Wisdom (2.30.9).

In 2.31, Irenaeus takes the arguments that he has made so far against the Valentinians and applies them to the wider world of other heretics. The axiomatic argument that God is one, all-powerful, and uncontained by anything (2.1–10) also works against "the disciples of Marcion, Simon, Menander, and any others who similarly try to separate our world from the Father" (2.31.1), as well as those like Saturninus, Basilides, Carpocrates, and Gnostics like them who agree that the Father contains all but deny that he created our world. Irenaeus also applies what he has said earlier about emanations, numerology, and the belittling of the Creator to these other opponents. He proceeds to a moral comparison between what it is like to be Christian and what it is like to be Gnostic (2.31) and challenges his opponents by the standards of the Sermon on the Mount, whose moral teachings they ignore, and the earthly Jesus, whom they consider the greatest of souls but still disdain as belonging to the "psychic" or middle state along with the Demiurge (2.32). He argues against the transmigration of souls (2.33–34), using both conventional philosophical arguments and reasoning of his own, some of it drawn from Scripture.

At the very end of Book 2, Irenaeus returns to the theme of the unity of God, as attested by all the prophets, since even the many names for God in Scripture refer to one and the same. Irenaeus asserts that he has shown that the apostles, the Lord, the prophets, the gospel, and the law all support his position, but he still promises another book, in which the abundant testimonies of Scripture will be set forth more fully and clearly.

WAS BOOK TWO PART OF A LARGER PLAN?

Earlier in this introduction I mentioned some of the discussions about whether Irenaeus had planned from early in his project to go on beyond Book 2 into further books of scriptural refutation of his opponents.

Irenaeus promises at the end of Book 2 a special book (*proprium librum*) devoted to the testimonies of Scripture, to complement the arguments he has just made. There are signs earlier in Book 2 of that intention. The first indication comes in 2.2.6, where Irenaeus says, "We have already shown that God is one; we shall go on to prove it from the apostles themselves and from the Lord's words." At this point, Irenaeus may still expect to get to Scripture in Book 2. In 2.9.1 he asserts, "all the Scriptures and the Lord teach this Father who is in heaven and no other, as we shall show as our argument continues." In 2.11.2, Irenaeus says that he has decided "to bring in the words of the Lord later, so that they [the Gnostics] will not be left to propose" their doctrines without competition. In 2.28.4, where he is apostrophizing his opponents, he says, "and since the Lord calls this one alone his Father and knows no other," but adds as if in parenthesis, "as we shall show from his own words." A broad promise is made in 2.31.1, where he says that his critique of Gnostic belittlement of the Demiurge applies against all the heretics, but adds, "and whatever will yet be said in the following books" (note the use of the plural). All that was prophesied of the Lord "will be narrated from the prophetic proofs" (2.32.5). "All the prophets preached one God and Lord, the same the maker of heaven and earth and all that is in them; and they indicated the coming of his son, as we shall prove from the Scriptures themselves in the following books" (2.35.2; note the plural again). From all these forward references, one may conclude that, while Irenaeus may originally have thought that he could do his task in two books only, by somewhere in Book 2 he has either discovered his mistake or expanded his vision of what he can and should accomplish in *Adversus haereses*.[29]

BIBLIOGRAPHY

Besides works referred to in the Introduction, this bibliography includes titles that have appeared since the publication of Book I in 1992 as well as a few earlier works to which that earlier volume did not refer, which are here for the sake of completeness.

Andia, Ysabel de. "Jérusalem, cité de Dieu, dans l'Adversus haereses d'Irénée de Lyon." In *Pléroma: Salus carnis. Homenaje a Antonio Orbe, S.J.*, edited by Eugenio Romero-Pose, 281–98. Santiago de Compostela: n.p., 1990.

Beatrice, Pier Franco. "Der Presbyter des Irenäus, Policarp von Smyrna und der Brief an Diognet." In *Pléroma: Salus carnis. Homenaje a Antonio Orbe, S.J.*, edited by Eugenio Romero-Pose, 179–202. Santiago de Compostela: n.p., 1990.

Bergmeier, Roland. "'Königlösigkeit' als nachvalentinianisches Heilsprädikat," *Novum Testamentum* 24 (1982): 316–39.

Consonantia salutis: studi su Ireneo di Lione. Edited by Enrico Cattaneo and Luigi Longobardo. Trapani: Il pozzo di Giacobbe, 2005.

Donovan, Mary Ann. *One Right Reading? A Guide to Irenaeus.* Collegeville, MN: Liturgical Press, 1997.

Grant, Robert M. *Irenaeus of Lyon.* Early Church Fathers. London: Routledge, 1997.

Greer, Rowan A. "The Dog and the Mushrooms: Irenaeus's View of the Valentinians Assessed." In *The Rediscovery of Gnosticism: Proceedings of the International Conference on Gnosticism at Yale, New Haven, Connecticut, March 28–31, 1978*, vol. 1: *The School of Valentinus*, edited by Bentley

Layton, 146–71. Studies in the History of Religions: Supplements to Numen 41. Leiden: E. J. Brill, 1980.

Irenaeus. *Adversus haereses = Gegen die Häresien.* Edited and translated by Norbert Brox. Buch II. Fontes Christiani, 8,2. Freiburg: Herder, 1993.

———. *Contra los herejes: exposición y refutación de la falsa gnosis.* Edited and translated by Carlos Ignacio González. Lima, Perú: Facultad de Teología Pontificia y Civil de Lima, 2000.

———. [Irénée de Lyon]. *Contre les hérésies,* Livre II: *Édition critique, traduction, introduction, notes justificatives, tables de Adelin Rousseau et Louis Doutreleau.* 2 vols. Sources Chrétiennes 293–94. Paris: Cerf, 1982.

———. *Contro le eresie e gli altri scritti.* Complementi alla *Storia della Chiesa.* Nuova edizione a cura di Giorgio Maschio. Milan: Jaca, 2003.

Kalvesmaki, Joel. "The Original Sequence of Irenaeus, *Against Heresies* 1: Another Suggestion." *Journal of Early Christian Studies* 15 (2007): 407–17.

May, Gerhard. *Creatio ex nihilo: The Doctrine of "Creation out of Nothing" in Early Christian Thought.* Translated by A. S. Worrall. Edinburgh: T & T Clark, 1994.

McCue, James F. "Conflicting Versions of Valentinianism? Irenaeus and the *Excerpta ex Theodoto.*" In *Rediscovery of Gnosticism: Proceedings of the International Conference on Gnosticism at Yale, New Haven, Connecticut, March 28–31, 1978,* vol. 1: *The School of Valentinus,* edited by Bentley Layton, 404–16. Leiden: E. J. Brill, 1980.

Meijering, Eginhard. *Irenaeus: Grondlegger van het christelijk denken.* [Amsterdam]: Balans, 2001.

Minns, Denis. *Irenaeus.* Outstanding Christian Thinkers Series. London: Geoffrey Chapman, 1994.

Norris, Richard A., Jr. "The Insufficiency of Scripture: *Adversus haereses* 2 and the Role of Scripture in Irenaeus's Anti-Gnostic Polemic." In *Reading in Christian Communities: Essays on Interpretation in the Early Church,* edited by Charles A. Bobertz and David Brakke, 63–79. Notre Dame: University of Notre Dame Press, 2002.

Pagels, Elaine. "Conflicting Versions of Valentinian Eschatology: Irenaeus and the *Excerpta ex Theodoto,*" *Harvard Theological Review* 67 (1974): 35–53.

Perkins, Pheme. "Ordering the Cosmos: Irenaeus and the Gnostics." In *Nag Hammadi, Gnosticism, and Early Christianity,* edited by Charles W. Hedrick and Robert Hodgson, Jr., 221–38. Peabody, MA: Hendrickson, 1986.

Schoedel, William R. "Enclosing, Not Enclosed: The Early Christian Doctrine of God." In *Early Christian Literature and the Classical Intellectual Tradition: In Honorem Robert M. Grant,* edited by William R. Schoedel and Robert L. Wilken, 75–86. Paris: Beauchesne, 1979.

———. "Theological Method in Irenaeus (*Adversus Haereses* 2.25–28)." *JThS* n.s. 35 (1984): 31–49.

———. "'Topological' Theology and Some Monistic Tendencies in Gnosticism." In *Essays on the Nag Hammadi Texts in Honour of Alexander Böhlig*, edited by Martin Krause, 88–108. Nag Hammadi Studies 3. Leiden: E. J. Brill, 1972.

Sesboüé, Bernard. *Tout récapituler dans le Christ: Christologie et sotériologie d'Irénée de Lyon*. Paris: Desclée, 2000.

van Unnik, W. C. "Theological Speculation and Its Limits." In *Early Christian Literature and the Classical Intellectual Tradition: In Honorem Robert M. Grant*, edited by William R. Schoedel and Robert L. Wilken, 33–43. Paris: Beauchesne, 1979.

ST. IRENAEUS OF LYONS: AGAINST THE HERESIES

BOOK 2

PREFACE
(SUMMARY OF BOOK ONE AND PLAN OF BOOK TWO)

1. In the previous Book,[1] we exposed the falsely so-called knowledge[2] and so showed you, dear friend, the entire falsehood[3] devised in many and contradictory ways by the followers of Valentinus. We also explained the opinions of their leaders[4] and showed that they differ among themselves and, much more so, from the Truth. With all carefulness we also explained the opinions and the deeds of Marcus the Magician, since he belongs to their number. Moreover, we carefully reported how much of the Scriptures they select and attempt to adapt to their fabrication. We went into great detail to show how they boldly attempt to state the truth by means of numbers and the twenty-four letters of the alphabet. We also told how they claim that creation was made after the image of their invisible Fullness, and what all they hold and teach about the Demiurge. We made known the doctrine of their progenitor, Simon the Magician of Samaria, and of all those who followed him. We spoke, too, of the multitude of Gnostics who descended from him, and we noted their differences and doctrines and successions (of Aeons).[5] We likewise explained all the heresies that were begun by them. We showed how all of these heretics, after getting their start from Simon, introduced godless and impious teachings into this life. We disclosed their redemption, how they initiate those who are being made perfect, and their invocations and mysteries. We showed, on the other hand, that there is but one God the Creator, and that he is not the fruit of degeneracy,[6] and that there is nothing either above him or after him.

2. In the present Book we shall build up (our own system) as far as we are able and as time will permit,[7] and we shall overthrow their entire system by main principles. And so, since this work is an exposé

15

and refutation of their doctrines, I have titled it such. For it is necessary to bring their hidden conjugal couples to naught in Profundity by exposing and overthrowing the manifest conjugal couples, and to give proof that he never existed in the past and does not exist at present.[8]

CHAPTER 1
THERE IS BUT ONE GOD:
IT CANNOT BE OTHERWISE.

1. It is necessary, then, that we begin with the first and greatest principle, with the Creator God who made heaven and earth and all things in them,[1] whom these individuals blasphemously call the fruit of degeneracy. [It is necessary] further that we show that there is nothing either above him or after him, and that he was influenced by no one but, rather, made all things by his own counsel and free will, since he alone is God, and he alone is Lord, and he alone is Creator, and he alone is Father, and he alone contains all things, and he himself gives existence to all things.[2]

2. Really, how would it be possible for another Fullness or Beginning or Power or another God to be above him, since God, the Fullness of all things, necessarily contains them all without limit and is not contained by anyone?[3] Now if there is anything outside of him, then he is no longer the Fullness of all things, and he does not contain all things, because whatever they say is outside of him will be lacking to the Fullness or to the God who is above all things. But what is lacking or taken away from something is not the Fullness of all things.

He would have a beginning, a middle, and an end in relation to the things outside of him.[4] Now if he is an end to the things below him, he is also a beginning to those above him. In the same manner, it is entirely necessary that he experience the very same in relation to the other sides and to be contained and limited and enclosed by the things that are outside of him. For anyone who is the end of the things below him necessarily and absolutely circumscribes and surrounds the thing of which he is the end. Again, according to them, Father of all, whom they style their Fullness and who is the good God of Marcion, will be contained, enclosed by something else, and surrounded from the outside by some other Authority[5] that must, of necessity, be greater, since what contains something must be greater than that which is contained. Moreover, what is greater is also more stable and more powerful; and what is greater and more stable and more powerful—that will be God.[6]

3. By way of explanation, since around themselves[7] there exists something else that they assert is outside the Fullness into which, they

17

believe, the Power on high that went astray also descended, one of the
following is by all means necessary: either what is outside does the
containing—but then Fullness is contained, otherwise it will not be
outside the Fullness, for if anything is outside the Fullness, the
Fullness will be within the very thing that they say is outside the
Fullness, and the Fullness will be contained by what is outside; but
they understand also the first God to be within the Fullness—or the
Fullness and what is outside of it are separated from each other by an
immeasurable distance. Now if they accept this, then there will be a
third something that immeasurably separates the Fullness from what
is outside of it. This third something will put bounds around and contain both,[8] and this third something will be greater than the Fullness
and what is outside of it, inasmuch as it will contain both within itself.

And so, talk about what is contained and what contains would go
on forever. For, if this third something would have a beginning in the
things above it and an end in the things below it, it is entirely necessary that it be limited also on the sides, either beginning or ending at
some other beings. And these in turn, and others above and below,
would have a beginning in relation to some other beings; and this
would go on forever, so that their speculation would never come to a
stop in the one God; but on the pretext of seeking after more than
exists, this speculation would fall away into what does not exist and
would separate itself from God.

4. These remarks are likewise appropriate against the followers
of Marcion, for his two Gods will be contained and limited by the
immeasurable interval that separates the one from the other. But then
it is necessary to devise many Gods on every side, Gods that would be
separated from one another by an immeasurable interval, beginning
from one another and ending in one another. And then, by the same
line of reasoning by which they attempt to teach that there is some
Fullness or God above the Creator of heaven and earth, one would
have to set up a Fullness above the first, and another above that, and
another sea of deity[9] above the Profundity. The same thing would
have to be set up on the sides. And so their opinion would go on
indefinitely, and it would always be necessary to think up other
Fullnesses and other Profundities; and one would never come to a
stop, always seeking others besides those mentioned. Moreover, it
would be uncertain whether the things of our world are below or
whether they are really above; and whether the things they call above

are above or below. Our mind would have no stopping place and no stability but would necessarily escape into innumerable worlds[10] and interminable Gods.

5. Since things are so, each God would be content with his own things and not curiously meddle into things alien to himself; otherwise, he would be unjust and greedy and would cease to be what God is. And each creation would praise its own Maker and be satisfied with him and not acknowledge any other; otherwise, it would be most justly condemned by all as a rebel and receive a deserved punishment.[11] For it is necessary either that there be one who contains all others and who made within his own realm each creature that was made, just as he willed; or that there be in turn many and interminable Makers and Gods, beginning with each other and ending in each other on every side; and that all others that are outside be contained by some other who is greater. And it would be necessary to acknowledge that each one of them be, as it were, enclosed and remaining in his own realm. However, none of all these would be God, for each one of them would be deficient since that one possesses only a very small portion in relation to all the rest. And so the name Omnipotent would be destroyed, and such an opinion would of necessity fall into impiety.

Chapter 2

The World Was Made Not by Angels but by the Father through the Word.

1. Those, however, sin who claim that the world was made by the Angels or by some other World-Maker apart from counsel with the Father who is above all things, first of all, by the very fact that they say that the Angels made such a great creation apart from the will of the First God. Really this would mean that the Angels are more concerned[1] than God, or that he is neglectful or inferior or cares nothing about things that happen in his realm, whether they turn out bad or good, so that he might demolish and forbid the one but praise and rejoice over the other. One would not even ascribe such an attitude to a man who is skillful; how much more, then, not to God?

2. Next, let them tell us whether these things were made among the things enclosed by him and in his own realm, or in a realm that

belongs to others and is outside of himself. Now, if they say that it was outside of himself, then all the incongruities mentioned will be against them, and the First God will be enclosed by what[2] is outside of him, and in whom he will necessarily have his end. If, on the contrary, it was in his own realm, then it will be very foolish to say that the world was made in his own realm apart from his counsel, by the Angels and those who are under his power or by someone else; as if either he would not have a view of all things in his domain or would be ignorant of what the Angels would do.

3. If, however, it was not apart from his will but, as some believe, with his will and knowledge, then the Angels or World-Maker would no longer be the cause of this creation, but God's will would be. For if he made the Maker of the world or the Angels,[3] or if he was also the cause of their creation, he will be regarded as having made the world, since he made in advance the causes of its formation. Even though they claim that the Angels were made by a long descending succession or that the Maker of the world [was made] by First-Father, as Basilides asserts, nevertheless, the thing that was the cause of the things that were made will be referred to him who was the First-Producer of such a succession, just as success[4] in war is ascribed to the king who prepared the things that were the cause of victory; and as the making of a certain city or of a certain work is ascribed to him who prepared the causes for finishing the things that were made under him. For this reason, too, we do not say that it was the ax that cut the wood or the saw that sawed it; rather, one would most properly say that the man who made the ax and saw for that very purpose is the one who does the cutting and sawing, and much more so the one who made all the tools by which the ax and saw were made. In the same way, according to their reasoning, the Father of all things will rightly be called the Maker of this world, and not the Angels, nor any other World-Maker besides him who is the Originator and the first one who made ready the cause of this creation.[5]

4. Perhaps such talk [of theirs] is persuasive[6] to those who are ignorant of God and who liken him to needy human beings and to such as cannot make something directly out of matter that was prepared but need many tools for making them. But such talk is entirely specious for those who know that God has no need of anything that exists[7] since he created all things and made them by his Word.[8] He did not need Angels as helpers to make the things that are made, nor did he need any Power much inferior to himself and ignorant of the Father;[9] neither any

degeneracy nor ignorance in order that he who would become man might know him. On the contrary, he predetermined in himself all things in advance according to his nature, which to us is ineffable and inscrutable, and he made them as he willed, bestowing on all things their form[10] and order, and the principle of their creation—giving to spiritual beings a spiritual and invisible substance; to supercelestial, a supercelestial;[11] to Angels, an angelic; to animals, an animal; to swimming creatures, an aquatic; to land creatures, one fitted for land; that is, giving to all a suitable substance.[12] But all beings that have been made he made through his indefatigable Word.

5. It is proper to God's preeminence not to be in need of other instruments for creating things to be made. His own Word is sufficient[13] for the formation of all things. Thus John, the Lord's disciple, says of him: All things were made by him and without him was made nothing.[14] Now in "all" is contained also this word of ours. It too was made by his Word, as Scripture tells us in Genesis; he made all things around us by his Word.[15] David in like manner says: For he spoke and they were made, he commanded and they were created.[16] Whom, then, will we believe more in regard to the making of the world—the heretics we mentioned above, who babble about foolish and incoherent things, or the disciples of the Lord, and Moses, God's faithful servant and prophet?[17] He it was who first narrated the origin of the world when he said: In the beginning God created the heavens and the earth,[18] and after that all the rest. But Gods and Angels did not create.

6. That this God is the Father of Our Lord Jesus Christ, Paul the Apostle asserted: One God, the Father, who is above all and throughout all and in us all.[19] We have already shown that there is one God. This we shall show further from the apostles themselves and from the Lord's words. For how can one disregard the utterances of the prophets and of the Lord and of the apostles but listen to these people who say nothing sound?

CHAPTER 3

THE VALENTINIAN PROFUNDITY AND FULLNESS AND MARCION'S GOD ARE ABSURDITIES. THE WORLD WAS CREATED BY THE SAME GOD WHO PLANNED IT: IT DID NOT RESULT FROM DEGENERACY OR IGNORANCE.

1. Their Profundity, then, and his Fullness and the God of Marcion are unfounded. If, as they assert, he has something below and outside of himself, which they call a void and a shadow, this void is then proved to be greater than their Fullness. It is unfounded, moreover, to say that although he contains all things that are below himself, the creation was made by someone else. For it is absolutely necessary that they admit some empty and formless being below the spiritual Fullness in which this totality was made. And this formless being was thus forsaken on purpose because either the First-Father foreknew what was going to happen in it, or he was ignorant of that. But if he was ignorant, he will no longer be the God who foreknows all things; nor will they be able to adduce a reason why he thus left this place empty for so long a time. If, on the one hand, he has foreknowledge and contemplated in his mind the creation that was to be made in that place, then he who planned it beforehand in himself also made it.[1]

2. Let them, therefore, cease to assert that the world was made by another. For as soon as God conceived something in his mind, what he had thus conceived was also made. For it was impossible that one conceive a thing in his mind, and another make what was conceived by the former in his mind. But according to these heretics, God conceived in his mind either an eternal world or a temporal one. Neither supposition is credible. For if he had conceived it mentally as eternal and spiritual and invisible,[2] it would also have been made such. If, however, it was made such as it is, he himself who conceived it such mentally made it such, or he willed it to be such in the Father's presence according to the mental conception, namely, composite and changeable and transitory. Now since it is such as the Father had planned it in himself, it is a formation worthy of the Father.[3] But to assert that what was mentally conceived by the Father of all and formed beforehand is, as it was made, the fruit of degeneracy or the emission of ignorance is a great blasphemy. For then according to them the Father of all things would be

generating in his breast, by the conception of his mind, the emissions of a degeneracy and the fruits of ignorance, since the very things he had conceived in his mind have been made.

CHAPTER 4

THE VOID AND DEGENERACY OF THE HERETICS ARE PROVED ABSURD.

1. It is necessary, therefore, to inquire about the reason for such a dispensation[1] from God, but the formation of the world is not to be ascribed to another. Besides, all things must be said to have been prepared beforehand by God to be made just as they were made; but the one must not invent a shadow or a void. For the rest, one might ask, from where would the void have come? Did it come from the Father of all and the Emitter, who, according to them, is himself emitted, and is it equal in honor and related to the rest of the Aeons, and perhaps more ancient than they?[2] Now, if it was emitted by him, it is like him who emitted it, and like those with whom it was emitted. It is, then, absolutely necessary that their Profundity, together with Silence, be like a void, that is, be himself a void. And the rest of the Aeons, since they are brothers of a void, must also have a voidlike substance. But if it is not emitted, it must have sprung from and been generated by itself, and must be equal in time to their Profundity, the Father of all. Then void would be of the same nature and have the same honor as their Father of all. For it must either have been emitted by someone or have been generated by itself and born of itself. But if that which is emitted is a void, then the Emitter, Valentinus, is also a void, and his followers are voids. If, on the other hand, it was not emitted but generated by itself, then what is a void is both like to, and the brother of, and equal in honor to, the Father whom Valentinus announced. He is more ancient, too, existing long before, and is more honorable than the rest of the Aeons of Ptolemaeus himself and Heracleon,[3] and all the rest who hold the same opinions.

2. But if they are also perplexed[4] by these things, let them acknowledge that the Father of all contains all things and outside of the Fullness there is nothing—for it is absolutely necessary that such a being would have to be bounded and circumscribed by someone

greater, and that they speak about what is "outside" and what is "within" according to knowledge and ignorance, but not according to local distance.[5] Within the Fullness, however, or in the things that are contained by Father, [let them acknowledge] that the things made by Demiurge or the Angels, and whatever we know were made, are contained by an unutterable Greatness, as the center in a circle or a stain in a garment. In that case, first of all, what sort of being will Profundity be who allows a stain to take place in his bosom and permits someone else to create or emit in his own realm apart from his counsel? That would no doubt bring impropriety[6] on the whole Fullness—since this was able from the first to prevent the degeneracy, and the emissions got their beginning from it[7]—and not allow the formation of a creature in ignorance or in passion or in degeneracy. For he who at a later date corrects a degeneracy and, as it were, washes away the stain, could have taken care much earlier that such a stain would not have taken place in his realm in the beginning. Or, if he permitted that in the beginning, because the things made could not be made any other way, then it is necessary that they happen thus always. For how can things that cannot be corrected in the beginning be corrected later? Or how can they say that men and women are called to perfection when the very things from which men and women were made, either Demiurge or the Angels, are themselves degenerate? And if he had pity on humanity in these last times and grants them perfection precisely because he is kind, then he ought to have had pity first on those who were the makers of men and women, and grant them perfection. Thus, truly men and women would have received mercy, having been made perfect from the perfect. For if he had pity on their work [men and women], much more ought he to have had pity on them [the makers] and not have permitted them to come to such great blindness.

Their talk, moreover, about a shadow and a void, in which they claim our creation was formed, will be shattered if these things were made in the realm that is contained by Father. For if they believe that Father's light is such that it can fill all things that are within him and can light up all of them, how can a void and a shadow exist in the realm that is contained by the Fullness and by Father's light? It is necessary that they point out a place in First-Father or within the Fullness that is not lighted up or limited by anyone, in which either the Angels or the Demiurge made whatever they willed. The place where so great a creation was made is not small. So it is absolutely necessary that they acknowledge[8] a place void and formless and darksome within the Fullness, in which were formed the things that were formed. Likewise, Father's light would incur a reproach, as if it would not be able to light up and fill the things that are within itself. Furthermore, if they say that these are the fruit of degeneracy and the work of error, they introduce degeneracy and error into the Fullness and into Father's bosom.

CHAPTER 5

OUR WORLD WAS NOT FORMED BY
OTHER BEINGS IN FATHER'S REALM.

1. What we have just now written makes a suitable argument against those who claim that this world was made outside of the Fullness or under the "good" God. And they will be enclosed with their Father by what is outside of the Fullness[1] and in which they must also find their end. Those, however, who assert that this world was made by certain others in the realm contained by Father will be faced by all the absurdities and incongruities of which we have just now written. They will be forced either to admit that all things that are within Father are luminous and full and active, or to blame Father's light for not being able to light up all things. Or they must admit that their entire Fullness is void and disordered and darksome, just as a part of it is. They blame all the rest of the things of creation as if these were temporal, terrestial, and earthly.[2] But[3] these ought to be blameless since they are within the Fullness and Father's bosom; or the blame will fall in a similar manner on the entire Fullness.

Their Christ will be found to be the cause of ignorance. For, as they say, when he had formed their Mother in accordance with substance,[4] he cast her out of the Fullness; that is, he separated her from knowledge.[5] Therefore, the one who separated her from knowledge caused ignorance in her. How, then, could the same one who is the cause of ignorance in their Mother[6] bestow knowledge on the rest of the Aeons, the ones who were more ancient than he?[7] Really, he caused her to be outside of knowledge by casting her out of the Fullness.

2. Moreover, if, as certain ones of them do, they will speak of "within the Fullness" and "outside of the Fullness" from the viewpoint of knowledge and ignorance, inasmuch as whoever is in knowledge is

within what he knows, then they must agree that Savior himself, whom
they claim to be the All, was in ignorance. For they say that when he
went out of the Fullness, he formed their Mother. If, therefore, they
call the ignorance of all things what is outside, and if Savior went outside to form their Mother, then he happened to be outside of the
knowledge of all things, that is, in ignorance. How, then, could he
bestow knowledge, when he himself was outside of knowledge? For
even we, they claim, since we are outside of their knowledge are outside of the Fullness. And again, if Savior went outside of the Fullness
in search of the lost sheep,[8] since the Fullness is knowledge, then he
happened to be outside of knowledge, that is, in ignorance. For either
they have to agree that what is outside of the Fullness is so in a local
sense, and then all that has been said will be against them; or if they
assert that what is "within" is so from the viewpoint of knowledge, and
what is "outside" is so from the· viewpoint of ignorance, then their
Savior and, long before him, Christ happened to be in ignorance
when for the formation of their Mother they went outside of the
Fullness, which means outside of knowledge.

3. These arguments can likewise be used against all those who in
any way maintain that the world was made either by the Angels or by
anyone else besides the true God. Really, whatever blame they level at
Demiurge and the things that were made material and temporal will
reflect on Father. Because, how were the things made in the bosom of
the Fullness that would soon again be dissolved by Father's permission
and good pleasure? The Maker is, then, no longer the cause of this
action, though he thinks that he makes things very well; yet he it is
who allows and approves that the emissions of degeneracy and the
works of error take place in his own realm; and the temporal things
in the eternal; the corruptible, in the incorruptible; and those that
belong to error, in those that belong to Truth. If, on the contrary,
these things were made without the permission and approval of the
Father of all, then the one who made these things in Father's realm
without Father's permission has more power and strength and dominion. On the other hand, if, as some claim, Father allowed this without
giving approval, then either he allowed this because of some necessity,
though he was able to prevent it, or he was not able. But if he was not
able, then he is weak;[9] but if he was able, then he is a deceiver and a
hypocrite and a slave of necessity, not indeed approving yet allowing
as if he did approve. And in the beginning by allowing he would estab-

lish error and make it increase; in later times he would attempt to destroy it, after many had already miserably perished because of the degeneracy.

4. It is not proper to assert that God, who is above all things, since he is free and has self-determining power, is a slave of necessity, inasmuch as something might be according to a concession of his but independent of his counsel. For then they would make necessity greater and more powerful than God, since whatever is more powerful is also more ancient than all. For immediately in the very beginning he would have had to do away with the cause of necessity and not bind himself to necessity by allowing something beyond what is becoming to him. Really, it would have been far better and more consistent and more godlike if he had cut off such a beginning of necessity from the start, than later, as if repentant, attempt to root out such a large crop of necessities. And if Father of all things would be a slave of necessity and fall under fate, unwillingly tolerating the things that happen, without being able to do anything against necessity or fate, he would be just like the Homeric Jupiter, who of necessity says, "For I gave to you, as if willing, yet with unwilling soul."[10] According to this reasoning, therefore, their Profundity will be found to be a slave of necessity and fate.

CHAPTER 6

THE ANGELS AND THE DEMIURGE COULD NOT HAVE BEEN IGNORANT OF THE SUPREME GOD.

1. How were the Angels of the Maker of the world ignorant of the First God, since they were in his realm and were his creation and were contained by him? He could indeed have been invisible to them because of his eminence, but he could by no means have been unknown to them because of his providence. For, as they say, though they were separated very much from him by reason of their subsequent coming into being,[1] nevertheless, since his dominion extends to all things, it was necessary to know their ruler, and to know this, too, that he who created all things is Lord of all. For, since the invisible reality that is God is powerful,[2] it bestows on all a profound mental intuition and perception of his most powerful, even all-powerful emi-

nence.[3] Hence, even though no one knows the Father except the Son, and the Son except the Father, and those to whom the Son may reveal,[4] nevertheless, all know this one fact that there is one God, the Lord of all, whenever the Word that is implanted in their minds moves them and reveals it to them.[5]

2. On this account, all things have been made subject to the Name of the Most High and of the Almighty. And by his Name even before the Lord's coming men were saved from the most wicked spirits and from all demons and from every rebel power. This was so, not as if the spirits of the earth or demons had seen him, but because they knew that he is the God who is above all things,[6] and so at his Name they trembled,[7] as also every creature and principality and power and every virtue that is subjected to him trembles. Or could not those who live under the empire of the Romans, although they have never seen the emperor but are separated from him by land and by sea, know, by reason of his dominion, who it is that possesses the supreme power of ruling? But would the Angels, who are superior to us, or even he whom they call the Maker of the world, not know the Almighty, when even the dumb animals tremble and submit to such a Name? Indeed, they have not seen him, yet all things are subject to the Lord's Name.[8] So, too, those are subject to the Name of him who made and created all things[9] by a word, since it was no one else than he who formed the world. For this reason, again, do the Jews to this day put demons to flight by means of this invocation, inasmuch as all beings fear the Name of him who created them.

3. If, then, they do not wish to hold that the Angels are more irrational than the dumb animals, they will find that it was necessary that these, though they had not seen God who is above all,[10] know his sovereignty and dominion. For it will appear truly ridiculous if they maintain that they themselves who are on the earth know God who is above all, whom they have never seen, but will not grant that he who formed them and their whole world knows those things that they themselves know, although he is on high, even above the heavens, whereas they are here below. Unless perhaps they maintain that their Profundity lives in Tartarus below the earth, and that on this account they knew him before the Angels who dwell on high! They arrive at so great a madness as to pronounce the Maker of the world devoid of understanding. Of a truth, they are deserving of pity when with so great folly they assert that he knew neither his Mother nor her off-

spring nor the Fullness of the Aeons nor First-Father nor what the things he made were, which were, however, images of the things within the Fullness made in honor of the things on high through the secret working of Savior.[11]

CHAPTER 7
CREATED THINGS ARE NOT IMAGES OF THE AEONS.

1. And so, while Demiurge was ignorant of all things, they claim, Savior conferred honor on the Fullness in the creation made through his Mother, inasmuch as he emitted likenesses and images of the things on high.[1] But we have shown that it was impossible for anything to exist outside the Fullness in which, they say, the images of the things within the Fullness were made, or that this world was made by anyone else than the First God. Now, if it is a pleasure to refute them from every angle and expose them as liars, we shall affirm against them that if these things were made by Savior according to the image of the things on high as an honor to them, then it is necessary that they continue always so that the things that have been honored might always be in honor. But if they pass away, of what use is this honor of a very short time, which once did not exist and will again cease? You blame Savior, therefore, for being ambitious for vainglory rather than that he honors the things on high. For what honor are temporal things to eternal things that exist always, transient to permanent, perishable to imperishable? Why, even among men and women, who are temporal, it is not an honor that quickly passes that is favored but one that endures as long as possible. On the other hand, the things that are destroyed shortly after having been made will rightly be said to be rather a dishonor to those whom they were thought to honor, and what is eternal [will be said] to be treated with dishonor when its image has perished and has been destroyed. What if their Mother had not wept and laughed and had been perplexed, would Savior not have had the means to honor the Fullness, since the extreme state of confusion [of Achamoth] did not have its own substance,[2] whereby he might honor First-Father?

2. O empty honor of vainglory that soon passes and no longer appears! There will come a time[3] when such honor will not be esteemed at all, and then the things on high will be without honor.

Or, it will again be necessary to emit for the honor of Fullness another Mother who weeps and is perplexed. What a dissimilar and at the same time blasphemous image.[4]

You tell me that the image of Only begotten,[5] whom you hold to be the Mind of Father of all things, was emitted by the Maker of the world, and yet (you) maintain that this image was ignorant of itself—ignorant too of the creation, ignorant likewise of its Mother and of all things that exist and were made by him.[6] And you do not blush on attributing even to Only begotten himself the ignorance that is against you? To be sure, if these things were made by Savior after the likeness of the things on high, while he [Demiurge] who was made after the likeness remained ignorant of so great things, it is necessary that such ignorance exist spiritually around and by virtue of the one after whose likeness the one who is ignorant was made. Really, it is impossible, since both were emitted spiritually and were not fashioned or composed, that they preserved the likeness in some parts but in others distorted the image of the likeness, which was emitted for the very purpose that it should be made after the likeness of the emission on high. But if it is not a similar image, then Savior will be accused of being a blameworthy craftsman for having made a dissimilar image. Nor can they say that Savior, whom they style the All, did not have the power of emission. Consequently, if the image is dissimilar, the craftsman is a poor one and their Savior is at fault. If, on the other hand, it is similar, then the same ignorance will be found in their First-Father's Mind, that is, in Only begotten. And so Father's Mind was ignorant of himself; ignorant, too, of Father, and ignorant of the things that were made by him. But if he has knowledge, it is necessary that also he who was made by Savior after his likeness know the things that are similar. And thus, according to their rule, their very great blasphemy is shattered.

3. But apart from this, how can the things of creation which are so varied[7] and numerous and innumerable be the image of the thirty Aeons that are in the Fullness, whose names, as given by these individuals, we have set down in the preceding Book? Not only will they not be able to fit the variety of the entire creation into their small Fullness, but not even a part of it, as that of the celestial or superterrestrial or aquatic beings. For they themselves testify that in their Fullness there are thirty Aeons; but anyone will agree[8] to show them that one part of the created beings mentioned number not thirty but

many thousands of kinds. How, then, can the things that belong to such a varied creation and consist of such contrary substances, and that are opposed to each other and kill one another—how can these be the images and likenesses of the thirty Aeons of the Fullness, if indeed, as they say, these [Aeons] are of one nature and consist of an equal and similar substance and differ in no way? Now if these beings [here below] are images of those [above], since some people are by nature bad and some good, it would be necessary to point out such differences in their Aeons, too, and to admit that some of them are by nature emitted good and some by nature bad, so that their fabrication about the image might match the Aeons. Still more, since in the world some beings are gentle and others wild; some harmless, some harmful, and destructive of the rest; some superterrestrial, some aquatic; some winged, some celestial, they are bound in the same manner to point out that the Aeons have the same properties—if indeed they are images of these. In addition, they must explain whose image among the Aeons on high the eternal fire that the Father prepared for the devil and his angels is![9] After all, it too belongs to creation.

4. If, however, they will say that these things are the images of the Intention of the Aeon who suffered passion, then, first, they would act impiously against their Mother by asserting that she is the initiator of evil and perishable images. Second, how can the things that are many and dissimilar and contrary in nature belong to one and the same image? Neither will their account be consistent if they would say that the Angels of the Fullness are many and that the many things [here below] are the images of them? For, first, they will be obliged to point out in the Angels of the Fullness differences that are opposed to each other, just as the pertinent images belong to natures that are opposed to each other. Now, surrounding the Creator there are many and innumerable Angels, as all the prophets profess: *Ten thousand times ten thousand stand before him, and many thousand thousands serve him.*[10] So according to them, the Angels of the Fullness will have the Angels of the Makers as images, and the entire creation remains in the image of the Fullness, in such a way that the thirty Aeons no longer correspond to the multiform variety of creation.[11]

5. Furthermore, if these things [here below] are made after the likeness of those [above], after the likeness of what things will those [above] be made? If the Creator of the world did not make them by himself, but, as a worthless architect and a boy who is taking his first

lesson, copied them from archetypes made by others, from where did Profundity get the image of the economy that he emitted first? It is logical that he got the model from someone else who is above him, and he in turn from someone else. And still the discourse about images would run on indefinitely, just as about the Gods, if we do not fix our mind on one Architect and on one God who by himself made the things that are made. When there is question of men and women, does one allow that they planned by themselves something useful for life, but one does not allow that the God who perfected the world made by himself the image of the things that he made and the plan of the beautiful economy?

6. Again, how can these things be images of those above, since they are opposed to them and have nothing in common with them? Really, things that are opposites can indeed destroy the things to which they are opposed but can by no means be their images; as, for instance, water of fire, light of darkness, and other such things can by no means be images of one another. Thus, neither can perishable and earthly and composite and transitory things be the images of their spiritual things, unless these, too, are acknowledged to be composite and circumscribed and formed and no longer spiritual, diffusive, and incomprehensible.[12] Certainly, it is necessary that they be formed and circumscribed if they are to be true images; and then it is settled that they are not spiritual. If, however, these men claim that those are spiritual and diffusive and incomprehensible, how can the things that are formed and circumscribed be images of those that are not formed and incomprehensible?

7. If, however, they claim that these things are images not in respect to form and shape but in respect to number and order of the emission, then, in the first place, these things cannot be styled the images and likenesses of the things on high that belong to the Aeons. For how can they be their images if they have neither their form nor their shape? Second, let them match the same and similar numbers and emissions of the Aeons on high with the things of this creation. But now, since they point out thirty Aeons and claim that so great a multitude of things in creation are their images, we rightly expose them as senseless.

CHAPTER 8

THE CREATED WORLD IS NOT A
SHADOW OF THE FULLNESS.

1. To continue, if, as some of them make bold to assert, they claim that these things [here below] are a shadow of those [above], in such a manner that they are images[1] in this respect, they must acknowledge that the things on high have bodies. For bodies that are above cast a shadow, but not spiritual bodies, since these can in no way darken anything. But if we concede also this to them—though it is something impossible—that spiritual and luminous beings have a shadow into which they claim their Mother descended, still since these are eternal, both the shadow caused by them continues to be eternal, and these things [below] are no longer transitory but continue along with those that cast their shadow on them. But if these [below] are transitory, it is necessary that also those [above], of which they are the shadow, be transitory; on the other hand, if those above continue, then likewise their shadow must continue.

2. If, on the other hand, they will claim that a shadow is such not because something is darkened but by the fact that these things [below] are far separated from those [above], they will charge Father's light with cowardice and weakness, as if it did not reach these things [below] and is unable to fill up the void and to dispel the shadow, and this, when no one places any hindrance. In fact, according to them, Father's light will be turned into darkness and will become obscure and will not reach the places of void, since it cannot fill up all things. And so let them no longer claim that their Profundity is the Fullness of all things, since he did not fill up or light up the void and the shadow. Or, on the contrary, let them stop talking about a shadow and a void, since the light of the Father fills up all things.

3. Neither, then, can there be some thing outside of First-Father, who is the God above all things, or outside of the Fullness—into which, they say, Intention of the Aeon that suffered passion descended—without the Fullness or First God being limited and circumscribed and contained by what is outside. Nor can there be a void or a shadow, since Father already exists, so that his light does not fail and does not come to an end in a void. It is, further, irrational and impious to think up a place in which their First-Father and First-

Beginning and Father of all things, even of this Fullness, should cease and come to an end. Nor is it allowed to assert, because of the reasons already mentioned, that a certain other being made so great a creation in Father's bosom, either with or without his consent. The fact is, it is impious and equally irrational to assert that so great a creation was made in Father's realm by the Angels, or by some emission that was ignorant of the true God. Nor is it possible that the things that are terrestrial and earthly were made within their Fullness, which is entirely spiritual. It is not even possible that the many things of creation that are opposed to each other were made after the image of those [above], since they are said to be few and of similar form and one [in nature].[2] False, too, in every respect has been shown their talk about the shadow of the void.[3] And so their fabrication has been shown to be a void, and their doctrine inconsistent. More yet, those who pay attention to these people are likewise a void and are really descending into a profundity of ruin.[4]

CHAPTER 9

THAT THERE IS ONLY ONE CREATOR, GOD THE FATHER, IS THE CONSTANT BELIEF OF HUMANKIND AND OF THE CHURCH.

1. That God is the Maker of the world is clear even to those people who talk against him in many ways, and they acknowledge him by calling him Maker and styling him an Angel, without mentioning that all the Scriptures acclaim [him], and the Lord teaches this *Father who is in heaven*[1] and not some other, as we shall show in the course of this treatise. For the present, the testimony of those who [in other areas] hold doctrines contrary to ours suffices; for in this matter all men and women are unanimous. On the one hand, the ancients guard this persuasion as a tradition coming from the First-formed-Man, and they hymn the one God as the Creator of heaven and earth. On the other hand, the people who come after them were reminded of this matter by God's prophets, whereas the heathens learned it from creation itself. Really, creation itself manifests him who created it, and the work itself suggests him who made it; and the world mani-

fests him who put order into it.[2] Moreover, the whole church throughout the world received this tradition from the apostles.[3]

2. Since, therefore, this God is stable, as we have said, and since all people testify to his existence, Father whom they invent is without doubt unstable and without witness. Simon Magus was the first to assert that he himself is the God above all things, and that the world was made by his Angels.[4] After this, his successors, as we showed in Book One, by various opinions spread around impious and irreligious doctrines against the Creator. Since these [heretics] are their disciples, they make those who assent to them worse than heathens. For, though the heathens *serve the creature rather than the Creator*,[5] and also *the things that are not gods*,[6] still they attribute the first place of the deity to God the Creator of this universe. But these heretics, because they assert that the Creator is the fruit of degeneracy and call him ensouled who is ignorant of the power that is above him, and who they claim lies when he says: *I am God, and there is no other God*,[7] though they themselves are the liars who attach all sorts of wickedness to him, by fabricating according to their opinion him who is not above this one who is,[8] expose themselves as blasphemers of him who really is God and, to their own condemnation, as fabricators of him who is not God. And so they who claim that they themselves are the perfect who have knowledge of all things are found to be worse than heathens and are more blasphemous in mind also toward their Creator.

CHAPTER 10

THE HERETICS INTERPRET SCRIPTURE PERVERSELY.
GOD CREATED ALL THINGS OUT OF NOTHING.

1. How most irrational it is, then, for them to pass him by who is truly God and who has testimony from all people, instead to go in search of one who does not exist but is supposed to be above him, and who has never been proclaimed by anyone. They themselves furnish testimony that nothing has even been openly said about him. It is manifest that they now generate another God, who was not sought after before, inasmuch as the parables, which themselves need to be studied for their meaning, they adapt incorrectly to the God whom they invented.[1] For, by the fact that they wish to explain ambiguous

scriptural passages—ambiguous not with regard to the economies of God[2]—they fabricated another God. And so, as we have said before, they braid ropes out of sand[3] and add a bigger difficulty to a smaller one. But no mystery is solved by another that itself needs a solution, nor is one ambiguity solved by another ambiguity by anyone who has sense, or one riddle by another greater riddle. But such difficulties are solved by things that are manifest and harmonious and clear.

2. These [heretics], while seeking to explain the Scriptures and parables, introduce another, greater God above the God who is Creator of the world. Thus, they do not solve the difficulties. How can they? Rather, they attach a greater difficulty to a smaller one and so tie a knot that cannot be untied. They make a collection of foolish discourses that they might come to this knowledge, [namely], to know that the Lord indeed came to the baptism of the truth at the age of thirty,[4] but without learning this [the meaning of the baptism], they impiously scorn the very God who is the Creator and who sent the Lord for the salvation of humankind; likewise, that they might be thought to be able to tell us from where the substance of matter came, without believing that God made those things that were made in order that all things might exist out of things that did not exist,[5] just as he willed, making use of matter by his own will and power. In this way they really manifest their unbelief, since they do not believe in the things that exist, but have fallen into what does not have existence.

3. For, when they tell us that from the tears of Achamoth come the moist substance; from her smile, the luminous; from her sadness, the solid; from her fear, the mobile; and that in these things they exercise profound wisdom, and that this is something proud,[6] how deserving of ridicule and really laughable are not these things! They do not believe that God created matter itself, though he is powerful and rich in all things, since they are ignorant of how powerful the spiritual and divine substance is. On the other hand, they believe that their Mother, whom they style a female from a female,[7] emitted this huge matter of creation from the passions mentioned. They question whence anyone provided the Creator with the matter of creation, but they do not question whence [were provided] to their Mother, whom they call Enthymesis and impulse of the wandering Aeon, such an amount of tears, or sweat, or sadness, or that which let loose the remainder of matter.

4. To attribute the substance of the things that were created to the power and the will of the God of all things is credible and accept-

able and stable. In this regard one might well say: *What is impossible with mortals is possible with God.*[8] The reason for this is that men and women cannot make anything out of nothing, only out of matter that exists; God, however, is far superior to humankind inasmuch as he himself invented the matter of his work, since previously it did not exist. On the contrary, to say that matter was emitted from Intention of the Aeon that went astray, and that the Aeon is far separated from her Intention, and again that Intention's passion and emotion were expelled from her in order to become matter[9] is both incredible and foolish and impossible and unstable.

Chapter 11
The Heretics Have Fallen into a Profundity of Error.

1. They [heretics] do not believe that this God who is above all things made, just as he willed, the diversified and dissimilar things in his own realm through the Word, since as a wise Architect[1] and a very great king he is the Maker of all things. They believe, on the contrary, that the Angels or some Power separate from God and ignorant of him made this universe.[2] And so, not believing the truth but wallowing in falsehood, they have lost the bread of true life and have fallen into the void and profundity of shadow. They are like Aesop's dog, who let go of his bread but made a dash for its shadow, and so lost its food.[3] From the Lord's very words, too, it is easy to prove that he acknowledges one Father,[4] Maker of the world, and Fashioner of the human being, who was announced by the law and the prophets; that he knows of no other; that this God is above all things; that he, moreover, teaches and confers by himself on all the righteous filial adoption with relationship to the Father, which is eternal life.[5]

2. Nevertheless, because these individuals delight in making accusations, and because, like calumniators, they assail the things that are above calumny, bringing against us many parables and difficulties, we thought it well,[6] first by way of opposition, to question them concerning their opinions, to show what in these is not probable, and to cut off their audacity; after that, to adduce the Lord's words, so that they will not only be devoid of means for proposing their theories but,

unable to give a rational answer to the questions put to them, they will
see their reasoning shattered and will either return to the Truth, hum-
ble themselves, and give up their manifold fantasy, appeasing God in
regard to the blasphemies they had uttered against him, and be saved;
or, if they should continue in the vainglory that preoccupied their
mind, they will change their reasoning.

Chapter 12
The Triacontad Is Erroneous
Both by Defect and by Excess:
Wisdom Could Not Have Emitted
without Her Consort.
Word and Silence Could Not
Have Been Contemporaries.

1. First, we shall say in regard to their Triacontad that the whole
of it will strangely fall to pieces on both sides: on the side of defect and
on the side of excess. They claim that the Lord came to baptism when
he was thirty years of age[1] for the sake of [indicating] the Triacontad.
When this collapses, the refutation of their entire doctrine will be
manifest.[2]

From the side of defect,[3] in this way: First, they class the First-
Father with the rest of the Aeons; but the Father of all things ought
not to be counted with the rest of the emissions; he who was not emitted with what was emitted; he who is unbegotten, with what was begotten; he whom no one comprehends with what is comprehended by
him;[4] he who was not formed with what was formed. For, inasmuch as
he is superior to the rest, he ought not to be classed with them; and
so he who is impassible and did not err with the Aeon that is passible
and was established in error. In the preceding Book, we have shown
that they begin counting their Triacontad from Profundity and go on
to Wisdom,[5] as they style the Aeon that went astray; we also set down
the names that they give to them. Now, if one does not count that one
[Profundity], there are no longer thirty emissions of Aeons as they
want, but only twenty-nine.

2. Second, when they speak of Thought or Silence as the first emission,[6] and when they say Mind and Truth were in turn emitted from her, they err on both points. For it is impossible to conceive of anyone's thought, or silence, apart from himself and as having its own form, if it has been emitted outside of himself. But if they say that she was not emitted outside but was united to First-Father, why do they class her with the rest of the Aeons, namely, with those who are not united and are on this account ignorant of his greatness? Or, if she is united (let us consider this too), it is absolutely necessary that from this united and inseparable conjugal couple, which exists as one, there should result an undivided and united emission, so that it might not be dissimilar to him who emitted it. Now, since this is so, Mind and Truth will become one and the same, just like Profundity and Silence, always adhering to each other. It is a fact that one cannot be conceived of without the other; for example, water without moisture, fire without heat, a stone without hardness, because these are united with each other and cannot be sep- arated from each other but must always coexist. So, too, Profundity must be united with Thought, and in the same manner Mind with Truth. Again, Word and Life, having been emitted by such as are united, must themselves be united and be one. And, according to this, Man too and Church, and every emission by a conjugal couple of the rest of the Aeons must be united and must always coexist with each other. For, in their view, a female of the Aeons must exist side by side with a male, since she is, so to say, a disposition of his.

3. Since these things are so, and since they are mentioned by [the heretics] themselves, they impudently dare to teach that the youngest Aeon of the Dodecad, whom they also style Wisdom, suf- fered passion without the embrace of her consort, whom they call Desired, and without him, alone, she generated offspring that they call a female from a female.[7] They have thus reached such a pitch of senselessness that they most clearly believe two contrary opinions about the same thing. To explain, if Profundity is united with Silence, and Mind with Truth, and Word with Life, and so on the rest, how could Wisdom suffer passion or generate without the embrace of her consort? But if she suffered passion without him, it is necessary that the rest of the conjugal couples, too, be divorced and separated from each other. But this is, as we said before, impossible. So it is impossi- ble for Wisdom on her part to have suffered passion without Desire. Consequently, their entire system is again shattered, because from the

passion that they say she suffered without the embrace of her consort, they fabricated all the rest of the tragedy, as one might call it.[8]

4. If, however, they impudently assert that also the other conjugal couples, having been divorced, are separated because of the latest conjugal couple, so that their vain babbling will not be shattered, then, first, they are insisting on an impossible thing. For how can they separate First-Father from his Thought, or Mind from Truth, or Word from Life, or the rest in like manner? How can they themselves, moreover, claim to return to unity and all be one, if the conjugal couples in the Fullness do not retain unity but separate from each other to the extent of suffering passion and generating without the embrace of the consort, as hens without roosters?

5. Second, their first and principal Ogdoad is, likewise, brought to naught. For Profundity and Silence, Mind and Truth, Word and Life, Man and Church, will have a specific existence in the same Fullness. Now, it is impossible for Silence to exist when Word is present, or for Word to manifest himself when Silence is present. For these are destructive of each other. For example, light and darkness can by no means exist in the same place; if light is present, there is no darkness;[9] but where there is darkness, there can be no light, for when light comes on the scene, darkness is dispelled. So, where Silence is, there Word cannot be present, and where Word is, there indeed Silence does not exist. But if they assert that Word is immanent, Silence too will be immanent, and will nonetheless be dispelled by the immanent Word! But the fact that the Word is not immanent is indicated by the very ordering of their emission.[10]

6. And so let them no longer maintain that the first and principal Ogdoad stems from Word and Silence; rather let them reject either Silence or Word.

And then their first and principal Ogdoad is dissolved. For if they say that the conjugal couples are united, their entire system is dissolved. Really, how, if they are united, did Wisdom generate Degeneracy without her consort? But if they would say that each of the Aeons has its own substance, as in the emission, how can Silence and Word be manifested in the same place? So far, then, on the side of defect.

7. Now on the side of excess, their Triacontad is likewise destroyed in the following manner. Limit, whom they call by many names, as we explained in the preceding Book, they claim was emitted

by Only-begotten just as the rest of the Aeons were. Now this Limit, who some claim was emitted by Only-begotten, others claim [was emitted] by First-Father himself after his own likeness. In addition, they assert that Only-begotten also emitted Christ and Holy Spirit,[11] and these they do not class with the number of the Fullness; nor Savior either, whom they also call the All.[12] It is clear, therefore, even to a blind person, that according to them not merely thirty emissions were emitted, but thirty plus four more. For they class First-Father himself in the Fullness, as well as those who were emitted successively from each other. Why, then, are those who had the same kind of emission not classed with those with whom they exist in the same Fullness? What just reason can they give for not classing with the rest of the Aeons either Christ, whom they claim Father willed to emit from Only-begotten, or Holy Spirit, or Limit, whom they also call Stake,[13] or even Savior himself, who came to help and form their Mother? Is it that these latter are weaker than those former and are, therefore, unworthy of the name and of the name of the number of the Aeons,[14] or that they are better and more excellent? Now, how can those become weak[15] who were emitted for the consolidation and correction of the others? On the other hand, they cannot be more excellent than the first and principal Tetrad, by which they were emitted; for these, too, are classed in the aforementioned number. So these latter ought also to have been classed in the Fullness of the Aeons, or else the honor of this name ought to be taken away from those former.[16]

8. As we have shown, their Triacontad has been dissolved from the viewpoint both of defect and excess. For in such a number, if more or less will make the number worthless, how much more will both together make it worthless.[17] The fable, consequently, about their Ogdoad and Dodecad is unstable, since their support itself has been demolished and brought to naught in Profundity, that is, in him who does not exist. So from now on let them seek other reasons why the Lord came to be baptized at the age of thirty, and for the number twelve of the apostles, and for her who suffered a hemorrhage,[18] and for all the rest of the points over which they labor uselessly and about which they babble nonsense.[19]

CHAPTER 13

THE FIRST ORDER OF EMISSION ESTABLISHED
BY THE HERETICS IS INDEFENSIBLE.

1. That the first order of their emissions is to be rejected we prove as follows. They say that Mind and Truth were emitted by Profundity and his Thought. This is shown to be a contradiction. For Mind is itself the directing element,[1] and, as it were, the beginning and the source of all understanding. But Thought is a particular activity, which comes from Mind and is relative to a definite object.[2] It is impossible, therefore, that Mind was emitted from Profundity and Thought. It would have been more plausible[3] to say that Thought was emitted as the daughter of First-Father and this Mind. Thought, really, is not the mother of Mind, as they assert; on the contrary, Mind becomes the father of Thought.

But how was Mind emitted by First-Father, who holds the direction[4] of the hidden and invisible inner development, from which are generated understanding, thought, and intention, and the like? None of these, however, is distinct from mind; they are, as we said before, particular activities of mind relating to a determined object and immanent to this very mind.[5] They get their different names because of continuance and development, but not because of a change.[6] These activities together tend toward interior discourse[7] and are co-emitters of a word, while understanding remains within, creating and governing in all independence,[8] just as it wills, as we said before.

2. By way of explanation, the first activity of the mind on some object is called thought. But when it continues and develops and takes possession of the soul, it is styled intention. This intention, when it dwells on the same object for a long time and is, as it were, approved, is called understanding. This understanding, when it has been continued for a long time, becomes counsel. When the development and activity of counsel have been very extensive, it becomes thought. This, even while continuing in the mind, can very correctly be called a word, from which the uttered word is emitted.[9] Now all these activities mentioned are one and the same thing: they have their origin in the mind and get their names because of development. To illustrate, the human body, which at one time is young, then mature, then aged, gets names because of the development and continuance, but not because

of a change of substance, or because of the loss of the body. The same holds for those acts [of mind]. For, a person thinks of the object he is contemplating; he understands what he thinks of, and also takes counsel about it; and he passes judgment on what he counsels about, then what he passed judgment on, he utters. But all of these activities, as we have said, the mind governs, though it is itself invisible, and it emits the word from itself by means of the activities mentioned, as by a ray, but itself is not emitted by someone.

3. These activities can be spoken of in men and women, since men and women are composite in nature, consisting of body and soul.[10] But whoever asserts that Thought is emitted from God, and Mind from Thought, and from these Word, are in the first place to be convicted of applying these emissions improperly. Second, although they are ignorant of [the nature of] God, they describe men's and women's actions and passions and intentions of the mind. They apply to the Father of all things, who, they assert, is unknown to all, the actions that occur in men and women that lead to the spoken word.[11] They deny that he made the world lest he be considered small, but they ascribe human actions and passions to him! Now, if they had known the Scriptures and had been taught by the Truth, they would indeed have known that God is not like men and women,[12] and that his thoughts are not like the thoughts of men and women.[13] For the Father of all things is far removed from the actions and passions that men and women experience. He is simple and not composite; with all members of similar nature, being entirely similar and equal to himself. He is all Mind, all Spirit, all Understanding, all Thought, all Word, all Hearing, all Eye, all Light, and the whole Source of all blessings. That is how devout people can speak properly of God.[14]

4. He is above all these things, and because of that, unutterable. He may well and correctly be called a Mind that comprehends all things; but his Mind is not like the mind of men and women. He may most correctly be called Light, but he is nothing like our light. In the same manner in regard to all the other points, the Father of all things is in no way similar to humankind's littleness. Indeed we speak of him in such [terms] because of love; but it is understood that he is above them by virtue of his greatness. If, then, even among men the mind itself is not emitted or separated from the living person who emits the rest, though its actions and passions are brought forth, much more

will the mind of God, who is all mind, be by no means separated from him, nor is one thing emitted in him as if from another.

5. To be sure, if he emitted Mind, he who emitted Mind, in their view, is considered composite and corporeal, so that God who emitted exists distinct from Mind who was emitted. But if they say that Mind was emitted from Mind, they cut up and divide God's Mind. To what, and from where, was he emitted? For whatever is emitted by someone is emitted to some receptacle. But what being, into which they claim Mind was emitted, existed prior to God's Mind? And how large was the place that it would receive and hold God's Mind? If, however, as an example, they speak of a ray proceeding from the sun, then just as in the one case there is the existent air as a receptacle[15] [of the ray] and it exists prior to the ray itself, so also in the other case let them show that there was something existent into which God's Mind was emitted, something capable of receiving him and older than God. Next, just as we notice that the sun, which is smaller than all things we see, emits rays far from itself, so we would have to say that the First-Father emitted a ray outside of and far from himself. But what can be conceived of outside and far from God, into which he emitted a ray?

6. If, on the other hand, they will say that Mind was not emitted outside of Father, but within Father himself, first, it will be useless to say that he was emitted at all. For how was he emitted if he was within Father? An emission is the manifestation of the one emitted outside of the one who emits. Second, when Mind was sent forth, Word who proceeds from Father will be within Father; in the same manner, the other emissions of Word. And so they will no longer be ignorant of Father, since they are within him. And since all are surrounded by Father equally and on all sides, no one will know him less because of the descending order of their emissions. All will continue to be equally incapable of passion since they are in Father's bosom; and none of them will be in degeneracy, for Father is not a degeneracy. Unless perhaps, as in a large circle, there is contained a smaller one, and in this a still smaller one; or they might say that, in resemblance to a sphere or a square, Father contains within himself on all sides all the other Aeons that have been emitted successively and have established themselves in the form of a sphere or a square—each one being surrounded by another above it and greater than it, and in turn surrounding the one smaller than itself and which comes after it, and thus the smallest and last of all was set in the center, far removed from

Father, and so would be ignorant of First-Father.[16] Now, if they would assert that, they would enclose their Profundity in a form or boundary, and he would then both surround and be surrounded. They would be forced, in other words, to admit that there is something also outside of him that would surround him. Nonetheless, the talk about the beings that contain and are contained would go on indefinitely, and all the Aeons would clearly appear enclosed as bodies.

7. Furthermore, they will acknowledge either that he is a void, or the all that he is exists within him, and so all will equally partake of Father. For example, if one makes circles in water or either round or square forms, they will all equally partake of the water. Just as those that are made in air would necessarily partake of the air; if in light, of light. Just so all who are in Father partake of Father equally, and ignorance can have no place among them. For where is the ignorance when Father fills up everything? For if he has filled up a place, ignorance will not exist there.[17] And so the work of degeneracy is brought to naught, as also the emission of matter and the rest of the making of the world, which they hold took its substance from passion and ignorance. If, however, they acknowledge that he is a void, they fall into the most grievous blasphemy and would deny his spiritual nature. For how can he be spiritual who cannot fill up even the things that are within him?

8. Now, these remarks that were made about the emissions of Mind are equally applicable against the followers of Basilides and all the Gnostics,[18] from whom these also got their principles for emissions. They were exposed in the First Book. We have already shown that their first emission, that of Mind, is untenable and impossible. Now let us look at the rest. From Mind they assert were emitted Word and Life, the makers of this Fullness. They get [their notion about] an emission from human activity and rashly divine against God,[19] as if they had discovered something great when they assert that Word was emitted by Mind. All indeed know that this can logically be said of men and women, but in the God who is above all things, and who is all Mind and all Word, as we have said, an emission with the type of order mentioned cannot exist, since he does not have in himself anything that is more ancient or of later origin, nor does he have in himself anything that belongs to another.[20] Moreover, he continues to be absolutely equal and similar and one. Just as one would not err if he said that God is all sight and all hearing—for he sees in the same way

that he hears, and he hears in the same way that he sees—so one who says that God is all Mind and all Word, and that as far as he is Mind, he is also Word, and that his Word is this Mind, would still have a low esteem of the Father of all things; but he would have a more becoming esteem than these heretics who transfer the generation of the uttered word[21] of humankind to the eternal Word of God, and mark a beginning and an origin in the uttering [of the Word] as they do in their own word. Now, in what would the Word of God, even God himself, since he is the Word, differ from the human word if he had the same order and emission of generation?[22]

9. They err, further, in regard to Life by saying that she was emitted sixth in line, though she ought to have been placed before all, since God[23] is Life and Incorruptibility and Truth. These, and like perfections, were not emitted according to a process of development,[24] but they are names of perfections that are always with God, as far as it is possible and proper for men to hear and speak of God. As a matter of fact, Mind, Word, Life, Incorruptibility, Truth, Wisdom, Goodness, and all other perfections are heard together with God's name.[25] Neither can anyone assert that Mind is more ancient than Life, for Mind itself is Life; or that Life is of later origin than Mind, lest he who is the Understanding [Mind] of all things—that is, God—should at any time be without Life. But if they should say that Life is in Father, but that she was emitted in sixth place so that Word might have life, she would necessarily have had to be emitted long before, in fourth place, so that Mind might have life; and even before Mind, with Profundity, so that their Profundity might have life. For, to class their Silence with the First-Father and give her to him as consort and not to count Life with them—what consummate foolishness!

10. In regard to the following emission, namely, of Man and of Church, the fathers themselves [of the Valentinians], the falsely called Gnostics, fight them [the Valentinians] in vindicating their own opinions and in accusing them of being evil thieves.[26] They claim that it is more in keeping with an emission, even plausible, that Word was emitted from Man, rather than Man from Word, and that Man is more ancient than Word, and is really the God who is above all things.

For that purpose, as we said, they throw together as plausible all human operations and activities of the mind, generations of the intentions, and emissions of words, but they certainly lied about God.[27] Really, when they ascribe to the divine Word the things that happen to people and whatever they recognize from their own experience, they seem to those who are ignorant of God to be saying things that are proper; just as when they drag Mind of theirs through these human passions, describing in fifth place the origin and emission of God's Word, they assert that they are teaching wonderful, ineffable, and profound mysteries, known to no one else—mysteries of which the Lord should have said: *Seek, and you will find,*[28] namely, that they should inquire as to how from Profundity and Silence came Mind and Truth; and then how Word and Life in turn came from them, and how Man and Church came from Word and Life.[29]

Chapter 14

The Valentinians Took Their Principles from the Pagans.

1. Aristophanes, one of the ancient comic poets, said much more plausible and more pleasing things about the generation of all things in a theogony.[1] He says that Chaos was emitted from Night and Silence; then from Chaos and Night came Love; from this came Light; and from this, according to him, sprang all the rest of the primary generation of gods. Next he introduces a secondary generation of gods and the formation of the world; then, as he tells it, from these secondary gods sprang humanity. In adopting the fable, these people [Valentinians][2] constructed their treatise of natural history, changing only the names;[3] thus they set forth the very same beginning and emission of the generation of all things. For Night and Silence they named Profundity and Silence; for Chaos, Mind; for Love—"Through which," the comic poet said: "all things were put in order"[4]—they proposed Word; and for the primary and greatest gods they dreamed up the Aeons. In place of the second gods, they tell of the series outside the Fullness made by their Mother. This series they call the second Ogdoad. From this series they, like the writer mentioned, proclaim the making of the world and the forming of humanity, while saying that they alone know of these unspeakable and unknown mysteries. And these mysteries, which are everywhere dramatized in the theaters by buffoons with the most pompous voices, they adapt to their own

system. Why, they even teach it with exactly the same reasoning, changing only the names.

2. These people are exposed not only as proposing as their own what the comic poets staged, but as gathering together whatever has been uttered by those who are ignorant of God and who are called philosophers. They sew these together into a kind of cento out of many and worst rags, and so, by a subtle style, they prepare for themselves a fictitious cloak.[5] They introduce a new doctrine in that it is now supported by a new craft; but it is old and useless because these things have been patched together from old opinions, redolent of ignorance and irreligion. Thales of Miletus, for instance, held that water was the genesis and beginning of all things.[6] But to speak of water is the same as to speak of Profundity.[7] Likewise, the poet Homer gave out as an opinion that Ocean with Thetis as mother was the origin of the gods.[8] The Valentinians have adapted that to Profundity and Silence. Anaximander[9] proposed that immensity is the beginning of all things, containing in itself as in a seed the genesis of all things, from which he says the immense world was constituted.[10] The Valentinians have transferred this to their Profundity and Aeons. Anaxagoras,[11] who was also called the Atheist, held the opinion that animals were formed from seeds that fell from heaven upon the earth.[12] The Valentinians have transferred this to the offspring of their Mother; also that they themselves are that offspring. Thus they admit directly among such as have understanding that they themselves are the offspring of the irreligious Anaxagoras.

3. They got their shadow and void from Democritus[13] and Epicurus[14] and adapted them to themselves, since these were the first to make a long discourse on void and atoms. They called the one [the atoms] "what is"; the other [void] "what is not." Those people spoke of atoms as "what are," so do the Valentinians of the things in the Fullness; those people spoke of void as "what is not," so do the Valentinians of the things outside the Fullness. Thus they assigned themselves a place in this world that "is not," since they are outside the Fullness. By saying that those things are images of "what are" [in the Fullness], they most evidently give expression to the doctrine of Democritus and Plato.[15] As proof, Democritus was the first to say that many and varied forms which had been expressed from the universe, descended into this world.[16] Plato in turn spoke of matter as both idea and God.[17] The Valentinians followed them. They named those[18]

forms and type the images of the things on high.[19] They boast of being originators and authors of this sort of imagined fabrication by changing the name.

4. Their assertion that the Creator made the world out of existent matter was already expressed before them by Anaxagoras,[20] Empedocles,[21] and Plato.[22] Thus, they would have us understand that these, too, were inspired by their Mother.[23] Moreover, their assertion that everything, of necessity, passes into the elements from which it was made; and that God is the slave of this necessity, so that he cannot give immortality to what is mortal, or bestow incorruptibility on what is corruptible; but that each being must pass into the substance that is similar to its own nature—this assertion is made by the Stoics, who were called such because of the portico [stoa]; and indeed by all poets and writers who are ignorant of God.[24] The Valentinians who follow the same unbelief assigned their own realm, the one within the Fullness, to the spiritual beings; but the middle realm to the ensouled beings; and the material to the corporeal beings. And they assert that God cannot make these things otherwise but that each one of the beings mentioned passes into the beings of identical nature.

5. Further, when they say that Savior was made out of all the Aeons, inasmuch as all deposited in him, as it were, their flower, they are not adding anything new to the Pandora of Hesiod.[25] For these Valentinians appropriate to Savior what was said of her, presenting him as a Pandoron [Gift-of-all], as if each of the Aeons had bestowed on him the best it had.[26] More yet, their opinion concerning[27] the indifferent quality of foods and other deeds—that they can in no way be defiled by anyone because of their noble lineage,[28] regardless of what they eat or do—they have acquired from the Cynics, since they belong to the same company as these.[29] Besides, they try to inject into the faith hairsplitting and subtle argumentation about difficulties, which is an Aristotelian trait.[30]

6. To continue, their wish to reduce this universe to numbers they have received from the Pythagoreans.[31] These were the first to introduce numbers as the beginning of all things, and their own beginning they suppose to have been an even and uneven [number],[32] from which both the perceptible and the intelligent substances got their origin. Some are indeed the principles of the material substratum, but others are those of intellection and substantial reality. It is from these two types of principles that everything has been made,

just as a statue [is made] from copper and a form.[33] Now this [system] these Valentinians adapted to the beings outside of the Fullness. Those Pythagoreans, however, spoke of the principle of the intellection insofar as the mind understands what is first apprehended and seeks until, worn out, it comes to the One and Indivisible Being.[34] [They held] that One is the beginning of all things and the essence of every generation. Then from this sprang Dyad, Tetrad, Pentad, and the varied generation of the rest of the beings. Those things these [Valentinians] give word for word in referring them to their Fullness and Profundity. And from this same source they try to introduce the conjugal couples, which sprang from One. Marcus, boasting that these things are his, seemed to have originated something more novel than the others, whereas he is telling of the Tetrad of Pythagoras as the origin and mother of all things.

7. Now, in opposition to these people we shall say this: Did all these whom I mentioned, with whose statements you [Valentinians] are convicted of agreeing, know the truth or did they not know it? And if they did know it, the descent of the Savior into this world is useless. For what was his reason for coming? Was it to bring the truth that was known to the knowledge of men who know it? If, on the other hand, they did not know it, how is it that you who hold the same things as those who do not know the truth, boast that you alone possess the knowledge that is above all things, which even those who are ignorant of God possess? So, by a contradiction, they style ignorance about truth knowledge. Well did Paul speak of *novelties of words of the false knowledge.*[35] For their knowledge is found to be truly false.

If, however, they act impudently and assert that men and women indeed did not know the truth, but that their Mother,[36] or Father's offspring, proclaimed the mysteries of the truth through such people, just as through the prophets, though Demiurge was ignorant of them, then, first, they are not speaking of things that have been predicted that cannot be understood by anyone; for those [prophets] themselves realized what they were saying, and so did their disciples and their followers. Second, if either their Mother of the offspring knew of and related the things that belonged to Truth, and if Father is Truth, then Savior, according to them, lied when he said: *No one knows the Father except the Son.*[37] For if he was known either by their Mother or his [Father's][38] offspring, this *No one knows the Father except the Son,* is made meaningless, unless they claim that the offspring of these or Mother is No one!

8. To this extent, then, they seemed speciously to mislead some people by illustrating with human activities and saying things similar to those of the many people who are ignorant of God. They attract them to a discourse about the Aeons[39] by terms with which they are familiar, expounding as they do the birth of God's Word and of Life and of Mind, and that they assist at the birth of the emissions from God. But since emissions from these have no plausibility or proof, they have fabricated all things out of all sorts of things. By way of illustration, people who wish to catch some animals will place customary food before them in order to attract them, gradually luring them by the customary food, until they capture them. But once they have taken them captive, they tie them up in a most painful manner and forcefully lead them away and drag them wherever they please. In like manner, do also these [Valentinians] gradually persuade [people] through notions already familiar to them by specious argumentation to accept the emissions mentioned,[40] the while offering neither rational nor plausible images of the other emissions.[41] Ten Aeons they assert were emitted from Word and Life; but twelve from Man and Church. For these matters, however, they have neither proof nor testimonies nor plausible argument, nor anything at all along these lines. Still they would have us believe that from Word and Life, who are actual Aeons, were emitted, uselessly and aimlessly, Profound and Mingling, also Ageless and Union, Self-producing and Pleasure, Immobile and Blending, Only-begotten and Happiness. But from Man and Church, also actual Aeons, were emitted Advocate and Faith, Paternal and Hope, Maternal and Love, Praise and Understanding, Ecclesiastic and Blessedness, Desired and Wisdom.[42]

9. When telling of the opinion of the heretics in the preceding Book, with all diligence we explained the passions suffered by this Wisdom and her going astray, and how they say she was in danger of perishing because of her search after Father, and her activity outside of the Fullness,[43] and out of what sort of degeneracy they teach that the Maker of the world was emitted.[44] Moreover, we explained Christ, who they say was generated later[45] and emitted after all those; Savior, too, who got his substance from the Aeons which were made within the Fullness.[46] It is necessary for us to recall their names here so that from them may be manifest their absurd lie and the confusion of their

fabricated nomenclature. They themselves dishonor their Aeons by so many names of that sort, whereas the heathens gave their twelve so-called gods names that are plausible and credible; besides, they hold that these gods are even images for the twelve Aeons. But the images have names that are much more becoming and more powerful to lead one to contemplate the divinity by the very meaning of the word.

CHAPTER 15
THESE EMISSIONS CANNOT BE ACCOUNTED FOR.

1. Let us return to the above-mentioned problem of the emissions. And first, let them tell us the reason for such an emission of Aeons, without relating them to things pertaining to creation. For they assert that these were not made for the sake of creation, but creation for their sake. And they claim that these things [below] are not the images of those [on high]; but those [on high], of these [below]. Therefore, just as they give a reason for the images when they say the month has thirty days because of the thirty Aeons, and the day has twelve hours and the year twelve months because of the twelve Aeons that are within the Fullness, and whatever other nonsense they babble—so let them now tell us this reason for the emission of the Aeons: Why was it made such? Why was a first and principal Ogdoad emitted and not a Pentad or a Triad or a Hebdomad, or any of the things that are determined by a different number? And why were ten Aeons emitted from Word and Life and not more or less; and again, why twelve from Man and Church when it was possible for these, too, to be more or less?

2. As for the entire Fullness, why indeed is it divided into three parts, namely, the Ogdoad, the Decad, and the Dodecad, and not some other number different from these? And the division itself, why are there just three, and not four or five or six, or some other number, without relating to numbers that belong to creation? For they say that those [on high] are older than these [beings below]. And so it is necessary for those [above] to have their own reason, namely, one [that holds] before creation, but not one according to creation.[1]

3. We, indeed, when we talk about the harmony of creation, are speaking about things that are well ordered; for this harmony is well

adapted to the things that have been made for this harmony. But these [Gnostics] are not able to talk about a proper reason for the things that are prior [to creation] and were made by themselves, and so they necessarily fall into the greatest perplexity. They ask us about the things of creation, as if we were ignorant of them; contrariwise, when they themselves are asked about the Fullness, either they will talk about human activities or they will descend to discourse on the harmony in creation. Thus they give an irrelevant answer in regard to secondary things and do not answer at all in regard to things that according to them are primary. For we do not ask them concerning the harmony in creation, or about what belongs to human activities. Since their Fullness, of which creation is the image, is in groups of eight, ten, and twelve Aeons,[2] they must affirm that their Father uselessly and aimlessly made the Fullness of such a form; but they will surround Father with deformity if he made anything irrationally. Or again, if they will claim that it was according to Father's foresight that the Fullness was so emitted for the sake of creation, in order that this be arranged well in order,[3] then the Fullness will no longer have been made for its own sake, but for the sake of the image which would be made after its [Fullness'] likeness. For example, a statue made out of clay is not made a mold for its own sake, but for the sake of the statue that would be made out of copper or gold or silver. And so if those things were emitted for the sake of creation, creation would be more honored than the Fullness.

CHAPTER 16

EITHER THE CREATOR PRODUCES BY HIMSELF THE IMAGES OF THE THINGS TO BE MADE, OR THE FULLNESS HAD TO BE PATTERNED AFTER SOME PREVIOUS SYSTEM, AND SO ON INDEFINITELY.

1. Now if they refuse to admit any of these conclusions, because they would be convicted by us, since they are not able to give a reason for such an emission of their Fullness, they will be forced to admit[1] that there is some other, more spiritual and more princely order above the Fullness, according to which their Fullness was patterned.

Of a truth, if Demiurge of himself did not make the form of creation such as it is, but made it after the form of the things on high, then from whom did their Profundity—he who made the Fullness to be of such a form—receive the form of the things made before him? For it is necessary either that one keep his mind set on the God who made the world, inasmuch as he got the exemplar for making the world by his own power and of himself; or, if one would depart from him, one would necessarily always have to ask, Whence did he who is above him get the form of the things that were made? What is the number of the emissions? What is the basis of the exemplar itself? Now, if it was in the power of Profundity to achieve such a form of the Fullness by himself, why was it not in the power of Demiurge to make such a world by himself? And so, again, if creation is the image of the things on high, what hinders one from saying that the things on high are the images of things above them, and again, that those which are above these are in turn images of others, so that the images of images run on endlessly?

2. That happened to Basilides, since he had in no way arrived at the truth, he thought that by an endless succession of things made one from the other, he could escape from such perplexity. When he spoke about the 365 heavens that were made by succession and likeness from one another, saying that proof of this was the number of days of the year, as we have stated before,[2] and that above these [heavens] there was a power, which they called Unnameable, and its system—not even in this way did he escape from the perplexity. Really, when he would be asked whence the image of the form came for the heaven that is above all the others, from which, as he held, the rest were made by succession, he would answer that it came from the system that belongs to the Unnameable. Then either he will say that the Unnameable made it of himself, or he will necessarily have to agree that there is some other power above him from which his Unnameable received his type of so great a form of things that exist.

3. How much safer, then, would it not be, and more careful, to admit the truth from the very beginning, namely, that this Creator God who made the world is the only God, and that there is no other God beside him, inasmuch as he himself received of himself the type and form of the things that were made—rather than after having wearied oneself by so much impiety and a roundabout way to be forced at some time to bring the mind to a halt with some one and to acknowledge that from him comes the form of the things that have been made?

4. The followers of Valentinus accuse us of remaining with the things of the Hebdomad [of Demiurge] here below, as if we did not raise our minds on high or understand the things that are above, just because we do not believe that monstrous story. The followers of Basilides, however, make the same accusation against those [Valentinians], that they are still wallowing in the things of this world as far as the primary and secondary Ogdoad goes, and stupidly think that they have found the Father of all things directly after the thirty Aeons, without making an intelligent investigation into the Fullness above the 365 heavens, which amounts to more than forty-five Ogdoads. Now, with reason, one could in turn throw blame on those [Basilidians]. One could, for instance, think up 4,380 heavens or Aeons, since the days of the year have that many hours. And if one were to add the hours of the nights, thus doubling the above hours, and then think he had originated a vast multitude of Ogdoads and a kind of innumerable activity of the Aeons, and would believe himself more perfect than all, he would have to make the same accusation [mentioned above] against Father, who is above all. For they [the hours] would not suffice for the height of the multitude of the heavens or Aeons, as that one [Basilides] styled them; but since they would be lacking, they would remain either in the realm here below, or in the middle one.

CHAPTER 17

THE EMISSION OF THE AEONS IS VERY ILLOGICAL, INVOLVING FATHER AND MIND IN IGNORANCE.

1. Since, therefore, the system of their Fullness, and especially concerning the primary Ogdoad, has such great contradictions and perplexities, let us look at the rest. Because of their unintelligible system, we too will be going in search of things that do not exist. But this is necessary because this task has been entrusted to us, who also *desire that all people...come to the knowledge of the truth.*[1] Besides, you yourself have requested to get from us many, even all, aids for refuting them.

2. So, we ask this question: How were the other Aeons emitted? Did they remain united to the one who emitted them, as the rays to the sun; or were they [emitted] as a distinct and separated work,[2] so

that each of them would exist separately and have its own form, just as human beings have their source from human beings, and cattle have their source from cattle? Or was it by sprouting, like branches from a tree? And were they of the same substance as those from whom they were emitted, or did they have substance from some other substance? And were they emitted at the same time so that they would be contemporary to some order so that some would be older and others younger? And were they simple and of one form, and in every way equal and similar, just as air and light are emitted; or were they composite and of different form, dissimilar to their fellow members?

3. If, however, each one of them was emitted as a distinct work and by its own generation after the likeness of human beings, either Father's generations will be of the same substance as he and they will be like the one who generated them, or if they appear to be dissimilar, they [Valentinians] must confess that these are from some other substance. And if Father's generations are similar to him who emitted them, those who were emitted will remain impassible, just as he is who emitted them. If, however, they are emitted from some other substance that is capable of passions, how did this dissimilar substance get into the Fullness that belongs to incorruptibility? Further, according to this reasoning each one of them will be understood to exist separately and divided from the other, like human beings, not mixed or united with one another; but each one, distinct in form and determined in space, will be patterned according to a particular size.[3] Such things are characteristic of a body, not of a spirit. They should, then, no longer speak of the Fullness as spiritual, nor of themselves as spiritual, since their Aeons, as if they were human beings, sit feasting with Father, and manifest him to be of the same form as they who were emitted by him.

4. If, however, the Aeons were emitted from Word, and Word from Mind, and Mind from Profundity, as lights are lit from a light— for example, torches from a torch—then they can perhaps differ from one another in generation and in size. But since they are of the same nature as the originator of their emission, either they will all remain impassible, or their Father will share in passions. For a torch that is lighted later will not have a different light from that which existed earlier. Wherefore, when the lights of these torches are brought together into one, they regain their original unity, since there results one light that existed even from the beginning. And one cannot tell that one is

younger or older by the light itself—for the whole is one light—or by the torches themselves that received the light (for these were contemporaneous in their material substance, since the matter of the torches is one and the same), but only according to the lighting, since one was lit a short while ago, but another just now.

5. Degeneracy, therefore, of the passion that resulted from ignorance will either pervade equally the entire Fullness of theirs, since it is of the same substance, and then First-Father will exist in degeneracy of ignorance—that is, he will be ignorant of himself—or all the lights that are in the Fullness will equally remain without passion. What is the source, then, of passion in the younger Aeon, if Father's light, which is by nature without passion, is the one from which all the lights have been made? For how can one Aeon be called younger or older among them, since the light of the whole Fullness is one? And if anyone should call them stars, still they will all manifestly share in the same nature. For if *star differs from star in glory*,[4] it is not by quality or substance, by which one would be with passion and another without passion; but either all, since they are from Father's light, must by nature be without passion and unchangeable, or all, together with Father's light, are capable of passion and of the changes of corruption.

6. The same conclusions follow even if they would assert that the emission of the Aeons came from Word as the branches from a tree, because Word is generated by their Father. All the Aeons, as a matter of fact, are found to be of one same substance with Father, differing from each other only in size but not in nature. They complete the greatness of Father as the fingers complete the hand. So if Father is said to be in passion and ignorance, then to be sure, the Aeons too will be, since they were generated from him. But if it is impious to impute ignorance and passion to the Father of all, how did he, according to them, emit an Aeon capable of passion, and how can they call themselves pious if they impute the same impiety to the very Wisdom of God?

7. If, however, they should claim that their Aeons were emitted as the rays of the sun, either all will be capable of passion, along with him who emitted them, since all are of the same substance and from the same Father, or all will remain without passion. To be sure, it is impossible to admit any longer that from such an emission some are with passion and some without passion. So if they claim that all are without passion, they demolish their own system. For how can a rather young Aeon have suffered if all are without passion? If, on the other

hand, all share in this passion, as certain ones make bold to assert, since it began with Word but continued onto Wisdom, they will be convicted of referring passion to Word, who is the Mind of this First-Father, and of acknowledging that Mind of First-Father, and Father himself, suffered passion.[5] Certainly, the Father of all things is not some composite, ensouled being, apart from Mind, as we have demonstrated before; but Mind is the Father, and the Father is Mind. And so the Word who springs from him, and much more so, Mind, since it is the Word, must necessarily be perfect and without passion; likewise, the emissions that sprang from him, being of the same substance as he, are perfect and without passion and must always remain like him who emitted them.

8. No longer, therefore, is the Word, being third in order of generation, ignorant of Father, as these [Gnostics] teach. Such a thing might be considered plausible in the generation of human beings, because they are often ignorant of their parents; but in Father's Word this is wholly impossible. For, since he is Father, he knows the one in whom he is; that is, he is not ignorant of himself. Furthermore, his emissions, since they are his powers and always assist him, will not be ignorant of him who emitted them, just as the rays are not [ignorant] of the sun. So God's Wisdom, who within the Fullness, since she is of such an emission, was not able to have fallen in passion and have conceived such ignorance. But it is possible for Valentinus's Achamoth (since she is from the devil's emission) to experience every passion and bring forth a depth of ignorance! For when they bear witness concerning their Mother [Achamoth], saying that she is the offspring of the Aeon [Wisdom] who went astray, it is no longer necessary to search for a reason why the sons of such a Mother always swim in the depth of ignorance!

9. I do not understand how they can speak of another emission besides those mentioned. In fact, we are not aware that they ever told us of any sort of emission, though we had a very long discussion with them about such forms.[6] This alone they affirm, that each one of them [Aeons] was emitted and that it had knowledge only of the one that emitted it, being ignorant of the one prior to that one. They do not, however, come forward with a proof as to how they were emitted or how it was possible for something like that to happen to spiritual beings. In whatever manner they might have come forth, they will get away from right reason, since they are so blind in regard to the truth[7] that they claim Word who was emitted by their First-Father's Mind was

emitted in degeneracy.[8] Mind, who was first generated perfect from the perfect Profundity, could not make the emission that sprang from himself perfect, but one that was blind in regard to the knowledge and greatness of Father. Savior manifested the symbol of this mystery in the man who was blind from birth.[9] Since, according to that, the Aeon [Word] was emitted blind by Only-begotten [Mind], that is, by ignorance,[10] they falsely attribute ignorance and blindness to God's Word, who, according to them, holds the second place in the emissions of First-Father. What admirable sophists, who both search out the heights of the unknown Father and report on the supercelestial mysteries *into which angels long to look*,[11] only to learn that Word was emitted blind by the Mind of Father who is above all things, that is, he was ignorant of Father who emitted him.

10. And how, O most empty sophists, could Father's Mind, even Father himself, since he is Mind and perfect in all things, emit his Word as an imperfect and blind Aeon, when he is able directly to emit together with him also the knowledge of Father? How do you claim Christ was begotten later than the rest, but perfect? Much more, then, Word, who is older, would certainly have had to be emitted perfect by the same Mind, and not blind. And he in turn would not emit Aeons blinder than himself, until your Wisdom, who was always blind, gave birth to such a great mass of evils! And it is your Father who is the cause of this sort of evil. For you say that the greatness and power of Father are the causes of ignorance; while you liken him to Profundity, you also attribute to him this name that belongs to the unnameable Father! Now if ignorance is an evil, and if you decree that all evil flowered from ignorance, while asserting that the cause of this ignorance was the greatness and power of Father, you show him up as the Maker of evils. Really, you assert that the cause of evils is the fact that he was not able to look upon his greatness. But if it was impossible for Father to make himself known from the beginning to those who were made by him, he cannot be blamed if he was not able to remove the ignorance of those who came after him! But if he, upon willing, could later remove the ignorance that increased with the progress of the emissions and was thus implanted in the Aeons, much more would he earlier, upon willing, not have permitted the ignorance, which did not yet exist, from coming into existence.

11. Since, therefore, when he willed, he became known not only to the Aeons but also to the men and women who lived in the last

times; since, however, when he did not will to reveal himself in the beginning, he was unknown, Father's will, according to you, is the cause of ignorance. For, if he foresaw that things would happen thus, why did he not prevent their ignorance before it took place, rather than afterwards, as if repentant, to take care of it through the emission of Christ? Really, the knowledge that he revealed to all through Christ, he could have revealed much earlier through Word who was also the firstborn of Only-begotten.[12] Or, if he foreknew and willed that these things should happen in that manner, the works of ignorance continue forever and never pass away. For the things that were made because of the will of your First-Father must continue to exist together with the will of him (First-Father) who willed them. Or, if they pass away, the will, too, of him who willed that they have subsistence would pass away together with him. And how did the Aeons, upon learning that Father is illimitable and incomprehensible, find rest and receive perfect knowledge? They could have had this knowledge before they suffered passion, for Father's greatness would not have been debased from the beginning by the fact that these knew that Father is illimitable and incomprehensible. For if he was not known because of his immense greatness, then on account of his immense love he ought to have preserved those passionless who were born of himself, since in the beginning there was nothing to impede their knowing; in fact, it was more useful [to know] that Father is illimitable and incomprehensible.[13]

Chapter 18

Their Account of Wisdom's Ignorance and Passion Is Full of Contradictions.

1. How can it be anything else but foolish for them to say that his Wisdom, too, was in ignorance, degeneracy, and passion? Such things are foreign and opposed to Wisdom: they are qualities that do not belong to her. Surely, where there is lack of intelligence and ignorance,[1] there Wisdom does not exist. So let them no longer call Wisdom the Aeon that suffered passion; on the contrary, let them avoid speaking of either her name or her passion. Neither let them call the entire Fullness spiritual if this Aeon who suffered so great pas-

sion had been dwelling in it. For such things not even a vigorous ensouled being, let alone a spiritual substance, can accept.

2. And again, how could her Intention that came forth together with passion become separated from it? An Intention is understood to have a relation to someone and never exists by itself. Really, a bad intention is destroyed and absorbed by a good one, as sickness by health. What sort of Intention existed before passion? [It was the Intention] to search for Father and contemplate his greatness! But what was she afterwards advised that she regained health? Of this, that Father is incomprehensible and unsearchable! So it was not a good thing that she wished to know Father, and for this reason she had passion. But when she was advised that Father was unsearchable, she also regained health. And Mind itself, who searched for Father, ceased to search further, according to them, when he learned that Father is incomprehensible.

3. How, then, could Intention, when separated, conceive passions that themselves were dispositions of hers? For a disposition has a relation to someone and cannot exist or subsist by itself. But this is not only unstable; it is also contrary to what our Lord said: *Search and you will find.*[2] For the Lord perfects his disciples by having them seek and find the Father. But Christ of these people [Valentinians], who is on high, perfected the Aeons by ordering them not to seek Father, advising them that they will not find him even though they expend much effort. Again, they affirm that they themselves have become perfect, as they claim, by having found their Profundity; but the Aeons [should have become perfect] by being advised that he for whom they searched is unsearchable!

4. Since, then, Intention itself could not exist separated from the Aeon, they add a still greater lie about her passion, dividing and separating it and asserting that it is the substance of matter—as if God were not light, and as if there were no Word with power to expose and refute their wickedness.[3] To be sure, whatever the Aeon thought of, that she also experienced in passion; and what she experienced in passion, that she also thought of. And with them her Intention was nothing else than the passion of one who pondered how she might comprehend the incomprehensible. And so Intention was the passion. Really, she thought of impossible things. How, then, could the disposition and passion be separated from Intention and become the substance of so much matter, when Intention herself was the passion,

and the passion was Intention? Therefore, neither Intention without the Aeon, nor the disposition without Intention can have a separate subsistence. And so again, their rule is destroyed in this case too.

5. But how could the Aeon both be destroyed and suffer passion? Surely, it was of the same substance as the Fullness, and the whole Fullness is from Father. What is similar will not be reduced to nothing in something similar to itself, nor will it be in danger of perishing; no, it will rather continue and increase, just as fire in fire, and air in air, and water in water. But things that are contrary to each other endure passion and undergo change and destruction by contraries. And so, if there had been an emission of light, it would not have endured passion or been endangered by similar light; no, it would have lit more and increased, as the day by the sun. Really, they claim that Profundity is the image of their Father.[4] Animals that are foreign and strange to each other, and contrary in nature, are endangered and destroyed [by each other]. Those, however, that are familiar and akin to each other are not endangered when living in the same place; even they derive therefrom both health and life. So, if this Aeon had been emitted from him [Profundity] with the same substance as that of the whole Fullness, she would never have undergone a change, since she would be living with such as are similar and familiar to herself—a spiritual being with spiritual beings. For, fear and consternation, passion and dissolution, and the like, may perhaps happen because of contraries among beings that are in our world and among corporeal beings; but in spiritual beings, diffused in light, such calamities cannot happen. Now it seems to me that these [Valentinians] have endowed their Aeon with the passion possessed by the very amorous but hated one in the comic poet Menander.[5] For these [Valentinians] who excogitated these things had more the idea and concept of some unhappy human lover than of a spiritual and divine being.

6. Yet more, to think about searching after the perfect Father and to desire to be within him and to have knowledge of him could not infect a being with ignorance and passion, especially not a spiritual Aeon. No, it rather leads to perfection, to lack of passion, and to the truth. In fact, these [Valentinians] themselves, human beings that they are, by thinking about him who existed prior to them, and, as it were, by already comprehending the perfect One and having been established in knowledge of him, do not claim that they are in the passion that spelled consternation,[6] but rather that they are in knowledge and in possession of the truth. For they say that Savior said to his dis-

ciples: *Search and you will find*,[7] for the reason that they might go in search of the unnameable Profundity, whom they excogitated and imagined to be above the Creator of all things. And they hold that they themselves are perfect, because by searching they have found the perfect One though they are still on earth. On the other hand, they claim that the Aeon who is still within the Fullness who is entirely spiritual, by searching after First-Father and attempting to be within his greatness and to comprehend Father's truth, fell back into passion; and the passion was such that unless she had met the Power that stabilizes all things, she would have been dissolved into the common substance and brought to naught.[8]

7. Such self-conceit is insane and really fits men and women who are destitute of a sense of truth. For they themselves confess, according to their own rule, that this Aeon is superior to and more ancient than they, by saying that they are the offspring of Intention of the Aeon who suffered passion, so that this Aeon is the father of their Mother,[9] that is, their own grandparent! Now, to their grandchildren, who are begotten later, the search after Father brings truth and perfection and stability and purification of fluid matter, as they say, and reconciliation with Father. On the other hand, this same search, they claim, infected their grandparent [wisdom] with ignorance, passion, consternation, fear, and perplexity, from which in turn the substance of matter was made. So, their saying that the search after and seeking for the perfect Father and the desire for communion and union with him brings well-being to themselves, but was the cause of dissolution and ruin for the Aeon from whom they had their origin—how totally inconsistent and senseless and irrational is it not? Those, likewise, who agree with them, are truly blind, making use of blind leaders. Rightly do they fall into a real profundity of ignorance.[10]

CHAPTER 19
ABSURD CONTRADICTIONS ABOUT THE OFFSPRING AND DEMIURGE.

1. What sort of talk, too, is this about their offspring, who was conceived by their Mother [Wisdom] after the form of the Angels who surround Savior? A formless, patternless, and imperfect offspring who

was deposited in Demiurge, without his knowledge, in order that by means of him he might be implanted in the soul that came from himself, and so receive perfection and form.[1] First, it must be noted that these Angels that surround Savior are imperfect, patternless, and formless, because the offspring that was conceived according to their pattern was generated such.

2. Second, when they say that the Creator was ignorant of the deposit of the offspring made in himself, and also of the implantation of the offspring made by him in humanity, they utter a futile and empty statement that can in no way be proved. For how was she ignorant of that if the offspring itself had any substance and its own certain nature?[2] If it was without substance or a certain nature, and so was nothing, he was, consequently, ignorant of it. For the things that have some activity of their own and a certain nature, either of heat or speed or sweetness or a variety of brightness, do not remain even from human beings— although they are only human beings.[3] Far be it, then, that these things [escape] the Creator God of this universe. He indeed does not know of their offspring since it is without a certain nature for any usefulness and without substance for any activity, even absolutely nonexistent. It is for this reason, it seems to us, that also the Lord said: *On the day of judgment you will have to give an account for every careless word you utter.*[4] For all individuals of this kind whatsoever who fill people's ears with idle talk will be present at the judgment to render an account of the things they have foolishly conjectured and lied against God, to the extent of claiming that they themselves have knowledge of the spiritual Fullness because of the substance of the offspring, inasmuch as the inner self shows them the true Father; for the ensouled person has need of sentient disciplinary measures.[5] But Demiurge, they say, who received in himself this total offspring, which his Mother [Achamoth] deposited [in him], was totally ignorant of all things and had no understanding of the things concerning the Fullness.

3. How more than irrational is not their assertion that they themselves are spiritual because a certain particle of the Father of all things was deposited in their souls, though they, so they claim, have souls of the same substance as Demiurge. He, on the contrary, though he received once for all the total offspring from his Mother and had it within himself, remained an ensouled being and understood nothing at all of the things on high. These [Valentinians], however, boast that they understand these things, though they are still on earth! For

to think that the very same offspring bestowed knowledge and perfection on the souls of these [Valentinians], but bestowed ignorance
on the God [Demiurge] who made them, is an act of persons who are
truly insane and totally destitute of understanding.

4. It is, furthermore, most senseless for them to say that this offspring, when the deposit was made, was given a pattern and grew and
was made ready to receive the perfect Word.[6] The fact is, it would have
a mixture of matter—this material substance they hold it received
from ignorance and degeneracy—which would be more suitable and
useful than their Father's light, if it was formless and patternless when
born by virtue of contemplating that [light], while from this [material substance] it received a form and a pattern and growth and perfection. If, as a fact, the light from the Fullness was the reason for the
spiritual being's not having its own form or pattern or size, and if the
descent into this [world] bestowed all these things on her and brought
her to perfection, it would seem that the sojourn here below, which
they even call darkness, is much more useful than their Father's light.[7]
And how ridiculous it is to say that their Mother was in danger of
almost suffocating in material substance and of nearly perishing if she
had not then, though with difficulty, extended herself beyond and
leaped outside of herself, having received aid from Father;[8] but that
her offspring grows and receives a form in this material substance and
is made fit and freed for receiving the perfect Word, and this, even
while bubbling over amid dissimilar and unfamiliar beings, since they
themselves say that the earthly is opposed to the spiritual, and the
spiritual to the earthly. How, then, could the small emission, as they
style it, grow and receive a form and attain perfection while with
beings who are of contrary nature and unfamiliar?[9]

5. Further, in addition to what has been said, one might ask: Did
their Mother, when she contemplated the Angels, give birth to the offspring all at one time or separately? If it was all together and at one
time, what was then conceived will no longer be an infant, and so its
[that offspring's] descent into men and women at present will be useless. If, however, it was conceived separately, then she no longer conceived according to the pattern of the Angels that she contemplated;
for, since she saw them all together and at one time, and thereupon
conceived, she ought to have given birth all at one time to those
whose patterns she had conceived.

6. How was it, moreover, that on seeing the Angels with Savior

she conceived the form of these but not of Savior, who is more beautiful than they? Was it that he did not please her, and so she did not conceive according to him?

How was it that Demiurge, whom they style an ensouled being,[10] since according to them he has his own size and form, was emitted perfect in regard to his substance, whereas the spiritual being, which must also be more active than the ensouled, was emitted imperfect and needed to descend into the ensouled being in order to receive a form there and, thus made perfect, it might be fit to receive the perfect Word? If, then, he receives form in earthly and ensouled persons, he is no longer after the likeness of Angels (whom they call lights), but of persons here below. For he will have the likeness and pattern not of Angels but of ensouled persons, in whom he also receives form—just as water that is put in a vessel will have the form of the vessel itself, and if it should freeze in the vessel, it will have the shape of the vessel in which it had frozen—since ensouled persons themselves have the shape of the bodies; for they are fit to the vessel, as we said before. If, therefore, that "seed" is composed and formed here below, it will have the shape of persons and will not have the form of Angels. How, then, can that "seed" which has been shaped after the likeness of persons be after the image of the Angels? And, since it is spiritual, why did it have to descend into the flesh? The flesh, it is true, if it is to be saved, has need of the spiritual, so as to be sanctified and glorified in it, and so that *the mortal may be swallowed up by immortality*.[11] The spiritual, however, in no way needs the things here below; for we do not make it better, but it makes us better.[12]

7. Still more clearly is their talk about the "seed" exposed to be false—and this can be grasped by all—by the fact, as they claim, that the ensouled persons who have their "seed" from their Mother become superior to all others, and for that reason they were honored by Demiurge and were appointed rulers and kings and priests. For, if this were true, first of all, Caiaphas, the high priest, and Annas and the rest of the high priests and the teachers of the Law, and the rulers of the people would have believed the Lord, since they belonged to that kinship,[13] and above all, King Herod. But as it is, neither he nor the high priests nor those who rule, nor the nobility among the people came to meet him; on the contrary, the beggars who sat along the wayside, the deaf and the blind, and those who were trampled on and despised by the rest [met him]. To this effect Paul said: *Consider your*

own call, brothers and sisters; not many of you were wise by human standards, not many were powerful, not many were of noble birth....God chose what is low and despised in the world.[14] And so, ensouled people of this sort were not superior because of the "seed" that was deposited in them, nor were they on this account honored by the Demiurge.

8. Enough has been said about the fact that their rule is weak and unstable and even futile. Nor need we recall the proverb: "One need not drain the whole ocean if one wishes to learn whether the water is salty."[15] To illustrate further, suppose a statue has been made out of clay and painted on the surface so as to make people think that it is gold, though it is clay; now anyone who takes off any little part from it and lays bare and brings to light the clay frees from a mistaken opinion those who are looking for the truth. In the same way, not by taking merely a little part, but by analyzing the most important principles of their rule, we have shown to all who do not wish knowingly to be led astray what is evil and deceptive and seductive and pernicious in the school of the followers of Valentinus and of the rest of the heretics, who give a false treatment to the Maker and Creator of this universe, the only God who exists. This we have done by manifesting their destructible method.[16]

9. Really, who that has intelligence and attains to only a modicum of truth will tolerate their asserting that there is another Father above the God who is the Creator, and that Only-begotten differs from the Word of God, who they claim was emitted in degeneracy, and that Christ, who they assert was made later than the rest of the Aeons together with the Holy Spirit, differs from Savior, who was put together,[17] not by the Father of all things but by the Aeons who were made in degeneracy, and who was necessarily emitted because of the degeneracy? Thus, unless the Aeons had been in ignorance and degeneracy, neither Christ nor Holy Spirit nor Limit nor Savior nor the Angels nor their Mother nor her offspring [Demiurge] nor the rest of the created world would have been emitted; but all would have been destitute of so many blessings.[18] They are, therefore, impious not only against so great a Creator, declaring him to be the fruit of degeneracy, but also against Christ and the Holy Spirit, asserting that these were emitted on account of the degeneracy; and in like manner, that Savior [was emitted] after the degeneracy. Really, who will tolerate the rest of their silly talk, which they have cunningly tried to fit into the parables,

and so have plunged themselves and those who believe them into the greatest impiety?[19]

CHAPTER 20

THE PASSION OF THE TWELFTH AEON CANNOT BE PROVED FROM CERTAIN GOSPEL PASSAGES.

1. We have shown that they apply improperly and illogically, in the following manner, both the parables and the deeds of the Lord to their fabrication.[1] The passion that the twelfth Aeon suffered they try to prove by the fact that the passion of the Savior was caused by the twelfth apostle and in the twelfth month. They hold, namely, that he preached one year after his baptism.[2] Likewise, they assert that it is clearly proved by the case of the woman who suffered from a hemorrhage, since the woman suffered for twelve years, and when she touched the hem of the Savior's robe, she was restored to health by the Power that went out from the Savior, which they claim was effective.[3] To explain, the Power that suffered was straining forward and flowing out profusely, so that she was in danger of being reduced to the total substance. But when she touched the primary Tetrad, which is indicated by the hem, she stopped and rested from her passion.[4]

2. Now in regard to their asserting that the passion of the twelfth Aeon is manifested by Judas, how can Judas be compared according to likeness [with her], since he was thrown out of the number of the Twelve and never restored to his place? For the Aeon, whose type they claim Judas is, was restored after her Intention had been separated; but Judas was demoted and thrown out, and in his place Matthias was appointed, as it is written: *Let another take his position of overseer.*[5] And so, they should have said that the twelfth Aeon was cast out of the Fullness and in her place another was emitted, if indeed she is pointed out to Judas. They claim, moreover, that the Aeon suffered but that Judas is the betrayer—for even they admit that the Christ came to the passion, and Judas did not.[6] How, then, could Judas, the betrayer of him who had to suffer for our salvation, be the type and image of the Aeon who suffered passion?

3. Neither is Christ's passion similar to the Aeon's passion, nor did it happen in similar circumstances. By way of explanation, the Aeon

suffered a passion of dissolution and destruction, so that the one who suffered was in danger of perishing. On the contrary, Christ Our Lord suffered an efficacious passion, one that would not fail.[7] He was not only not in danger of perishing, but by his strength he strengthened man who had suffered corruption and recalled him to incorruption. Besides, the Aeon suffered passion when she was in search of Father and lacked the power to find him. The Lord, however, endured the passion that he might lead back to the knowledge of and union with the Father those who had strayed from him. Again, for her, search for the Father's greatness became the passion of destruction; but the Lord by his passion brought the knowledge of the Father and so bestowed salvation. Her passion produced the feminine fruit, as they say, weak,[8] formless, and inefficacious; but his passion produced the fruit of fortitude and power. The Lord, namely, by means of his passion: *When he ascended on high he made captivity itself a captive; he gave gifts to his people;*[9] and he conferred on those who believe in him [the power] *to tread on snakes and scorpions, and over all the power of the enemy,*[10] that is, of the prince of the rebellion. By his passion Our Lord likewise destroyed death, dispelled error, put an end to corruption, and destroyed ignorance; on the other hand, he manifested life, displayed the truth, and bestowed incorruption. Their Aeon, on the contrary, when she had suffered passion, was the cause of ignorance[11] and gave birth to a formless substance, from which, according to them, all the material works were brought forth—death, corruption, error, and such like.

4. Judas, therefore, the twelfth disciple, was not the type of the Aeon who suffered passion, nor was Our Lord's passion. Certainly we have proved that these are totally dissimilar and disagree with each other, not only in regard to the circumstances mentioned but also in regard to the number. That Judas was the twelfth among the twelve apostles named in the Gospel is clear to all. But this Aeon is not the twelfth but the thirtieth; for, according to their view, not merely twelve Aeons were emitted by Father's will, nor was she emitted twelfth in line, since they class her as emitted in the thirtieth place. How, then, can Judas, who is twelfth in line, be the type and image of the Aeon who is thirtieth in line?

5. Now, if they say that Judas's perishing is the image of her Intention, neither in this way will the image be similar to the truth about him. To explain, Intention was separated from the Aeon, then given a form by Christ; next she was given knowledge by Savior; and

finally, after she had made all things outside the Fullness after the image of the Aeons in the Fullness, she is said at last to have been received into the Fullness by those [Aeons] and united by conjugal union with Savior who was made out of all the Aeons.[12] But Judas, when once he was cast out, never returned to the company of the disciples, else another would not have been appointed in his place. Besides, the Lord said of him: *Woe to that one by whom the Son of man is betrayed;*[13] and: *It would have been better for that one not to have been born.* He also called him *Son of destruction.*[14] But if they say that Judas is the type of Intention, not as separated from the Aeon, but as the passion that embraced her [the Aeon], neither in this way can the number two[15] be a type of the number three. For here Judas was cast out, and Matthias was appointed in his stead; but there the Aeon is in danger of being destroyed and was ruined; and so were Intention and passion. For they distinctly separate also Intention from passion. The Aeon they present as restored, but Intention as receiving a form; passion, however, as a substance separated from these. So Judas and Matthias, being two, cannot be the type of the Aeon and Intention and passion, who are three.

CHAPTER 21

THE TWELVE APOSTLES WERE
NOT TYPES OF THE AEONS.

1. If they claim that the twelve apostles are a type of the emissions of only the twelve Aeons that Man, together with Church, emitted, then they should set up ten other apostles as a type of the other ten Aeons, who, in their own words, were emitted by Word and Life. It is irrational to say that the younger and, for that reason, inferior Aeons were manifested by Savior through the choice of the apostles, whereas the elder and, for that reason, superior [Aeons] were not manifested previously. Though the Savior (that is, if he chose the apostles in order through them to manifest the Aeons in the Fullness) could choose ten other apostles in order to manifest the second Decad, and even prior to these, eight others, in order to manifest the principal and primary Ogdoad set up as a type.[1] The reason is this: after the twelve apostles, Our Lord is found to have sent in advance of himself seventy others;[2] but seventy cannot be the type of the number

of eight or ten or thirty. For what reason, then, as we have mentioned before, are the inferior Aeons manifested by the apostles, while the superior Aeons, from which also the former were made, have no previous pattern? If the twelve apostles were chosen in order to manifest the number twelve of the Aeons, then the seventy ought in turn to have been chosen as a type of seventy Aeons. So they should no longer speak of thirty Aeons but of eighty-two. Certainly, one who makes a choice of the apostles according to the type of the Aeons in the Fullness would never make a choice of some [apostles] and not make it of others; rather, he would have tried to preserve the image in all the apostles and to manifest the type of the Aeons in the Fullness.

2. Nor may we be silent about Paul. We must demand of them of what Aeon the Apostle is said to be the type. Perhaps he is the type of their composite Savior, who exists as the aggregate of all the Aeons, and whom they also call All-Things, since he is from all the Aeons.[3] The poet Hesiod, too, has strikingly pointed him out, naming him Pandora, that is, the Gift-of-all, because from all of them the best gift was collected in him.[4] In them is verified this saying: "Hermes implanted words of fraud and thievish habits in their minds," in order to deceive the fools among men and women so that they would believe their fabrications. For the mother, that is, Leto, secretly stirred them up, without the knowledge of Demiurge, to give forth profound and unspeakable mysteries for people who have *itching ears*.[5] Now, their Mother brought it about that this mystery should be told not only by Hesiod but also very wisely in the lyrics of the poet Pindar.[6] So that he might keep Demiurge in ignorance, he pointed out Pandora in Pelops in this manner: his flesh was divided into parts by his father, then it was gathered up by all the gods and brought together and fashioned together.[7] Now, these [heretics], having been aroused because of this [Mother], say the same things as they, and are also of the same race and spirit as they.[8]

CHAPTER 22
CHRIST'S THIRTY YEARS BEFORE HIS BAPTISM ARE NOT A TYPE OF THE THIRTY AEONS.

1. We have shown that the number thirty of theirs is entirely deficient, since, according to them, sometimes a few Aeons were found in

the Fullness, sometimes again many. And so there are not thirty
Aeons. Nor did the Savior come to be baptized at the age of thirty in
order to disclose their thirty silent Aeons,[1] otherwise they must first
separate and cast him [Savior] out of the Fullness of all.

Now, they claim that he suffered in the twelfth month so that he
preached one year after baptism; and they make an attempt to confirm
this from the prophet; for it is written: *To proclaim the year of the Lord's
favor, and the day of vengeance of our God.*[2] They are really blind persons;
they boast that they discovered the depths of Profundity, and yet they do
not understand the *acceptable year of the Lord*, and *the day of vengeance* of
which Isaiah spoke. In truth, in the prophet there is no question of a day
with twelve hours, or of a year with twelve months. They themselves
admit that the prophets spoke many things in parables and allegories,
and not according to the literal meaning of the words themselves.[3]

2. So *the day of vengeance* spoken of is a day on which the Lord will
render to each one according to his deeds,[4] that is, the judgment. *The
acceptable year of the Lord*, however, is the present time, in which those
who believe in him are called and become acceptable to God; that is,
the entire time from his coming until the consummation, during which
he acquires as his fruit those who are saved. For, according to the
prophet's phrase, *the day of vengeance* follows the year; and so the
prophet would have lied if the Lord had preached only one year, and if
the prophet were speaking of that. Where is *the day of vengeance*? For the
year (according to them) has passed, and *the day of vengeance* has not yet
come; no, *he makes his sun to rise on the evil and on the good, and sends rain
on the righteous and on the unrighteous.*[5] Besides, the righteous suffer persecution and are afflicted and killed, whereas the sinners have abun-
dance, *whose feasts consist of lyre and harp, tambourine and flute and wine,
but who do not regard the deeds of the Lord.*[6] Now, according to the
[prophet's] statement about *the year* and *the day of vengeance*, they ought
to be joined together and *the day of vengeance* ought to follow *the year*. It
was said, namely, *to proclaim the acceptable year of the Lord, and the day of
vengeance.* And so the present time in which people are called and saved
by the Lord is well understood to be *the acceptable year of the Lord*; and this
is followed by *the day of vengeance*, that is, the judgment. This present
time, moreover, is not only called year but also day, both by the prophet
and by Paul. Of these things the Apostle, mindful of the Scriptures,
wrote in his Epistle to the Romans: *As it is written, "For your sake we are
being killed all day long; we are accounted as sheep to be slaughtered."*[7] Here *all*

the day long is said of the present time in which we suffer persecution and are killed as sheep. So, just as this *day* does not mean a day made up of twelve hours but the entire time in which those who believe in Christ suffer and are put to death for his sake, so also the year is not one of twelve months but is the entire time of faith in which people who hear the preaching believe and become acceptable to the Lord by uniting themselves with him.

3. It is very surprising how they claim to have found the depths[8] of God and have not searched the Gospels to see how often after his baptism the Lord went up to Jerusalem at the time of the Passover according to the custom of the Jews from every country to assemble every year at this time in Jerusalem and there celebrate the feast of the Passover. The first time he went up to the feast of the Passover was after he had made wine out of water in Cana of Galilee.[9] Of that occasion this was written: *For many believed in him, when they saw his signs which he did.*[10] That is what John, the disciple of the Lord, recorded. After withdrawing himself, he is found in Samaria, where, too, he disputed with the Samaritan woman[11] and healed the centurion's son, who was absent, by just a word. *Go*, he said: *Your son will live.*[12] After that he went up to Jerusalem for the feast of Passover the second time[13] At that time he healed the paralytic who had been lying beside the pool for thirty-eight years. He commanded him to rise and take up his bed and go home.[14] Again he departed to the other side of Lake Tiberias, where, when a large crowd had followed him, he satisfied that entire multitude with five loaves of bread; and twelve baskets of fragments were left over.[15] Next, when he had raised Lazarus from the dead,[16] and the Pharisees were in ambush plotting against him, he withdrew to the city of Ephraim.[17] Then it is written that six days before the day of the Passover he came to Bethany.[18] From Bethany he went up to Jerusalem and ate the pasch and suffered on the following day.[19] Now, everyone will admit that these three times[20] of the Passover do not make one year. Besides, the month itself in which the Passover is celebrated and in which the Lord suffered is not the twelfth but the first. These [Gnostics] who boast that they know all things can, if they are ignorant of this, learn it from Moses.[21] So their solution about the year and the twelfth month has been shown false, and they must reject their solution or the Gospel; otherwise how did the Lord preach only one year?

4. He was thirty years old when he came up to be baptized. Then, when he had the mature age of a teacher, he came to Jerusalem, so that

all would reasonably accept him as a teacher. For he did not appear to be one thing while he was another, as those say who introduce him as a man only in appearance. He actually was what he appeared to be. So, when he was teacher, he also had the age of a teacher. He did not reject human nature or exalt himself above it, nor did he abrogate in himself his own law [given in behalf] of the human race; but he sanctified every age by a likeness to himself. Surely, he came to save all people through himself; I say all who would again be born to God—infants, children, youth, young adults, elderly.[22] Therefore, he passed through every age. Becoming an infant among infants, he sanctified infants; becoming a child among children, he sanctified those having this age and at the same time became for them an example of piety and righteousness and obedience; becoming a young adult among young adults, he was an example for young adults and sanctified them to the Lord. In the same way, he became also an elderly person among the elderly, so that he might be a mature teacher for all, not merely by explaining the truth but also by his age, that is, by at the same time sanctifying the elderly and being an example for them. Lastly, he came even to death so that he might be *the Firstborn from the dead*, himself *holding the primacy in all things*,[23] the Author of life,[24] prior to all and going before all.

5. These [Gnostics], however, in order to maintain their fabrication about the passage, *to proclaim the acceptable year of the Lord*, claim that he preached one year and suffered in the twelfth month. It is to their disadvantage that they are forgetful [in speaking thus], destroying his [Christ's] entire work and taking away from him the age that is more necessary and more honorable—that more advanced age, I say, in which he has priority over all, even by teaching. Really, how did he have disciples if he did not teach? How did he teach if he did not have the age of a teacher? For he came to be baptized as one who had not completed his thirtieth year but who had only begun to be about the age of thirty. For so Luke, who noted his age, wrote: Jesus *was beginning about the age of thirty years*[25] when he came to be baptized. And if from his baptism he preached only one year,[26] then when he completed the thirtieth year, he suffered, being still a young adult, not having as yet the more advanced age. But everyone will acknowledge that the age of thirty is the first sign of a young adult, and it extends till the fortieth year.[27] From the fortieth and fiftieth year one already declines to old age. When Our Lord reached this age he taught.

Witnesses of this are the Gospels and all the presbyters in Asia who were united with John, the Lord's disciple. They [claim] that John handed the same tradition down to them. Now John continued among them till the time of Trajan.[28] Moreover, some of them saw not only John but other apostles, and they heard these same things from them and bear witness to this account. Whom must we rather believe? Men like these, or Ptolemaeus, who never saw the apostles, and who not even in dreams came near to a footprint of an apostle?

6. Even the Jews who at that time argued with the Lord Jesus Christ most clearly pointed out the same thing. To explain, when the Lord said to them: *Your ancestor Abraham rejoiced that he would see my day; he saw it and was glad*, they answered him: *You are not yet fifty years old, and have you seen Abraham?*[29] Now this is fittingly said of one who is past the age of forty but has not yet reached the age of fifty, though he is not far from fifty. Of one who is thirty years old one might say, "You are not yet forty years old." Certainly, those who wished to show him up as a liar would not greatly increase the age which they noticed him to have; but they would keep close to his real age, either because they knew it from the public tax register or took a guess according to the years over forty that they saw him to have, but not the age of thirty. For it is altogether irrational that they would lie by twenty years, since they wished show that he was younger than Abraham's times. They spoke of what they saw; he, however, whom they saw was not putative, but the Truth. So he was not far from fifty years, and for this reason they said: *You are not yet fifty years old, and have you seen Abraham?* Therefore, he preached not only for one year, nor did he suffer in the twelfth month. To be sure, the time from the thirtieth till the fiftieth year can never be one year,[30] unless perhaps among their Aeons such long years have been assigned to those who sit in the Fullness with Profundity according to rank! The poet Homer spoke of these, since he too was inspired by their Mother who had gone astray: "The gods sat beside Jove and held court on the golden floor."[31]

CHAPTER 23

THE WOMAN SUFFERING FROM THE HEMORRHAGE
WAS NOT A TYPE OF THE AEON IN PASSION.

1. Their ignorance, moreover, is evident also in regard to the woman who, suffering from hemorrhage, touched the tassel of the Lord's cloak and was healed.[1] They assert that through her is manifested the twelfth Power, that is, the twelfth Aeon, who suffered passion and was overflowing without limit.[2] Now, first of all, as we have shown, this Aeon is not the twelfth according to their system. For good measure, however, let us add also this. There were twelve Aeons; eleven are said to have remained without passion but the twelfth suffered passion. Contrariwise, the woman who was healed in the twelfth year clearly suffered continuously for eleven years but was healed in the twelfth. If it were said that the eleven Aeons suffered incurable passion, while the twelfth was healed, it would have been plausible to say that the woman was a type of those eleven. However, since she suffered for eleven years without being healed but was healed in the twelfth year, in what way can she be the type of the twelfth Aeon, when this one alone suffered passion, while the other eleven in no way suffered passion? True, at times a type and an image depart from the truth in regard to matter, but in regard to the shape they must retain the likeness; likewise, by what is present they must manifest what is not present.[3]

2. The number of the years of the illness which they claim to adapt to their fabrication has been mentioned not only in the case of this woman, mark well, but also in the case of another woman who, after being ill for eighteen years, was likewise healed. Of her the Lord said: *And ought not this woman, a daughter of Abraham whom Satan bound for eighteen long years, be set free…on the sabbath day?*[4] So if the first woman was a type of the twelfth Aeon who suffered passion, then this one ought to be the type of an eighteenth Aeon who suffered passion. But this they cannot prove; for then their primary and principal Ogdoad would be numbered with the Aeons who suffered passion. Still another person was healed by the Lord, who had suffered for thirty-eight years.[5] Let them, then, speak of a thirty-eighth Aeon that suffered passion. For, if they claim that the Lord's deeds are types of the things in the Fullness, then the typology must be retained in all of them. But neither can the woman who was healed after eighteen years nor the man who was

healed after thirty-eight years be fit into their fabrication. It is stupid and entirely inconsistent to say that the Savior preserved the type in some of them but did not preserve it in others. And so the type of the woman is unlike the arrangement of the Aeons.[6]

CHAPTER 24
THE GNOSTIC ARGUMENTS, LETTERS, AND SYLLABLES ARE ABSURD.

1. Again, the very fact that they attempt to adduce proofs at times from numbers, at times from syllables of names, at times from letters of syllables, at times by numbers that are represented by the Greek letters[1]—that demonstrates their machination and unstable fabrication to be false. This shows up most clearly, too, the perplexity and instability of their "knowledge" and its twisted character. To explain, they translate the name Jesus, which is of a foreign language, by a number of the Greek language. Sometimes they call it "symbol," having six letters; sometimes it has the number 888, which is the full-ness of the Ogdoads.[2] But they kept silent about the Greek name of Jesus, which is *Sōtēr*, because it does not fit their fabrication, either in regard to number or in regard to letters. And, truly, if by divine fore-sight the Lord's names were given the power of numbers and letters to signify a number of the Fullness, then *Sōtēr*, being a Greek name, ought to have manifested the mystery of the Fullness both by letters and by numbers, according to the Greek language. That, however, is not the case, because it consists of five letters, and its numerical value is 1408.[3] But these have nothing in common with their Fullness. So this arrangement in the Fullness about which they speak is not true.

2. The name Jesus, moreover, according to the language of the Hebrews, consists of two and a half letters, as the learned among them say.[4] It points out the Lord who contains heaven and earth, because according to the ancient Hebrew language Jesus means heaven (and earth; heaven indeed is called *shemaim)* and the earth *ueres.*[5] So *Jesus* itself is the word that contains heaven and earth. False, too, therefore, is their explanation of the Symbol. And so their number is clearly refuted. To clarify, according to their own language, the Greek word *Sōtēr* has five letters; but according to the Hebrew language *Jesus* has

two and a half letters. Hence, the number of the calculation that is 888 also collapses. Above all, the Hebrew letters do not agree with the number of the Greek [letters]; but these [the Hebrew letters] ought especially to preserve the calculation of the names since they are the more ancient and more powerful. The ancient and first Hebrew letters, also called priestly,[6] are indeed ten in number; but some [of these] are written for [the number] fifteen, namely, the last letter is joined to the first.[7] On this account they write some letters in the sequence we do; but others in the reverse order, lining the letters up from right to left.[8]

Besides, the name Christ, who according to what they say, was emitted for stabilizing and correcting their Fullness, ought also to have a calculation corresponding to the Aeons of their Fullness. Likewise, even Father, both as to letters and number, ought to have contained the number of Aeons who were emitted by him. Furthermore, even Profundity, and no less Only-begotten, but chiefly and above all, the name that is called God—which in Hebrew is also called Baruch—and has two and a half letters.[9] And now, from the fact that these more secure names of the Hebrew and Greek languages do not agree with their fabrication either in number or in calculation of the letters, the calculation about the rest appears impudently forced.

3. To explain, they attempt by force to manufacture proofs from the law by choosing whatever agrees with the number in their heresy. Now, if it had been planned for their Mother, or Savior, to manifest types of things in the Fullness through Demiurge, they would have taken care that there be types in truer and holier things, most of all in the ark of the covenant itself, on account of which the entire tabernacle of the covenant was built. Now the ark was made two and a half cubits long, one and a half cubits wide, and one and a half cubits high.[10] This number of cubits, however, in no way agrees with their fabrication, though the types should have been manifested chiefly through it. Likewise, the propitiatory in no way agrees with their explanations.[11] Moreover, the table of proposition was two cubits long, one cubit wide, and one and a half cubits high. It stood before the Holy of Holies,[12] and yet throughout this [Holy of Holies] there is not even one numerical quantity that contains an indication of a Tetrad or an Ogdoad or of the rest of their Fullness.[13] But what of the candelabrum, which has (six) branches but seven lamps?[14] To be sure, if they had been made to serve as a type, the candelabrum should have

eight branches and just as many lamps, to typify the primary Ogdoad that shines for the Aeons and lights up the entire Fullness. They have carefully counted up the ten curtains, claiming these are a type of the ten Aeons.[15] But they did not count the skin coverings, which were eleven in number.[16] Nor did they measure the size of the curtains—each one was twenty-eight cubits long.[17] The planks that were ten cubits long they explain of the ten Aeons. *But the width of each plank was one and a half cubits*;[18] this they do not explain, nor the number of all the planks, nor the bars of the planks, because these have nothing in common with their system. But what of the oil of anointing, which consecrated the whole tabernacle?[19] Perhaps Savior did not know of this, or while their Mother slept, Demiurge of his own accord gave orders as to its weight; hence it does not harmonize with their Fullness. It contains, besides the oil, 500 shekels of myrrh, 500 of cassia, 250 of cinnamon, 250 of aromatic cane, so that it is a mixture of five ingredients.[20] In like manner, the incense was made of stacte, onycha, galbanum, mint, and frankincense.[21] These have nothing in common with their system, neither in [number of ingredients], nor in weight. The types, then, were not preserved in these sublime and more beautiful institutions of the law, whereas in the rest, namely, wherever a number agrees with what they say, there is a type of the beings in the Fullness. This is inconsistent and entirely stupid, because every number occurs in the Scriptures in a variety of ways, so that, if anyone would so wish, he could construct from the Scriptures not only an Ogdoad, a Decad, and a Dodecad, but any number, and assert this to be a type of the error devised by him.

4. That this is true will be shown as follows from the Scriptures by the number called five, which, however, has nothing in common with their system, does not agree with their fabrication, and is not suitable for them to prove a type of beings in the Fullness. *Sōtēr* is a name of five letters and so is *Patēr*. *Agapē* too has five letters. Likewise Our Lord blessed five loaves of bread and fed five thousand men;[22] five prudent virgins were mentioned by the Lord, and also five foolish ones.[23] Again, five men were said to have been with the Lord when he received the testimony from the Father, namely, Peter, James, John, Moses, and Elijah.[24] Moreover, the Lord was the fifth to enter the house of the dead girl when he raised her to life. For *he did not allow anyone to enter...except Peter...and James and the child's father and mother.*[25] The famous rich man, too, who was in hell, said he had five brothers,

to whom he begged someone should go who had risen from the dead.[26] The swimming pool where the Lord ordered the paralytic who had been healed to go to his house had five porches.[27] The form of the cross itself has five extremities, two on the length, two on the width, and one in the middle, on which the person rested who was fastened with the nails.[28] Each of our hands has five fingers, and we have five senses; our internal organs, too, are five in number—the heart, the liver, the lungs, the spleen, the kidneys. Further, the whole man can be divided into that number of parts—the head, the breast, the belly, the thighs, the feet. The human being passes through five ages—first he is an infant, then a child, then a youth, then a young adult, finally an elderly man.[29] Moses handed down the law in five books. Each of the tables he received from God had five commandments.[30] The veil covering the Holy of Holies had five pillars.[31] And the altar of the holocaust was five cubits wide.[32] In the desert five priests were chosen—Aaron, Nadab, Abiud, Eleazar, and Ithamar.[33] The tunic and the breastplate and other priestly vestments were woven out of five materials: they consisted of gold, violet, purple, scarlet, and fine linen.[34] And Joshua, the son of Nun, shut up in a cave five kings of the Amorites and gave their heads to the people to trample on.[35] Many other thousands like things with this number, or if one wishes, with any number, can be collected either from the Scriptures or from the surrounding works of nature. In spite of all this, we do not say that there are five Aeons above Demiurge, nor do we consecrate the number five as if it were some divine being. We attempt to confirm neither unstable tenets nor silly talk by such useless labor. Nor do we force the creation, which was well ordered by God, to be badly applied to types of things that do not exist, and to introduce impious and evil opinions, because an exposé and refutation can be worked out by everyone who has intelligence.[36]

5. For example, who would concede to them that the reason why the year has only 365 days is that twelve months of thirty days each might be a type of the twelve Aeons, even though the type is not in agreement?[37] For in that case each of the Aeons is a thirtieth part of the entire Fullness, but they themselves say that the month is a twelfth of a year. If the year were divided into thirty months and the month into twelve days, then the type might be considered in agreement with their falsehood. But actually, contrariwise, their Fullness is divided into thirty Aeons and a part of it into twelve; while in this case [of the

year] every year is divided into twelve parts, and a part of it into thirty [days]. And so Savior stupidly made the month a type of the entire Fullness, but the year, of the Dodecad that is in the Fullness. Really, it would have been more congruous to divide the year into thirty [parts], as the entire Fullness; but the month into twelve parts, as the Aeons in their Fullness. Besides these [Gnostics] divide the entire Fullness into three parts, that is, the Ogdoad, the Decad, and the Dodecad; but the year here [below] is divided into four parts, namely, spring, summer, autumn, and winter. Nor do the months, which they claim are a type of the Triacontad, have a preestablished thirty days; some have more and some have less, since there are five days super-added to them.[38] Nor do the days always have a preestablished twelve hours, but all the way from nine to fifteen, and in reverse, from fifteen to nine.[39] And so the months of thirty days were not made on account of the thirty Aeons, for then they would have a preestablished thirty days. Nor were the days of the months made so that they [Gnostics] might pattern the twelve Aeons on the twelve hours, for then the days would always have a preestablished pattern of twelve hours.

6. Furthermore, if they call material substances left hand, and claim that those who belong to the left hand necessarily tend to cor-ruption, but that Savior came to the lost sheep that he might transfer it to the right side, that is, to the ninety-nine sheep that were on the saved side, which had not been lost but remained in the sheepfold; in that case they would have to agree that the ninety-nine were not on the side of the saved, since they belonged to the raising of the left hand.[40] They are forced, too, to confess that whatever does not in like manner have the same number belongs to the left hand, that is, to corruption.[41] So the Greek word *agapē*, according to the Greek letters by which they make their computation, having as it does the numeri-cal value of ninety-three, also belongs to the raising of the left hand. *Aleithia*, too, according to the above method, has the numeric value of sixty-four and so takes its place on the side of material substances. According to that, they will be compelled to admit that absolutely all the names of sacred things that do not reach the numeric value of one hundred, but have only the numbers that are counted on the left hand, are corruptible and material.

Chapter 25

Investigations about God Must Be Rational and Humble.

1. If someone should reply, what then? Are the giving of names and the choice of apostles, and the Lord's activity, and the arrangement of created things something empty and aimless?[1] We would answer: Certainly not! On the contrary, all things have clearly been made by God harmonious and beautiful with great wisdom and care, both the ancient things and whatever his Word has made in this last epoch. One must, however, not connect these things with the number thirty, but with an existing system.[2] Nor should one make an inquiry into God by means of numbers and syllables and letters. For that would be a weak system because of the multitude and variety [of numbers, syllables, letters], and because at the present day every kind of system that has been similarly devised by someone can draw from these numbers testimonies contrary to the truth, since they [numbers] can be adapted to many things. On the contrary, the numbers themselves and all created things must be harmonized with the existing system of truth. For a rule does not come from numbers, but numbers from a rule; neither does God [come] from created things, but created things come from God. For all things are from the one and same God.

2. There are many and varied things in creation, and they are well ordered and harmonious in relation to the whole creation, though considered individually they are opposed to each other and discordant. By way of illustration, the sound of the harp, though it consists of many and opposite notes, forms one harmonious melody by the intervals between the notes. So the lover of truth should not be deceived by the interval between the notes; nor should he suspect one artist and author for the one, another for the other; nor that one arranged the high notes, another the low, and still another those in the middle. No, there is one and the same [author] for displaying the wisdom, the justice, the goodness, and the artistry of the total work.[3] Rather, those who listen to the melody ought to praise and extol the artist; and admire the high pitch of some notes; and pay attention to the low pitch of others; and listen to the middle pitch of still others;[4] and consider the type of some notes and to what each one is related; and find out the reason for each one. But they should never change

the rule, or stray from the Artist, or reject the faith in the one God who made all things, or blaspheme our Creator.[5]

3. If, however, anyone should not find the reason for all things about which he inquired, let him remember that man is infinitely inferior to God, and that man has received grace only in part and is not yet equal or like to the Creator; and, unlike God, he cannot experience and know all things. On the contrary, to the degree that he who today was made and began to exist as creature is inferior to him who was not made and who is always the same, to that degree he is inferior to him who made him, in knowledge and for investigating the reasons of all things. For you, O man, are not increate, nor did you always exist along with God, as his own Word did; but because of his preeminent goodness you now begin to exist as a creature and gradually learn from the Word the economies of God who made you.[6]

4. So, keep order in your knowledge and, ignorant as you are of what is good, do not go beyond God himself; for no one can go beyond him. Neither go in search of what is above the Creator; you will not find it, for your Artificer is without limits. Even though you were like one who had measured this entire universe and had traversed through its every creature and had considered its every depth or height or length, you will not excogitate another Father above the Creator. As a matter of fact, you cannot excogitate such a one; on the contrary, by reasoning contrary to nature, you will be unwise; and if you continue in this, you will go mad, esteeming yourself superior to and better than your Creator, and as one who will go beyond his kingdoms.

Chapter 26
Knowledge Puffs Up; Charity Builds Up.

1. It is, therefore, better and more useful that they be unlettered and know very little and come near to God through love than that, thinking they know much and have much experience, they be found among the blasphemers of their Sovereign,[1] by having fabricated another God the Father. In view of this, Paul exclaimed: *Knowledge puffs up, but love builds up.*[2] He did not find blame with true knowledge about God—in that he would blame himself first—but because he was aware that certain ones would be puffed up under pretense of knowl-

edge and so fall away from the love of God, and because of that they would think themselves perfect, the while introducing the imperfect Demiurge. It was to cut down their pride due to such knowledge that Paul said: *Knowledge puffs up, but love builds up.* Now, there is no greater conceit than to think that one is better and more perfect than he who created and formed us,[3] and gave us the breath of life,[4] and bestowed existence itself. And so it is better, as I have said, for one who knows nothing at all, not even one reason for anything created as to why it was created, to believe God and continue in his love,[5] than by knowledge of this kind to be puffed up and fall away from love, which gives life to man.[6] [It is better] not to go in search of knowledge about anything else than Jesus Christ the Son of God, who was crucified for us,[7] than through subtle questions and hairsplitting to fall into impiety.

2. To illustrate, suppose someone was puffed up a little by attempts such as those mentioned and would wish, because of this saying of the Lord—*And even the hairs of your head are all counted*[8]—to investigate out of curiosity and find out the number of hairs on each head and also the reason why one has this amount of hair and another that amount. Really, not all have an equal number, but many thousands upon thousands varying numbers have been found, due to the fact that some have larger heads and others smaller heads; some have always a thick head of hair, others a thin head, while still others have very little hair. Now what if those who think they have found the number of hairs try to apply that as a testimony for their heresy that they have excogitated! Or again, suppose someone, on account of this Gospel saying—*Are not two sparrows sold for a penny? Yet not one of them will fall to the ground apart from your Father,*[9]—would wish to count the sparrows that were caught each day the world over or in one country and discover the reason why so many were caught yesterday, so many the day before, and so many today, and would fit the number of sparrows to his system. Would he not utterly deceive himself and drive those who agree with him into madness? There are, of course, always men around who want to be thought of as having found something bigger in such matters than their teachers have.[10]

3. To continue, suppose someone were to put this question to us: Is every number of all things that have been or will be made known to God, and was it by God's foresight that each of these received the size it actually has? [And suppose] that, upon our admitting[11] that absolutely nothing of the things that have been made or are being

made or will be made escapes God's knowledge, but that each one of them, because of his foresight, receives and had received its shape and order and number and proper size, and that absolutely nothing was or is made uselessly and aimlessly,[12] but with great harmony and sublime insight, and that it takes a marvelous and truly divine "Word" even to distinguish all of them and tell their proper reasons.[13] Now, suppose he accepts this testimony from us and agrees to it, and then proceeds to count the sand and the pebbles of the earth, and also the waves of the sea, and the stars of the heavens, and think up the reasons for the numbers he has discovered. Would not all who have understanding rightly say that such a one labors uselessly and is senseless and irrational? And the more (than others) that he occupies himself with questions of this sort, and the more he thinks that he has found more than others, calling the rest inexperienced, unlettered, and ensouled because they do not admit his quite useless work, so much the more is he mad and stupid, as if struck by lightning, since he yields to God in nothing. And by the knowledge that he thinks to have found he changes God himself and extols his own mind above the greatness of the Creator.

CHAPTER 27

THE CORRECT INTERPRETATION OF THE
PARABLES AND OTHER PASSAGES OF SCRIPTURE.

1. The sound and safe and religious and truth-loving mind will readily apply itself to the things God placed within the power of men and granted to our knowledge. It will make progress in them because by daily exercise it will make easy for itself the acquisition of knowledge.[1] These are the things that come under our eyes and are expressed in the Sacred Scriptures clearly and unambiguously by the words themselves.[2] And so the parables may not be adapted to ambiguous matters. That way both he who interprets them will interpret them safely, and the parables will be explained by all in a similar manner. Thus, the body of Truth will continue entire, harmonious in its members and unshaken.[3] But to combine things that are not expressed openly or placed under our eyes with the explanations of the parables,[4] explanations that anyone excogitates at will, is unrea-

sonable. It would result in no one's having a Rule of the Truth.[5] On the contrary, as many interpreters of the parables as there would be, just so many truths would be seen at war with each other and setting up contradictory opinions, as is the case with the questions of the pagan philosophers.

2. According to that reasoning, then, man would always be in search without ever finding, because he had rejected the very method of investigation. And when the Bridegroom comes, one who has not prepared his lamp, with the result that it does not shine with the brightness of a clear light, will run back to those who parcel out the explanations of the parables in darkness. Since he forsakes him who by his clear preaching gratuitously grants him entrance, he is also excluded from his wedding hall.[6]

Since, therefore, the entire Scriptures, both the Prophets and the Gospels,[7] clearly and unambiguously—so they can equally be heard by all, even though all do not believe that there is only one God to the exclusion of others—preach that through his own Word God made all things, whether visible or invisible, whether heavenly or earthly, whether aquatic or subterranean creatures, as we have demonstrated from the very words of the Scriptures. Furthermore, since the very creation in which we are testifies, by the things that come under our eyes, to this same thing, namely, that there is one who made it [creation] and governs it, those persons will seem very dull who blind their eyes in the face of such clear manifestations and refuse to see the light of the preaching.[8] They put themselves in fetters, and each one of them thinks that he has discovered his own god by obscure explanations of the parables. They themselves testify that in none of the Scriptures is anything said openly and by the words themselves and indisputably about Father who was thought up by those who themselves hold contradictory opinions. In fact, they themselves bear witness to these things when they say that it was in secret that Savior taught these things not to all but to those disciples capable of grasping them,[9] who understand what he pointed out through enigmas and parables.

They arrive at the point where they say that the God who is preached differs from the one who is presented as Father in the parables and enigmas.[10]

3. Since, however, the parables can be given many interpretations, what lover of the Truth will not acknowledge that for these individuals to affirm that God is to be discovered by means of parables,

while forsaking what is certain and indubitable and true, this behavior is characteristic of people who very rashly hurl themselves into danger and act as if they are irrational?

And does this not amount to building one's house not on solid and strong rock set in the open but on the uncertainty of shifting sand?[11] That makes the overthrow of such a building easy.

CHAPTER 28

PERFECT KNOWLEDGE CANNOT BE ATTAINED IN THE PRESENT LIFE.

1. Since, then, we possess the Rule of Truth[1] itself and the manifest testimony about God, we ought not to cast out the solid and true knowledge about God by running from one solution to another. No, it is proper to direct the solution of difficulties toward that standard [the Rule], and to discipline ourselves by investigating the mystery and economy of the existent God, and to grow in the love of him who has done and does so much for our sakes. Never should we, however, give up the conviction that most clearly preaches that he alone is truly God and Father who both made this world and fashioned humanity and endowed his creation with [the power of] developing and gave the call [of rising] from his lesser [stages] to greater ones that are within himself.[2] To illustrate, he brings the infant that was conceived in the womb out into the light of day; and the wheat, after it has matured on the stem, he places in the granary.[3] Still one and the same Creator fashioned the womb and created the sun; one and the same Lord brought forth the stem, made the wheat grow and multiply[4] and prepared the granary.

2. If, however, we cannot find a solution for all things in the Scriptures, nevertheless let us not look for another God besides the one who exists. That is the greatest impiety. Such matters we must leave to God who created us, since we know very well that the Scriptures are perfect, inasmuch as they were given by God's Word and Spirit.[5] We, however, precisely inasmuch as we are inferior to God's Word and his Spirit, have need of a knowledge of his mysteries.[6] It should be no surprise if, in matters spiritual and heavenly and such as need to be revealed, we experience this, because even matters that

are at our feet—I mean, that are in this creation, and that we can touch and see that are with us—many of these matters escape our knowledge, and we leave even these to God. The fact is, he must be more excellent than all things. What happens when we try to explain the reason for the rise of the Nile? We give many answers, perhaps plausible, perhaps not plausible, but what actually is true, certain, and secure is in God's keeping. Another example, the habitat of the birds that come to our regions in spring and suddenly leave in autumn escapes our knowledge, though this takes place in this world. And what can we explain about the tide and ebb of the ocean, though it is evident that there is a certain case for it? Or what can we say about the things that lie beyond it, of what nature they are?[7] Or what can we say about the rains and lightnings and thunders and gathering of clouds and fogs and the issuing of the winds and other similar things, how they are brought about? Or what can we tell about the storehouses of snow and hail,[8] and other things like these? What kind of preparation is made for the clouds, and what is the nature of fog? What causes the moon to increase and decrease? What is the reason for the difference in waters and metals and stones and things of that sort? While trying to find the causes of such things we can really be loquacious; yet God alone, who made them, can tell the truth.

3. If, therefore, even among things of the created world some are in God's keeping, while we, too, have knowledge of others, why should it be irksome if while searching the Scriptures—since all the Scriptures are spiritual—we, with God's grace, explain some of the things, though we leave others in God's keeping—and that not only in this world but also in the next—so that God may always teach and man may always learn from God?[9] Just as the Apostle said, when all other things have been destroyed, these will continue, namely: faith, hope, and love.[10] For *faith* in our teacher continues firm, assuring us that there is only one who is truly God and that we should really *love* God always, since he alone is Father; and that consequently we should *hope* to receive something more and to learn from God that he is good and possesses unlimited riches, an eternal kingdom, and infinite knowledge.[11] So if, according to the method stated, we leave some of the questions in God's hands, we shall keep our faith, and we our-selves shall persevere without danger; and we will find that all the Scripture given us by God harmonizes, and the parables harmonize with the things that are expressly stated, and the plain statements

explain the parables. Thus, through the many voices of the passages there will be heard among us one harmonious melody[12] that hymns praises to God who made all things. If, for example, anyone should ask us what God did before he created the world, we reply that the answer to this is in God's keeping. The Scriptures do teach us that this world was made complete[13] by God when it began in time; but no Scripture reveals what God did before this. So the answer to this is in God's keeping; and you should not desire to discover foolish, sense-less,[14] and blasphemous emissions, nor reject God himself who made all things, by thinking you have discovered the emission of matter.[15]

4. All you who excogitate such things should do some thinking! The Father alone is called God, as he truly is, whom you call Demiurge. The Scriptures know only this God; and the Lord acknowledges only him as his own Father[16] and knows of no other, as we shall prove from his very words. In view of that, when you claim that this very God is the fruit of degeneracy and the emission of ignorance who is ignorant of the things above himself, and whatever else you might say of him, reflect on the gravity of the blasphemy against him who is truly God. You seem to assert solemnly[17] that you believe in God, but then, though you cannot prove another god, you declare that this very God whom you claim to believe in is the fruit of degeneracy and the emis-sion of ignorance. The result for you is such blindness and foolish talk that you leave nothing to God. No, you wish to preach about the gen-erations and the emissions of God himself and of his Thought, of Word and Life and Christ too. You get these things from nowhere else than the activities of women and men. You do not understand that in man, who is a composite ensouled being, as we said above,[18] one might speak of such things, namely, of man's mind and of man's thought, and that from the mind came thought, and from the thought the intention, and from the intention the word. Really, according to the Greeks, the word is the directing power that develops thought; that is something else from the organ by which the word is uttered.[19] So at times man rests and is silent; at times he speaks and acts. But since God is all mind, all intelligence, all spirit who is active, all light, and always existing the same and unchangeable,[20] things beneficial for us to know about God, as we also learn from the Scriptures, such activi-ties and parts cannot properly belong to God. The tongue, being fleshy, is not able to keep up with the speed of the human mind, which is spiritual; hence our word is held back within and is not

instantaneously uttered as it was conceived by the mind, but piece-
meal, as the tongue can minister to it.

5. Since, however, God is all Mind and all Word, what he thinks
he speaks, and what he speaks he thinks. For his thought is his Word,
and what he speaks he thinks. For his thought is his Word, and his
Word is his Mind; and the Mind that contains all things is the Father
himself. Whoever, therefore, speaks of God's Mind and gives to this
Mind an emission of its own proclaims him [God] to be a composite
being, as if God were one thing and Mind, his principal [emission]
another.[21] Again, [if anyone speaks] of the Word in the same manner,
making it the third emission in line from Father, which means that he
is ignorant of his [Father's] greatness, he has separated the Word very
far from God. The Prophet, indeed, said of him: *Who shall declare his
generation?*[22] But you who divine his origin from Father and apply to
God's Word the emission of the human word made with the tongue
are with good reason exposed by your own selves as ignorant of both
human and divine matters.

6. Puffed up in an irrational manner, you impudently assert that
you know all the ineffable mysteries of God; whereas the Lord, God's
very Son, admitted that the Father alone knows the very day of judgment and the hour. He said clearly: *But about that day and hour no one
knows...nor the Son, but only the Father.*[23] So if the Son was not ashamed to
refer the knowledge of that day to the Father, but told the truth, neither
should we be ashamed to leave to God the more important questions
we encounter. Really, no one is above the teacher.[24] If, then, anyone
should ask us, How was the Son emitted by the Father? we reply, No one
understands this emission, or generation, or calling, or manifestation,
whatever name one might call his ineffable generation.[25] Valentinus
does not understand it, nor do Marcion, Saturninus, Basilides, the
Angels, the Archangels, the Principalities, or the Powers.[26] Only the
Father who begot him does, and the Son who was born. And so since
his generation is ineffable, those who attempt to explain the generations and emissions are not in their right mind, since they promise to
declare things that are unutterable. All people certainly know that the
word is emitted by thought and understanding. So those who thought
up the emissions discovered neither anything great nor a hidden mystery, if they applied to God's Only-begotten Word what is understood by
all. And though they call him Unspeakable and Unnameable, they set
forth the emission and generation of his first offspring,[27] as if they them-

selves had been midwives at his birth. Thus, they liken him to the word emitted by men and women.

7. We shall, moreover, not go wrong if we follow the same procedure in regard to material substance, since God produced it. To be sure, we have learned from the Scriptures that God has dominion over all things; but from what source and how God produced matter no passage of Scripture has explained. Nor ought we to make an imaginary picture of it by conjecturing out of our own opinions an infinite number of things about God. We must cede this knowledge to God.

In like manner, why, since all things were made by God, certain creatures were guilty of transgression and withdrew from submission to God, while certain others, even the majority, continued and still continue to be submissive to him who made them;[28] also what the nature is of those who transgressed, and what the nature of those who persevered, we must leave up to God and to his Word, to whom alone he has said: *Sit at my right hand until I make your enemies your footstool.*[29] We, however, are still sojourning on this earth and are not yet seated near his throne.[30] And even though the Spirit of the Savior, who is in him, *searches everything, even the depths of God;*[31] nevertheless, *Now there are varieties of gifts…and there are varieties of services,…and there are varieties of activities…;*[32] and on earth, as Paul said: *For we know only in part, and we prophesy only in part.*[33] So in proportion to our partial knowledge we ought to leave all difficulties up to him who grants a portion of grace.

The Lord told us plainly, and the rest of the Scriptures prove, that eternal fire is prepared for sinners.[34] The Scriptures likewise prove that God foreknew that this would happen, just as in the beginning he prepared the eternal fire for those who would sin. But neither does any Scripture relate, nor does the Apostle tell us, nor did the Lord teach what the cause of the nature itself of sinners is. And so we ought to leave the knowledge of this to God, just as the Lord did the knowledge of the hour and day;[35] we ought not to endanger ourselves to the extent of leaving nothing to God—we who receive only a portion of grace. Moreover, in seeking after the things that are above us and that we cannot attain, we ought not[36] to be so bold as to unveil God and the things that have not yet been discovered as if we had already discovered God, the very Creator of all things, by our senseless talk about emissions. Nor [ought] we to assert that he got his substance from degeneracy and ignorance, and in this way fabricate an impious system against God.

8. Next, they have no witness to the fabrication that was recently originated by them, sometimes by the aid of all sorts of numbers, sometimes by syllables, and sometimes also by names. There are occasions when they try to establish their fabulous account, which was made up by them, by means of the characters that are in the [name of the] letters, sometimes by parables that they explain incorrectly, or by certain conjectures.[37]

If, then, anyone asks the reason why the Father, who has all things in common with the Son, was manifested by the Lord as the only one who knew the hour and the day,[38] he will find no more fitting, proper, or safe answer in the present life than this, namely, that we might learn through the Lord, who alone is the truthful teacher, that the Father is above all things. Truly, he said: *The Father is greater than I.*[39] Thus, Our Lord proclaimed that the Father excels in regard to knowledge, so that we too, as long as we live in the form of this world,[40] might leave perfect knowledge and such questions to God; and that we should not, while investigating the depths[41] of the Father, fall into so great a danger as to question whether there is another god above the God.

9. Now if anyone likes to pick a fight and contradict what we have stated and what the Apostle has said, namely, that *we know only in part, and we prophesy only in part*,[42] and thinks that he has received not only partial knowledge but absolutely real knowledge of all things that exist—he is really another Valentinus, or Ptolemaeus, or Basilides, or any other of those who claim that they have searched out the depths[43] of God. Decorating himself with vainglory, let him not boast that he knows more than the rest about the things that are invisible or that cannot be proved. Let him rather make a careful investigation about the causes of things in this world that we do not know, as, for example, about the number of the hairs on his head, and about the sparrows that are taken captive every day, and about the rest of the things of which we have no knowledge. When he learns these things from his "Father," let him tell us so that we in turn might give him credence in regard to more important things. But if "the perfect" do not yet know the things that are in their hands and at their feet and before their eyes and on the earth, and especially the matter of the hairs on their head, how are we to believe them about spiritual and supercelestial things and things above God, which they establish by an empty plausibility? We have said a good deal concerning numbers and names and

syllables and questions about things above us and concerning the fact that these individuals explain parables incorrectly. Let that suffice, since you can say more concerning them.

CHAPTER 29
HERETICAL NOTIONS ABOUT THE FUTURE DESTINY OF HUMANITY ARE REFUTED.

1. Let us return to the remaining points of their system. They hold that at the consummation [of all things] their Mother will return into the Fullness and receive Savior her spouse. They themselves, since they claim to be spiritual, having put off their souls and become intellectual spirits, will be the spouses of the spiritual angels. Demiurge, however, since they claim he is an ensouled being, will pass on to his Mother's realm. The souls of the righteous will repose in the intermediate realm in an ensouled manner. Likes must be gathered to likes, they say, and so spiritual to spiritual, but the material will continue in the material. But they set up contradictions by saying that the souls of the righteous return to the substance similar to themselves not because of their nature but because of their actions, since they hold that the "souls" of the just go there [to the intermediate realm], whereas the "souls" of the wicked remain in the fire. Really, if all the "souls" go to the place of rest by virtue of their nature, and all are in the intermediate realm by the fact that they are "souls," namely, because they are of the same nature, then it is useless to have faith, and the descent[1] of the Savior was useless. But if they go there because of their righteousness, they no longer go there because they are souls, but because they are righteous. Now if the souls would have perished unless they had been righteous,[2] righteousness has the power to save also the bodies. Why should it not save them, since they, too, partook of righteousness? Certainly, if nature and substance save, then all souls will be saved; if, on the other hand, righteousness and faith save, why do they not save the bodies that are condemned to destruction just as much as the souls?[3] Surely, in such a case, righteousness would manifest itself either powerless or unjust, if it saved some on account of itself, but not others.

2. It is manifest that the deeds of righteousness are achieved in the bodies; and so either all the souls will go into the intermediate

realm and nowhere will there be judgment; or the bodies, too, which
partook of righteousness, will get to the place of rest together with the
souls, which likewise partook of the righteousness, if righteousness has
the power to transfer to that place those who partook of itself. And
then the doctrine about the resurrection of the body, which, we
believe, will emerge as true and firm; namely, that God will revive our
mortal bodies,[4] which have safeguarded righteousness, and make them
incorrupt and immortal. The reason is: God is superior to nature, having within himself the power to will because he is good and to do
because he is mighty, and to perfect because he is rich and perfect.[5]

3. These [Gnostics], however, contradict themselves in every
respect when they decree that not all the "souls" will go to the intermediate realm, but only those of the righteous. That is, they say that
three types of beings were emitted by their Mother according to
nature and substance. The first, which sprang from perplexity, weari-
ness, and fear, is matter; the second, which sprang from impulse,[6] is
ensouled; but what she gave birth to when she gazed on the Angels
that surround Christ is spiritual.[7] So if what she gave birth to enters
the Fullness in any case because it is spiritual,[8] but what is material
dwells here below because it is material and will be consumed by the
fire that burns within it, why should not every soul go to the intermediate realm to which they send Demiurge as well?

And what is it that enters their Fullness? For they claim that the
souls remain in the intermediate realm, but the bodies, since they
have material substance, will be received into matter and burned by
the fire that is in it. Now if their body is thus destroyed and their soul
remains in the intermediate realm, no part of man will be left to go
into the Fullness. For the mind of man and reason, thought, and
mind's intention, and things like these, are not something distinct
from the soul, but are activities and actions of the soul itself that have
no subsistence apart from the soul. So what part of them is left to go
into the Fullness? Really, they too, inasmuch as they are souls, remain
in the intermediate realm; but inasmuch as they are a body, they will
burn with the rest of matter!

CHAPTER 30
THE GNOSTICS ARE NOT SPIRITUAL,
NOR IS THE CREATOR ENSOULED.

1. Such being the state of the question, these senseless men claim that they ascend above the Creator. They proclaim themselves superior to the God who made and adorned the heavens, the earth, the seas, and all things in them.[1] They hold, too, that they themselves are spiritual, though they are shamefully carnal because of their great impiety.[2] They claim that the Creator and Lord of all spiritual substance has an ensouled nature—he who made the winds his messengers,[3] and who is clothed with light as with a mantle,[4] and who holds the globe of the earth in his hand, as it were, and to whom its inhabitants are counted as grasshoppers.[5] In this they undoubtedly and truly manifest their madness, really struck by a thunderbolt,[6] even more so than the giants spoken of in fables. Swollen with vain presumption and unstable glory, they extol their opinions against God. The hellebore of the entire earth does not suffice as a purge for them, to vomit up their extreme foolishness.[7]

2. A superior being is to be proved by his or her deeds.[8] How, then, do they show themselves superior to the Creator—they to whom many stupid people bow in admiration, as if they could learn more from them than from Truth itself? We, too, because of the necessity of a discussion, would come down to their impiety and make a comparison between God and these mad individuals. While thus descending to their system, we might often expose them with their own opinions. May God be merciful to us, because we are really not comparing him to them; we merely say such things to expose and refute their madness.[9] The scriptural saying *Search, and you will find*[10] was said, according to their interpretation, that they might find themselves above Demiurge, calling themselves greater and better than God, and spiritual; but Demiurge, ensouled; and that for this reason they ascend above God; and that they go into the Fullness, but God, into the intermediate realm. So by their deeds let them show themselves superior to Demiurge. Certainly, a superior being must be proved not by what he says but by what he is.[11]

3. What work, then, will they point out as having been made by themselves either through Savior or their Mother, and which is greater

or more splendid or more intellectual than those which were made by
him who arranged all these things?[12] What heavens have they established?[13] What earth have they consolidated? What stars have they produced? To what luminaries have they given light, and what orbs have
they determined for these? Or what rivers, or frosts, or snows fitting
into each season and region, have they brought forth to earth?[14] What
heat or dryness have they set up against these? Or what rivers have
they made to overflow? What springs have they brought forth? With
what flowers and trees have they adorned the earth that lies below the
heavens? What multitude of animals have they formed, some rational,
others irrational, all decked out in beauty? And all the rest of the
things that were established by God's power and governed by his wisdom, who can count them up singly, or investigate the greatness of
the wisdom of him who made them?[15] And what can be said of the
beings above the heavens, which do not pass away—how great are
they?[16] The innumerable Angels, Thrones, Dominations, Powers?
With which one of these works, then, will they compare themselves?
What similar work can they show as having been made through themselves or by themselves, since they too are a creation and handiwork
of God? For whether Savior or their Mother (to use their own terms
in order to expose these liars with their own terms) used this Being
[Demiurge], as they say, for making the image of the beings that are
within the Fullness and of all the [angels] that she saw surrounding
Savior and which she contemplated[17]—in any case she used him as
one superior and more suitable for carrying out her will through him;
she did not pattern the images of such important beings from one
inferior but superior.

4. For these individuals were then already, as they themselves
affirm, a spiritual conception by virtue of the contemplation of the
satellite arranged around Pandora [Savior].[18] And those [Angels]
remained useless, since their Mother and Savior achieved nothing
through them.[19] Their conception was useless and suited to nothing,
because nothing, as is clear, has been made through them. Their God,
however, who was emitted, though inferior to themselves, according
to their system—they hold that he was an ensouled being—was the
artificer of all things, both efficacious and suitable for the images of
the Aeons to be made through him.[20] Not only were visible things here
below made through him but also the invisible, the Angels,
Archangels, Dominations, Powers, and Virtues[21]—all were made

through him, that is, as through one superior and capable of doing her will. But it is clear that the Mother made nothing whatever through these [angelic powers], as they themselves confess. Consequently, one rightly judges them to be abortive children of their Mother who had a miscarriage. Really, there were no midwives present to assist her in labor, and so they were brought forth abortive, as it were, since they were of no use for anything and were made for no work for [the use of] their Mother.[22] Although by their own system they are found to be very much inferior, they style themselves superior to him through whom so great and marvelous things have been made and arranged.

5. Suppose there are two iron instruments or tools. The artisan has the one tool always in his hands and puts it to use and makes with it whatever he wishes, and demonstrates his wisdom and skill. The other tool remains useless and idle, never in operation; the artisan appears to have made nothing at all with it and to have used it to no purpose. Now, if someone were to say that this useless, impractical, and idle tool is better and of more value than the one the artisan used to make things, which is to his praise, would not such a one be rightly considered a dullard and not in his right mind? The same is true of these [Gnostics] if, without offering any proof, they claim to be spiritual and superior, and Demiurge is ensouled; and that for this reason they ascend above him and penetrate into the Fullness to their spouses (to be sure, they are women, as they admit!), but that God is inferior and so remains in the intermediate realm. Of course, one who is superior is shown such by his works.[23] Certainly, all the works were made by Demiurge. They, however, have nothing worthy of intelligence to point to as made through themselves. They are mad with extreme and incurable madness.

6. Now if they should contend that all the material things—for instance, the heavens and the entire world below them—were made by Demiurge, but that all the more spiritual things, those above the Heavens—for instance, the Principalities, Powers, Angels, Archangels, Dominations, Virtues—were made through a spiritual offspring, which they claim to be, we proved first of all from the Lord's Scriptures that all the things mentioned above, the visible and the invisible,[24] were made by the one God. These [Gnostics], certainly, are not worthy of more credence than the Scriptures. So we ought not to forsake the words of the Lord, and of Moses, and the rest of the prophets, who her-

alded the Truth, and believe these men who say nothing rational, but rave senselessly about inconsistent things. Besides, if the things that are above the heavens were really made by them, let them tell us what the nature of the invisible beings is; let them count the number of the Angels and the rank of the Archangels; let them manifest the mysteries of the Thrones; let them teach us the difference between the Dominations, Principalities, Powers, and Virtues. They cannot give an answer; therefore, these things were not made by them. But if these things were made by the Creator, as they actually were, and are spiritual and holy, then He who made them spiritual is himself not ensouled. So their great blasphemy is destroyed.

7. All the Scriptures loudly proclaim that there are spiritual creatures in heaven. Paul, too, testifies that these are spiritual beings; he points out that he was rapt to the third heaven and that he was carried up to paradise and heard unutterable words that humankind is not allowed to utter.[25] What did either his entry into paradise or his being taken up to the third heaven profit him, since all those things are in the power of Demiurge, if, as some make bold to assert, he was to be a contemplator and hearer of the mysteries that are said to be above Demiurge? Certainly, to learn the dispensation that is above Demiurge, he would by no means have remained in the realm of Demiurge—he had not even explored all of this yet; according to their explanation he still had four heavens before he would come near Demiurge and thus see the seventh, which was subject to him. However, he would perhaps have been taken all the way to the intermediate realm, that is, to the Mother, so that he might learn from her what is within the Fullness. Surely, it was possible for his inner self,[26] since it was invisible, as they say, and spoke within him, to reach not only the third heaven but all the way to their Mother. For if they claim that they, that is, their inner selves, immediately pass beyond Demiurge and go up to the Mother, then certainly much more so would this have happened to the inner self of the Apostle. Demiurge would not have hindered him, since he himself is already subject to Savior, as they claim. But even if he had [tried to] hinder him, it would have been of no avail; it is impossible that he should be stronger than the foresight of Father, since the inner self is said to be invisible even to Demiurge. Now since he [the Apostle] narrated his being taken up to the third heaven as something great and marvelous, these [Gnostics] surely do not ascend above the seventh heaven; for they are no better than the

Apostle. If they should maintain that they are more excellent than he, they will be refuted by the deeds, for they have never gloried in such an event [ascending to the third heaven]. The Apostle adds: *Whether in the body or out of the body…God knows*,[27] so that one would not think that the body did not partake of the vision, since it, too, would share in the things that he had seen and heard; and that one would not say that he was not taken higher because of the weight of the body. Surely, those who, like the Apostle, are very perfect in the love of God are permitted to be contemplators and to go there even without the body, to view the spiritual mysteries, which are the activities of God who made the heavens and the earth[28] and fashioned man[29] and placed him in paradise.[30]

8. This God, therefore, made the spiritual things of which the Apostle became a contemplator even to the third heaven.[31] This God, according as he wills, since paradise belongs to him,[32] grants to those worthy ineffable messages, which man is not allowed to repeat, because they are spiritual. And this God is truly the Spirit of God[33] and not ensouled, else he would never have made the spiritual beings. But if he is ensouled, let them tell us by whom the spiritual beings were made. Nor are they able to show that anything was made through their Mother's offspring, which they claim they are. For these [Gnostics] are not only unable to make any of the spiritual beings but not even a fly or a louse or any other similar contemptible small animal. Only according to the law that is from God in the beginning, namely, by a deposit of "seed" in those of the same genus, have they and do they become animals by nature. Nor was anything made by the Mother alone. They claim that this Demiurge was emitted, and that he is the Lord of the whole creation. Now he who is the Maker of the whole creation, and the Lord, they claim is ensouled; whereas they claim that they themselves are spiritual, who are not makers or lords of any creation, not merely not of things outside of themselves, but not even of their own bodies. Finally, they who often suffer many things in their bodies against their will style themselves spiritual and better than the Maker.

9. Rightly, then, do we expose them as having strayed far and wide from the Truth. Certainly, if Savior made the things that have been made through him [Demiurge], this one is proved to be superior to them [Gnostics], not inferior, since he is recognized as their Maker; after all, they too belong to the things that have been made.

How, then, is it logical to say that these [Gnostics] are spiritual, but he through whom they were made is ensouled? Or, if—and this alone is true, as we have shown in many ways by clearest proofs—he by himself, by his own will and self-determination, made and ordered all things, and if his will is the [cause of the] substance of all things,[34] then he alone will be acknowledged as the God who made all things; he alone is omnipotent and alone the Father who, by the Word of his power,[35] created and made all things, both the visible and the invisible, the intellectual and the sentient, the heavenly and the earthly. He ordered all things by his Wisdom.[36] He comprehended all things, but himself alone cannot be comprehended by anyone. He is the Builder, he is the Creator, he is the Originator, he is the Maker, he is the Lord of all things. Neither is there anyone beside him nor above him; neither a mother, as they falsely assert, nor another God, whom Marcion imagined; neither a Fullness of thirty Aeons, which has been imagined empty; nor Profundity, nor First-Beginning, nor heavens, nor a virginal light [Barbelo],[37] nor an unnameable Aeon, nor absolutely anything of the things which these or all heretics senselessly rave about. No, there is only one God the Builder, he who is above every Principality and Authority and Dominion and Power;[38] he who is the Father, God, Creator, Maker, Builder, made them by himself, that is, by his Word and Wisdom,[39] namely, the heavens and the earth and the sea, and all things that are in them.[40] He it is who is just and good.[41] He it is who fashioned man,[42] planted paradise,[43] made the world, and brought on the flood that saved Noah. He is the God of Abraham, the God of Isaac, the God of Jacob, the God...of the living,[44] whom the Law announces, whom the Prophets herald, whom Christ reveals, whom the apostles hand down, whom the church believes.[45] This is the Father of Our Lord Jesus Christ.[46] Through his Word, who is his Son, he is revealed and manifested to all to whom he is revealed; for those know him to whom the Son has made the revelation. But the Son, always coexisting with the Father,[47] of old and from the beginning always reveals the Father, both to the Angels and the Archangels and the Authorities and the Powers,[48] and to whom God wishes to make the revelation.

CHAPTER 31
A SUMMARY OF THE HERETICAL SPECULATIONS,
MAGIC POWER, AND EVIL PRACTICES.

1. So, then, since we have disproved the followers of Valentinus, the entire crowd of heretics is refuted. We leveled many and varied points against their Fullness and beings outside it. We proved, namely, that the Father of all things would be limited and circumscribed by something outside of him—if there is really anything outside of him— and that there would have to be many Fathers and many Fullnesses, and on all sides there would have to be many creations of worlds that would each begin in one world and terminate in another; and that all beings would have to remain in their own realms and not curiously meddle with others with which they have no part or communion; and that there is no other God of all things. No, the name of God belongs only to the Omnipotent. All these things can equally be applied to the followers of Marcion and Simon and Menander, or anyone else who, in like manner, separates our creation from the Father.[1]

Again, we aimed many proofs against those who maintain that the Father of all things comprehends all things but that our creation was made not by him but by some other Power, or by the Angels who are ignorant of First-Father, which [creation] is circumscribed[2] as a center by the immense universe—somewhat like a stain in a mantle. We proved that it is not plausible that anyone else but the Father made our creation. The same can equally be said against the followers of Saturninus and Basilides and Carpocrates, and the rest of the Gnostics who say the same things in the same way.[3]

What has been said about the emissions and the Aeons and the degeneracy, and how unstable their Mother was, equally refutes Basilides and all those falsely so-called Gnostics who say the same things with different names, but who to a greater extent than those [Valentinians] transfer things that are outside of the Truth to the standard of their own doctrine.[4] Further, what we said about numbers can also be urged against all those who drag what belongs to the Truth down to this sort of standard. Likewise, what was said about the Creator, proving that He alone is God and the Father of all things, and what else will yet be said in the following Books, we state against all heretics. Those who are more gentle and humane you will turn away [from error] and put to shame so that they do not blaspheme their Creator and Maker and Nourisher and Lord, and that they do not imagine that his origin was from degeneracy and ignorance. Those who are fierce and dreadful and irrational you will drive far from you, so that you will no longer tolerate their loquacity.[5]

2. Besides, the followers of Simon and of Carpocrates and anyone else who claims to work miracles will be exposed, because the things they do they do not perform through God's power or in truth, or for the benefit of humankind, but through magical deceptions and total fraud for ruining and misleading them. By misleading them they do more harm than good to those who believe in them. For they cannot give sight to the blind or hearing to the deaf; nor can they drive out any demons, except the ones sent into others by themselves, if nevertheless they do that; nor can they heal the maimed and crippled and paralyzed, or others who have any other bodily ailment, as has often happened in regard to bodily ailment; nor can they restore health that was lost through external accidents. They are so far from raising the dead that they do not even believe this at all possible, but claim that the resurrection from the dead is the knowledge of what they call truth.[6] And yet the Lord did raise people, and through prayer the apostles did too; and, because of necessity, very often in our brotherhood, when the whole church, which is in every place, made petition through much fasting and supplication, the soul of a dead person returned[7] and the man was given back through the entreaties of the saintly people.[8]

3. These individuals are truly exposed also by this standard as total strangers to the divine nature and the goodness of God, and the spiritual excellence; namely, by the fact that among them error and deception and magical, illusory visions wickedly take place in full view of people; whereas in the church sympathy and mercy[9] and assurance and truth for aiding people are performed not only without reward and gratis, but we ourselves give away our own goods for the health of the people; and since those who are cured very often are in need of things, they receive them from us.[10] These [Gnostics], inasmuch as they are filled completely with all deceitfulness and rebellious inspiration and demoniacal energy and illusory vision of idolatry,[11] are indeed the precursors of the dragon that, because of such an illusory vision, will with its tail make a third of the stars rebel and hurl them to the earth.[12] These, as well as he, must be avoided; and the greater

the illusory vision by which they are said to operate, the more carefully must they be watched, inasmuch as they have received the
greater spirit of wickedness.[13] And for that reason, if anyone takes note
of the daily activity in their conduct,[14] he will find that it is the very
same as the conduct of the demons.

CHAPTER 32

JESUS' DOCTRINE AND DEEDS DISPROVE THE
GNOSTICS' MAGICAL PRACTICES AND WICKED DEEDS.

1. Their wicked doctrine about actions, namely, that it is necessary for them to have experience in every kind of deed, even in all the
bad ones,[1] is refuted by the Lord's doctrine. According to him, not
only the adulterer is thrown out but also one who desires to commit
adultery;[2] not only one who commits murder and deserves condemnation but also one who is unreasonably angry with his brother.[3] He
commanded men and women not only not to hate people but also to
love their enemies;[4] not only not to perjure themselves but not to
swear at them at all;[5] not only not to say evil things of one's neighbor
but not even to call anyone Racha and fool, or else they would be
guilty of hell fire;[6] and not only not to strike others, but those who had
been struck should turn the other cheek;[7] and not only not to steal
what belongs to others but not to demand back one's own goods that
have been taken away;[8] not only not to injure one's neighbors and do
them any kind of harm, but those who are mistreated should be for-
giving and show kindness toward their enemies and pray for them, so
that these might repent and be saved.[9] In no way should they imitate
the contumely, lust, and pride of others.[10] When, therefore, the
Lord—of whom they boast as their teacher and claim he has a much
better and stronger soul than the rest—commanded that certain
things must be done with great care, inasmuch as they are good and
excellent, but that one must abstain not only from certain actions but
also from the thoughts that lead to these actions, as something evil
and harmful and wicked—how are they not confounded who call him
their Teacher and better and stronger than the rest, and then com-
mand things that are openly contrary to his doctrine? Besides, if nothing would really be bad or good, but if only in human judgment some

things would be unrighteous and others righteous, he would certainly not have given out this decree: *Then the righteous will shine like the sun in the kingdom of their Father.*[11] But the unrighteous and those who do not perform deeds of righteousness, he will *hurl into the eternal fire,*[12]*...where their worm never dies, and the fire is never quenched.*[13]

2. Furthermore, they maintain that it is necessary for them to have experience in every kind of deed and in every kind of conduct, and if possible to accomplish this in one coming in this life and thus pass over to perfection.[14] But one does not find them trying to do those things that pertain to virtue and require effort and bring honor and demand skill, which are also approved by all people as good. Assuredly, if it is necessary that they go through every sort of deed and every activity, first of all, it would have been necessary that they learn all the arts, whether these be achieved by intellectual methods or labors,[15] whether they are taught through discipline or are acquired by work, by exercise,[16] and by endurance; as, for example, every branch of music, arithmetic, geometry, astronomy, and all arts that deal with intellectual methods; furthermore, all medicine, the science of herbs, other sciences that are studied for the health of humankind; painting and sculpturing, working in bronze and marble, and similar arts; besides these, every kind of farming, the veterinary skill, and shepherding; also the crafts, which are said to be involved in all the arts; also those [skills] pertaining to maritime life, physical culture, hunting, military life, life at court, and whatever others there are. Of these they cannot learn even the ten-thousandth part,[17] though they labor for a lifetime. And of these things they make no attempt to learn anything, though they maintain that they must have experience in every kind of deed. But they do turn to pleasures, lusts, and immoral acts. And so they are condemned by themselves,[18] according to their own teachings. To be sure, since they lack all the things just mentioned, they will endure the punishment of fire! These individuals, who really emulate the philosophy of Epicurus and the indifference of the Cynics, boast of Jesus as their Teacher, but he turns his disciples not only from evil deeds but, as we have shown, from words and thoughts as well.

3. These individuals maintain, moreover, that they have souls from the same realm as Jesus and so are similar to him, at times even better. Still, when they are brought forward to perform works that he did for the benefit and assurance of humankind, these are found

doing nothing of the kind, nothing that one can begin to compare with his. And if they do perform anything, it is done through magic, as we have said, by which they fraudulently try to deceive the stupid. They confer no advantage or benefit on those over whom they claim to exercise their powers. But they bring forward little boys,[19] whose eyes they can deceive by showing them illusory visions that cease immediately and do not last even for one moment. In this way they are proved to be not like Jesus Our Lord, but like Simon the magician. By the fact, on the one hand, that the Lord rose from the dead on the third day and appeared to the disciples and was taken up into heaven while these looked on; and, on the other hand, that they upon dying do not rise and do not appear to anyone, they are exposed as not having souls like that of Jesus.

4. If, however, they claim that the Lord performed these things only apparently, we shall take them back to the prophetic [writings] and prove from these that all of these things were predicted of him in that manner and that they have certainly taken place, and that he alone is the Son of God.[20] Wherefore, his *true* disciples receive the grace from him, and in his name perform [favors] for the benefit of the rest of humanity, according to the gift each one has received from him.[21] For instance, there are some who certainly and really drive out demons, so that very often those who were cleansed of the most wicked spirits become believers and are in the church. Others have foreknowledge of future things and have visions and make prophetic utterances. Others through imposition of hands heal those who have some illness and restore them to health. Why even, as we have already said, the dead have been raised and have remained with us many years. What more can we say? It is impossible to count up all the favors that the church performs daily throughout the whole world for the help of the peoples with the grace received from God in the name of Christ Jesus who was crucified under Pontius Pilate. In this she neither misleads them nor accepts bribes from them.[22] For, just as she has received gratuitously from God, so she renders service gratuitously.[23]

5. Nor does the church perform anything by calling upon Angels,[24] or through incantations, or through any other depraved superstition. But by directing prayers to the God[25] who made all things, and by calling upon the name of Our Lord Jesus Christ, she does perform miracles with a clean and pure intention and openly for the benefit of humankind, not to lead people astray. So, if even now the name

of Our Lord Jesus Christ bestows benefits and certainly and truly heals all who everywhere believe in him—but not the name of Simon, Menander, Carpocrates, or anyone else—it is evident that, having become man, he lived with his handiwork [men and women][26] and truly performed all things through God's power according to the good pleasure of the Father of all things,[27] as the prophets had foretold. What these things were will be told in the proofs from the prophetic writings.

CHAPTER 33

THE DOCTRINE OF TRANSMIGRATION OF SOULS IS ABSURD.

1. [Their opinion] about the transmigration of souls from one body to another we can overthrow by the fact that the souls have no recollection whatever of their previous status.[1] Certainly, if they would be sent forth in order that they might have experience in every activity, they ought to remember what took place in the previous state, so that they could supply what was lacking and would not always be occupied with the same activities, and thus continuously endure miserable toil. To be sure, the [soul's] union with the body could not obliterate entirely the memory and contemplation of the previous state, especially since they came for that purpose.[2] By way of illustration, when the body is asleep and at rest, whatever things the soul itself sees within itself, and whatever it does in vision, many of these it remembers and communicates to the body. And so it happens that upon waking one relates, even after a long time, what he or she has seen in a dream.[3] In the same manner, one would remember also the things he did before coming into the body. For if it keeps in mind what was seen only for the slightest moment, or received in a vision, and that by the soul alone in sleep when it is united with the body and dispersed in every member of the body, it would much more remember the things with which it lived for so long a time, even for the whole span of a past life.

2. In regard to these things, that ancient Athenian Plato, who first introduced this doctrine,[4] when he could find no excuse for it thought up the idea of a cup of forgetfulness, thinking that he could thus avoid such perplexity. Without offering any proof, he gave out dogmatically that when the souls enter this life the demon who stands

above the entrance gives them a drink of this forgetfulness before they enter the body.[5] He was unaware that he fell into a still greater perplexity. Really, if the cup of forgetfulness, namely, upon having been drained, can obliterate all deeds from the memory, how, O Plato, do you know that, since at present your soul is in the body, and before it entered the body it was given a drink of this drug of forgetfulness? Certainly, if you can remember the demon and the cup upon entry, you ought also to remember the rest of things! But if you are ignorant of those, neither is the demon real, nor was the rest of this specious theory of the cup of forgetfulness.[6]

3. Against those who claim that the body itself is the drug of forgetfulness, this comes to mind: How, then, does it happen that the soul remembers and tells neighbors whatever it sees by itself while the body is resting, both in dreams and in thought?[7] If the body were forgetfulness, the soul, when dwelling in the body, would not remember also the things that it once knew either through sight or through hearing; but immediately after the eye would be taken off the objects looked at, the memory of these objects would vanish. For while the soul would remain in that forgetfulness, it could not know anything else than what it saw for the moment. How, moreover, could it learn divine things and remember them while in the body, when, as they say, the body itself is the forgetfulness? Moreover, the prophets themselves while on earth remembered, when they returned to themselves,[8] whatever they saw or heard spiritually in visions of heavenly things while they were on earth, and they announced them to the rest. So the body does not cause a state of oblivion for the soul in regard to the things that were seen spiritually; no, the soul teaches the body, and it [the body] shares in the spiritual vision that the soul had.

4. In truth, the body is not more powerful than the soul. The body is given breath and life and growth and movement by the soul, and the soul controls and moves the body. The soul is indeed hindered in its speed in proportion as the body shares in the motion, but it does not lose its knowledge. For the body is similar to a tool, whereas the soul rules an artisan's mind. For example, an artisan quickly thinks out the blueprint of a work by himself, but he is slower in working it out with the tool, because of the immobility of what he is working with. The speed of his mind, then, linked to the slowness of the tool accomplishes a work with moderate movement. In like manner, since the soul shares in its body, it is slightly hindered because its speed is tied down to the

slowness of the body. Still it does not lose its powers altogether; in a sense it communicates life to the body, but itself does not cease to live. Similarly, while sharing other things with the body, it loses neither the knowledge of them nor the memory of things it had seen.

5. If, therefore, the soul has no recollection of things in the past but does know about things that exist here below, it was never in other bodies. Neither did it ever do things that it does not even know about; nor did it ever know things that it does not even see. On the contrary, just as every one of us receives his body through God's art, in the same way does he receive his soul. For God is not so poor and so destitute that he would not give to each body its own soul as well as its proper form. And so, when the number [of the elect] that God himself ordained beforehand is complete, all who are enrolled for life[9] will rise with their own bodies and souls and spirits[10] with which they pleased God. Those, however, who deserve punishment will depart into it; they too will have their souls and their bodies with which they rebelled against God's goodness. Both classes will cease to beget and to be begotten, to marry and to be given in marriage,[11] so that the calculated multitude of humankind, predetermined by God, might when completed preserve the harmony of the Father.[12]

Chapter 34

The Disembodied Soul Is Recognizable and Immortal.

1. That the souls not only continue to exist and do not transmigrate from one body to another, but also retain the same form as the body to which they were fitted, and that they remember the deeds they did here below from which they have ceased,[1] the Lord taught in most clear terms in the history of the rich man and Lazarus, namely, the Lazarus who rested in Abraham's bosom.[2] There he said that the rich man recognized Lazarus after death, and also Abraham; and that both remain, each in his own class; and that the rich man asked that Lazarus, with whom he himself had not shared even the crumbs from the table be permitted to bring him some relief. He spoke likewise of Abraham's answer, that he knew not only his own status but also the status of the rich man. He also urged those who do not wish to come

to that place of punishment to listen to Moses and the prophets and accept the preaching of him who rose from the dead. In truth, in these [writings] it has most clearly been said that the souls continue to exist; that they do not transmigrate from body to body; that they have the form of a human being so that they might also be recognized, and they remember the things that happened on earth; that Abraham possessed the prophetic spirit;[3] and that each soul receives, even before the judgment, the dwelling it deserves.[4]

2. If at this point anyone should object that souls, which shortly before began to exist, cannot continue to exist indefinitely[5] but must either be ingenerate if they are to be immortal or, if they had a beginning through being made,[6] must die with the body, let such a one learn that God alone, who is the Lord of all things, is without beginning and without end, truly and forever the same and acting in the same manner.[7] However, all things that came from him—namely, whatever things have been made and are being made—have their beginning through being made and on this account are inferior to him who made them, because they are not ingenerate. Still, by the will of God the Creator, they continue to exist and extend themselves through the long course of the ages.[8] He thus bestows on them the beginning of existence and thereafter continued existence.[9]

3. For example, the heavens and the firmament that is over us, the sun, the moon, all stars,[10] and all their ornaments,[11] since they did not exist before, have been made and continue to exist for a long time by God's will. Whoever thinks in the same way about souls and spirits and absolutely all things that have been created will not err, since all things that have been made have their beginning through being made, but they continue to exist as long as God wills them to do so. The prophetic Spirit testifies to these assertions when he says: *For he spoke and they were made, he commanded and they were created. He has established them forever and ever.*[12] Further, about saving humankind he spoke thus: *He asked you for life; you gave it to him—length of days forever and ever,*[13] inasmuch as the Father of all things bestows that gift, even of continuing forever and ever, on those who are saved. For life is not from ourselves or from our nature, but it is given according to God's grace.[14] Therefore, he who preserved the gift of life and gave thanks to him who bestowed it will in turn receive *length of days forever and ever.* He who rejects it, however, and so is ungrateful to his Maker for having been made and does not acknowledge him who bestowed it deprives himself of continuing *forever*

and ever.[15] Hence, the Lord said to those who are grateful to him: *If you have not been faithful in that which is least, who will entrust you with that which is great?*[16] By this he indicated that those who, in this short temporal life, were ungrateful to him who bestowed it will rightly not receive from him length of days *forever and ever.*[17]

4. Now, just as the ensouled body is itself not the soul but partakes of the soul as long as God wills, so too the soul itself is not life but partakes of life bestowed on it by God.[18] Hence also the prophetic word said to the first-formed Man that *he became a living being.*[19] By that he taught us that the "soul" became living by sharing in life, so that the "soul" is understood as distinct from the life that exists in its behalf. If, then, God bestows the gift of life and perpetual continuance, it is possible that the "souls" that first did not exist will continue to exist, since God willed them to have being and existence. For God's will ought to have rule and dominion over all things, whereas all other things ought to yield to it and be submissive and devoted to its service. Let this much, then, be said about the creation and continuation of the soul.

CHAPTER 35

VARIOUS GNOSTIC NOTIONS ARE REJECTED.

1. In addition to what has been said, Basilides will be compelled to maintain by force of his own rule that not only 365 heavens were made, one succeeding the other, but a certain immeasurable and innumerable multitude of heavens were always made and are being made and will be made, and this sort of making of heavens will never cease.[1] For if from the overflowing of the first heaven a second heaven was made according to its pattern, and a third according to the second, and so on all the subsequent [heavens], then it is necessary that also from our present heaven, which he calls the last, another heaven must be made like, and from, the present one; and from that still another; and so neither the overflowing of the heavens already made nor the making of new heavens will ever cease, but must run on into an immeasurable number of heavens, and not into a predetermined number.

2. The rest of the falsely so-called Gnostics, too, who claim that the prophets gave out prophecies from the various gods[2] will be easily overthrown by the fact that all the prophets preached one God and

Lord, and that he is the Creator of heaven and earth and of all things in them, and that they pointed out the coming of his Son. This we will demonstrate from the Scriptures themselves in subsequent Books.

3. If certain ones of them counter that according to the Hebrew language various names are given to God in the Scriptures, as, for instance, Sabaoth, Eloae, Adonae, and many like them, and endeavor to prove from this that there are various Powers and Gods, let them learn that all of these names are manifestations and titles of one and the same God. To explain, the name *Eloe*, according to the Jewish word, means "true God." But *Elloeuth*, according to the Hebrew language, means "that which contains all things."[3] The name *Adonae* sometimes means that which is nameable and admirable;[4] but sometimes, namely, with *delta* [in Hebrew *daleth*] doubled and with aspiration, thus *[H]addonai*, it means, "One who sets bounds and separates the land from the water," so that water should not afterwards rise over it.[5] Likewise, *Sabaōth*, the last vowel written with the Greek *omega*, means Voluntary; but when written with the Greek *omicron*, thus *Sabaoth*, it indicates the first heaven.[6] In the same manner, *Yaōth*, with the last syllable long and aspirate, means "a predetermined measure," with the last syllable shortened to the Greek *omicron*, thus *Yaoth*, it denotes "He who puts evils to flight."[7] All the other titles belong to one and the same name, for example, Lord of hosts, Father of all things, God Almighty, the Highest, Lord of the Heavens, Creator, Builder, and others like them. These do not belong to different gods, but they are names and titles of one and the same God by which the one God and Father is manifested, who contains all things and bestows on all the gift of existence.

4. We believe that we have sufficiently proved that the preaching of the apostles, the teaching of the Lord, the announcement of the prophets, the spoken message of the apostles,[8] and the service of the law[9] all harmonize with what we have said and prove that there is one and the same God of all things, which praise the Father, and not various gods; that he is not a being that has his substance from various gods and Powers; but all things are from one and the same Father who, in accordance with the natures of (beings) placed under (him), rules also the disposition (of their beings).[10] The visible and invisible things, and absolutely everything that has been made,[11] were not made by Angels or some other Power, but by God the Father alone. By the many things, therefore, that we have said, we have proved that there is one God the

Father and Creator of all things. But lest we seem to be avoiding the proof from the Lord's Scriptures, since the Scriptures themselves preach this very doctrine much more obviously and clearly, for such as do not have a depraved mind toward them, we will supply a special book, which will utilize these Scriptures, and so, for all who love the truth, we will bring into clear light proofs from the divine Scriptures.

NOTES

INTRODUCTION

1. Eginhard Meijering, *Irenaeus: Grondlegger van het christelijk denken* ([Amsterdam]: Uitgeverij Balans, 2001), 230.

2. Three of the quotations are found in Eusebius of Caesarea's *Historia ecclesiastica;* seven are in the large florilegium known as the *Sacra Parallela* of John of Damascus; and the other two appear in other florilegia. See Adelin Rousseau, "Les Fragments Grecs," in Adelin Rousseau et al., *Irénée de Lyons Contre les heresies Livres I–V*, 10 vols. (Book I = SC 263–64; Book II = SC 293–94; Book III = SC 210–11; Book IV [2 vols.] = SC 100*–SC 100**; Book V = SC 152–53) (Paris: Cerf, 1965–82), SC 293.83–100.

3. Adelin Rousseau, "Les Fragments Arméniens," SC 293.101–11.

4. Louis Doutreleau, "Les Fragments Syriaques," SC 293.113–15.

5. When he declares in 2.2.6, "We have already shown that God is one; we shall go on to show it from the apostles and the Lord's own sayings," he may be foreshadowing the agenda of Books III–V.

6. These two terms are contrasted in six places in the *Against heresies*: 2.13.4 and 2.17.11; 3.24.2; and three times in 4.20.

7. Richard A. Norris, Jr., "The Insufficiency of Scripture: *Adversus haereses* 2 and the Role of Scripture in Irenaeus's Anti-Gnostic Polemic," in *Reading in Early Christian Communities: Essays on Interpretation in the Early Church*, ed. Charles A. Bobertz and David Brakke (Notre Dame: University of Notre Dame Press, 2002), 66. Some corroboration of Norris's view may be seen in 2.11.2.

8. Denis Minns, *Irenaeus*, Outstanding Christian Thinkers Series (London: Geoffrey Chapman, 1994), 6. The same observation has been made by other writers, including Dominic J. Unger in his introduction to Book I of this series (p. 3).

9. Bernard Sesboüé (*Tout récapituler dans le Christ: Christologie et sotériologie d'Irénée de Lyon* [Paris: Desclée, 2000], 32) suggests that Irenaeus thought that a third book would be enough to contain his refutation of the Gnostic use of Scripture, but found that it was not.

10. Joel Kalvesmaki, "The Original Sequence of Irenaeus, *Against Heresies* I: Another Suggestion," *Journal of Early Christian Studies* 15 (2007): 416.

11. A.H. 1.praef.2: "To the best of our ability we will give you a concise and clear report on the doctrine of these people who are at present spreading false teaching. We are speaking of the disciples of Ptolemaeus, an offshoot of the Valentinian school" (Unger translation).

12. See A.H. 1.10.1; 1.22.1.

13. The word translated "syzygies" here in 2.praef.2 is *coniugationes*. The Gnostic syzygies were male–female pairings of spiritual beings that played a role in the origin and meaning of everything, according to Gnostic belief. Here Irenaeus is probably using the term by metonymy to refer to Gnostic doctrines in general, but he may also have in mind secret rituals such as those hinted at in A.H. 1.21.3.

14. Norris, "Insufficiency of Scripture," 74. For an excellent, clear exposition of the meaning of "hypothesis" in this sense and in Irenaeus, see John Behr, *The Way to Nicaea* (Crestwood, NY: St. Vladimir's Seminary Press, 2001), 32–34.

15. Irénée de Lyon, *Contre les hérésies*, Livre II: Édition critique par Adelin Rousseau et Louis Doutreleau, vol. 1: *Introduction, notes justificatives, tables*, SC 293 (Paris: Cerf, 1982), 118–20 (my translation).

16. Rowan A. Greer, "The Dog and the Mushrooms: Irenaeus's View of the Valentinians Assessed," in *The Rediscovery of Gnosticism: Proceedings of the International Conference on Gnosticism at Yale, New Haven, Connecticut, March 28–31, 1978*, vol.1: *The School of Valentinus*, ed. Bentley Layton, Studies in the History of Religions: Supplements to Numen 41 (Leiden: E. J. Brill, 1980), 151, 154.

17. Ibid., 156.

18. Irenaeus has already referred to this axiom in 1.15.5, cited it in 1.22.1, and he will appeal to it again in 2.4.2. It may be implied in 4.6.2, where Irenaeus is quoting from Justin Martyr. For an excellent analysis of where this axiom comes from and how Irenaeus's use of it goes beyond that of his predecessors, see William R. Schoedel, "'Topological' Theology and Some Monistic Tendencies in Gnosticism," in *Essays on the Nag Hammadi Texts in Honour of Alexander Böhlig*, ed. Martin Krause, Nag Hammadi Studies 3 (Leiden: E. J. Brill, 1972), 88–108, especially 101–2, and idem, "Enclosing, Not Enclosed: The Early Christian Doctrine of God," in *Early Christian Literature and the Classical Intellectual Tradition: In honorem Robert M. Grant*, ed. William R. Schoedel and Robert L. Wilken (Paris: Beauchesne, 1979), 75–86.

19. For example, Ps 50:12; 2 Macc 14:35; Acts 17:24–25. For philosophers on the subject, see Alcinous, *Epitome* 10.3.32–33, in *The Handbook of Platonism*, translated with introduction and commentary by John Dillon (Oxford: Clarendon, 1993), 18, and Dillon's commentary on this passage on p. 104, where he cites parallels from Plato, Plutarch, Calcidius, and Apuleius.

20. This is not the "dog" referred to in the title of Rowan Greer's essay cited earlier; that dog comes from an image used by Irenaeus in 1.8.1.

21. For early Christian use of Xenophanes, see Robert M. Grant, *After the New Testament* (Philadelphia: Fortress, 1967), 103–7, and his *Jesus after the Gospels* (Louisville: Westminster John Knox, 1990), 96–98.

22. See Book I, chapters 5–7.

23. Marcus is one of the principal targets of Irenaeus's polemic; see Book I, chapters 13–20.

24. It should be remembered that in languages like Greek and Hebrew, the same alphabetical characters served also to indicate numbers. There are too many examples of Gnostic practice in Book I to list here; the reader is referred to the notes to this translation.

25. William R. Schoedel, "Theological Method in Irenaeus (*Adversus Haereses* 2.25–28)," *JThS* n.s. 35 (1984): 31–49.

26. Matt 7:7–8 and 25:1–12.

27. William R. Schoedel, "Philosophy and Rhetoric in the *Adv. Haer.* of Irenaeus," *VC* 13 (1959): 22–32.

28. Elaine Pagels ("Conflicting Versions of Valentinian Eschatology: Irenaeus and the *Excerpta ex Theodoto*," *HTR* 67 [1974]: 35–53) attempts to show that not all Valentinians held that the three natures of people had distinct destinies. Her arguments are rebutted by James F. McCue, "Conflicting Versions of Valentinianism? Irenaeus and the *Excerpta ex Theodoto*," in *Rediscovery of Gnosticism: Proceedings of the International Conference on Gnosticism at Yale, New Haven, Connecticut, March 28–31, 1978*, vol. 1: *The School of Valentinus*, ed. Bentley Layton (Leiden: E. J. Brill, 1980), 404–16; and Roland Bergmeier, "'Königlösigkeit' als nachvalentinianisches Heilsprädikat," *Novum Testamentum* 24 (1982): 316–39, especially 328–36, "Anhang A," which is entirely devoted to refuting the Pagels article. See also ACW 55.168.

29. The two instances where the plural "books" is used may come from a correction, made either after Irenaeus had extended that scriptural exposition beyond Book III or by the Latin translator, who knew that there were five books in all.

PREFACE

1. I accept Rousseau's view (SC 293.199 [SC 294.23 n. 1]) that the Latin should be restored to *in eo quidem libro qui ante hunc est.*

2. Cf. 1 Tim 6:20.

3. Translation follows Rousseau's correction (SC 293.200 [SC 294.23 n. 3]) of the Latin to *omne…(quod) ab his qui sunt a Valentino…adinuentum es(t) falsiloquium.*

4. This is based on Rousseau's argument (SC 293.200 [SC 294.23 n. 4])
that *priores* refers to Valentinian leaders and not to earlier Gnostics like Simon
Magus or the Nicolaitans as Massuet (MG 7.707–8 n. 82) believed.

5. "Successions" is *successiones* in Lat. Iren., where it is used consistently
for the Gnostic line of Aeonic emissions by succession of one from the other,
and like the other, and also for the succession of bishops from the apostles.
On *succession*, see B. Reynders, *Lexique comparé du texte grec et des versions latine,
arménienne, et syriaque de l' "Adversus haereses" de saint Irénée*, vol. 2: *Index des mots
latins*, CSCO 142 Subsidia Tome 6 (Louvain: L. Durbecq, 1954), 315. It is in
the plural here and again in the preface to Book III after the word *doctrina* of
the Gnostics. Here it could therefore mean a line of Aeons being emitted one
after the other, which I followed in the translation. But since the verb *succedere*
is used for the succeeding of one Gnostic after a predecessor, as also for one
bishop following another, it seems possible that *successiones* here refers to the
Gnostic line of followers, about whom Irenaeus actually wrote in Book I.

6. On this expression, see Sagnard *Gnose*, 433-35. See also A.H. 1.17.2;
1.19.1; 2.1.1; 2.3.2; 2.4.3; 2.9.2; 2.19.9; 2.28.4 (twice); 3.5.1; 3.10.1; 3.25.5;
4.33.3. Rousseau (SC 293.201-2 [SC 294.25 n. 2]) notes that this expression is
used of the bread and the wine in the Eucharist, which to the Gnostics is an
earthly, and therefore evil, work of the Demiurge.

7. "Build up" stands for *instruemus*, which here does not mean to
instruct, but to build up the catholic system over against the Gnostic system,
which he will overthrow. But what does the object (*quae nobis apta sunt*) mean?
Since it is parallel to *et quae permittit tempus*, it seems to mean "according to our
ability." But I did wonder whether it could mean "whatever is fitting to us,"
namely, to our purpose in this book.

8. For the title indicated in this paragraph see ACW 55.2-3. This last
sentence is given in the MSS as follows: *Oportet enim absconditas ipsorum coniugationes per manifestarum coniugationum indicium et euersionem Bythum dissoluere, et
quoniam neque fuerit aliquando neque sit accipere ostensionem.* That Latin is certainly defective, because *dissoluere* would have a double accusative, namely,
coniugationes and *Bythum*. That would not be changed by Harvey's suggestion
(Harvey 250 n. 2) that *et* be restored before *Bythum*. Grabe (Grabe 113 note
g) had suggested moving *dissoluere* after *euersionem* and *et* before *Bythum*, in the
sense that conjugal couples would be brought to naught and Profundity
would be proved nonexistent. Rousseau (SC 293.202 [SC 294.25 n. 4])
accepts Grabe's solution. That would make sense, but a simpler solution presents itself, and seems certain from parallel cases. "In" seems to have fallen
out before *Bythum;* namely, their conjugal couples are annihilated *in*
Profundity, not having any basis without him who does not exist. See 2.8.3: *in
profundum perditionis descendentes;* and 2.12.8: *instabilis autem et uniuersa illorum
regula, ipso firmamento ipsorum dissipato et in Bythum, hoc est in id quod non est, dis-
soluto.*

CHAPTER 1

1. Cf. Exod 20:11; Ps 145 (146):6; John 1:3; Acts 4:24; 14:15.

2. Rousseau (SC 293.202-3 [SC 294.27 n. 1]) remarks that this is a new formulation of the Rule of Truth and that Irenaeus would view the Gnostic refusal to acknowledge the true divinity of God the Creator as their most fundamental error.

3. "Without limit" seems correct for *in immenso*, rather than "in his immensity." See Tertullian, *Adv. Marc.* 1.11 (CCL 1.451–53), who has a similar argument. Rousseau (SC 293.203–4 [SC 294.27 n. 2]) believes that the repetition of "another" suggests that Irenaeus has two distinct adversaries in mind: the Valentinians and Marcion.

4. "Beginning" is *terminus* in Lat. Iren., which I took as the *terminus a quo*, or the beginning, since it is in contrast to *finem*. That is the interpretation given in the next sentence. Rousseau (SC 293.204–5 [SC 294.29 n. 1]) thinks that *terminus* is a copyist's mistake for *initium*.

5. I accept Rousseau's argument (SC 293.205 [SC 294.29 n. 2]) that *conditus* is a corruption of *contentus*. "By some other authority" is *ab altera principalitate*. *Principalitas* can translate either αὐθεντία or ἐξουσία. "More powerful" is *magis dominus*, which is an extremely slavish attempt to give κυριώτερον, which is found in A.H. 1.13.4.

6. That is, if Fullness is contained by what is outside of it, then the first God who is within Fullness will also be contained by what is outside Fullness, and he will be limited and really not God at all.

7. "Around themselves" is *secundum eos*, which one might wish at first sight to give as "according to them," but then *esse dicunt* would be a kind of duplication. So this expression has adjectival force, as it does so often in Lat. Iren. Another example occurs only a few lines below in 2.1.4, where *secundum nos* seems to mean "the things of our world."

8. Even though the Latin MSS have *circumfinit*, in the present, the other verb in the pair is in the future: *continebit*. Thus, I translate *circumfinit* by "will put bonds around."

9. Rousseau (SC 293.206 [SC 294.33 n. 1]) wonders whether the expression *aliud pelagus Dei* (translated in English as "another sea of deity") is a free translation of the Greek ἄλλον βυθόν or whether *Dei* has been added inappropriately by a copyist in the course of transmitting the text.

10. "Innumerable worlds" is *immensos mundos*, which in itself could refer to the large size of the worlds, but here it rather expresses that they are immeasurable in number, just as the Gods are "interminable" in number.

11. "Condemned" is *iudicata*, which is accepted by Massuet (MG 7.712 n. 8) as modifying *conditio*. It is a correct complement to *poenam*. The Clermont and Voss Codices have *apostatam...iudicatam*, which is certainly faulty, but it confirms *iudicata* rather than *iudicatus*, the reading of the

Salamanca Codex. Harvey's guess (1.253 n. 5) that *iudicata* might be a corrupt reading for *indicata*, supposing ἐλεγχθεῖσα, and meaning "having been exposed," is therefore useless.

CHAPTER 2

1. "More concerned" is *efficaciores*. At first sight one might think that this means something like "more powerful." See 2.30.4, where *efficax* means "efficacious," and 4.38.3, where it means capable of effecting. In 5.26.1, too, it means capable of effecting. In that case it is a synonym for *agiles* and is probably a gloss. On *agiles sive efficaces*, see SC 152.324 [SC 153.325 n. 1]. Yet the rest of the ideas in this sentence have to do with negligence (*negligens sit*) and not caring (*nullam curam habens*). It seems probable, then, that "more concerned" is a better translation here.

2. This translation is based on Rousseau's argument (SC 293.207 [SC 294.37 n. 1]) that the context indicates that it is not really a question of who is outside the First God but of what reality is outside him.

3. This is based on Rousseau's and Doutreleau's reading: *Fabricatorem (vel) Angelos* (SC 294.37). Rousseau argues that this reading fits well with the context of the whole chapter, in which Irenaeus argues against those who claim that the world was made by the Angels or some other Creator of the world. See SC 293.207 (SC 294.37 n. 2).

4. "Success" is for *correctio* in Lat. Iren., which, according to J. de Billy (see Harvey 1.255 n. 1), supposes either κατόρθωμα or κατόρθωσις, but *correctio* was not a good choice; it was simply a very literal translation that can be understood only through the Greek original.

5. The translation for the last part of this sentence is based on Rousseau's and Doutreleau's restoration (SC 293.209 [SC 294.39 n. 1]) of it: *...et non Angeli neque alius quis mundi Fabricator praeter illum qui fuit prolator et primus causa e factionis huiusmodi praeparat <or> exsistens.*

6. The translation here reflects acceptance of Rousseau's argument (SC 293.209 [SC 294.39 n. 2]) that *suasorius siue seductorius* seems to be a doublet to express πιθανός.

7. The translation "God has no need of anything that exists" is based on Rousseau's restoration (SC 293.209 [SC 294.39 n. 2]) of the Greek original for this phrase: ὁ τῶν ἁπάντων ἀπροσδεὴς Θεός. For more on this expression, see SC 263.280–81 [SC 264.309 n. 4]).

8. Cf. Hermas, *Mand.* 1.1.

9. Rousseau (SC 293.210 [SC 294.39 n. 2]) notes that "much inferior to himself and ignorant of the Father" is a phrase that practically repeats what

Irenaeus said in A.H. 1.25.1 and 1.26.1 when he discussed the teaching of Carpocrates and Cerinthus.

10. The translation of "form" for *consonantiam* is based on Rousseau's argument (SC 293.210 [SC 294.32 n. 2]) that the underlying Greek word would be ῥυθμός, which would mean here the form of something.

11. The translation "to supercelestial, a supercelestial" is based on our agreement with Rousseau's proposal (SC 293.210 [SC 294.32 n. 2]) that the primitive Latin text perhaps would have been *et supercaelestibus<super>caelestem.*

12. The translation is based on our acceptance of Rousseau's suggestion (SC 293.211 [SC 294.32 n. 2]) that the Latin originally had instead of *(ae)qualitatis* a participle like *praebens* or *praestans.*

13. "Sufficient" is based on Rousseau's observation (SC 293.212 [SC 294.41 n. 1]) that the Latin *idoneus...et sufficiens* is a repetitious way to express the Greek ἱκανός.

14. John 1:3.

15. The reference is to Gen 1:3, 6, 9, 11, 14, 20, 24, 26, where God is said to have created by his Word. Other ancient Christian writers made the same deduction. See Tertullian, *Adv. Prax.* 5, 7 (CCL 2.1163–64, 1165–67).

16. Pss 32 (33):9; 148:5.

17. Cf. Num 12:7; Heb 3:5.

18. Gen 1:1.

19. Eph 4:6. Here and in other places where Irenaeus cites this passage (cf. A.H. 4.20.2; 5.18.2; and Proof 5), he omits the words καί and πάντων. He must have found it so in his Bible MSS. See ACW 16.140 n. 34.

CHAPTER 3

1. Lat. Iren. had a double question, which is obscure. Grabe (118 note k) correctly noted that the translator missed the supposed Greek construction, which should have been rendered by *aut...aut*, not *utrum... an.*

2. Lat. Iren. has *uisibilem*, which most authors correct to *inuisibilem.* Harvey's idea (1.257–58 n. 5) that the author wrote *visibilem*, in the sense of "eternal, though visible," does not seem correct.

3. Cf. Tertullian, *Adv. Marc.* 1.13 (CCL 1.454).

CHAPTER 4

1. Rousseau (SC 293.213 [SC 294.45 n. 2]) points out that Irenaeus has previously mentioned in A.H. 1.22.1 that if God created things that were con-

signed to last but a season, it is because of some dispensation that is destined to be realized in the course of history.

2. The Latin text is faulty. The adjectives *prolatum, aequale, cognatum*, and *antiquius* are neuter, obviously because in Greek their noun κένωμα is neuter. In Latin *uacuitas* is feminine.

3. Heracleon was not mentioned by Irenaeus in Book I. Little is known of him. Heresiologists mention him after Ptolemaeus as a follower of Valentinus. Clement of Alexandria speaks of him as the most esteemed of Valentinus's followers (*Strom.* 4.9.71 [GCS 52{15}.280]). He wrote a commentary on John's Gospel, of which some forty-eight quotations are preserved in Origen's commentary on John. These fragments are published in *The Fragments of Heracleon*, ed. A. E. Brooke, vol. 1 no. 4 of *Texts and Studies*, ed. J. A. Robinson (Cambridge [England]: University Press, 1891), 1-112. On Heracleon, see also C. Gianotto, "Heracleon," EEC 1.374; Rudolph *Gnosis* 17, 323–24.

4. "Perplexed" is *aporiati* in Lat. Iren., transliterated from the Greek, just as the noun *aporia* was also transliterated. It is also used in A.H. 2.7.1 and 2.7.2. The long sentence here is rather involved in construction, with a number of infinitives. Not all scholars note the correct dependence. *Confiteantur* is the main verb, which governs the infinitives *continere* and *contineri*, expressing something about what is outside the Fullness and then what is within the Fullness. But in between there is a long parenthesis, as indicated by Harvey (1.259). And so *necessitas* of this parenthesis governs *definiri* and *circumscribi* and *dicere*. *Dicere* is not controlled by *confiteantur*.

5. "Distance" is witnessed by the Clermont MS, and it must be correct. In A.H. 2.5.2 *localiter* is put in opposition to knowledge or ignorance. And so here we have the same opposites. If one speaks about something within or without the Fullness, that is a distinction of place, and not of knowledge, as if the Fullness were knowledge, and what is without were ignorance.

6. We accept Grabe's (120) reading of *indecibilitatem*.

7. "From it" is *ab eo*. Grabe (120 n. 5), Massuet (MG 7.720 n. 74), and Stieren (1.287 n. 11) take Demiurge to be the antecedent. Harvey's (1.260 n. 1) suggestion, however, seems certain—that *eo* is neuter and refers to *labe*, which is neuter in Greek (ὑστέρημα).

8. "Acknowledge" supposes *confiteri*. Lat. Iren. has *fieri*, and Massuet (MG 7.720–21 n. 77) thinks that supposes ποιεῖσθαι, which is in the middle voice and should have been translated with *facere*. But Lundström (Lundström *Studien* 72) thinks that the original was *confiteri*. This verb occurs in A.H. 2.3.1; 2.4.2; and 2.5.1. Since *con-* was often written simply *c*, the corruption to *fieri* was rather simple. It makes better sense here.

CHAPTER 5

1. We accept Rousseau's contention (SC 293.215 [SC 294.53 n. 1]) that the Latin translator has not got the force of the underlying Greek ὑπὸ ἐκτὸς τοῦ Πληρώματος. The context indicates that it is not a question of who is outside of the Fullness, but rather of what is outside of it.

2. Our translation is based on Grabe's emendation (121 n. 6) *quasi temporalia sint ac terrena et choica.*

3. The MSS have *aut...aut....* So does Massuet (MG 7.721) without any remark. Harvey (1.261) inserts *at* after the first *aut* in brackets, but gives no explanation. We used *at* in place of *aut*, but *aut* would also seem to read well.

4. Cf. A.H. 1.2.4; 1.4.5.

5. Rousseau (SC 293.216 [SC 294.55 n. 1]) remarks that Irenaeus is directing these remarks against the system of Ptolemaeus.

6. Our translation has been influenced by Rousseau's remarks (SC 293.216 [SC 294.55 n. 2]) that the Latin translator may have substituted αὐτοῦ for αὐτῶν.

7. For their Christ giving knowledge, see A.H. 1.6.1.

8. Cf. Luke 15:3–7.

9. We agree with Rousseau (SC 293.217 [SC 294.59 n. 1]) that the Latin *inualidus et infirmus* is a doublet translating ἀσθενής

10. Homer, *Il.* 4.43.

CHAPTER 6

1. For the rationale of this translation, see SC 293.218 (SC 294.61 n. 2).

2. Rousseau notes (SC 293.218–19 [SC 294.61 n. 2]) that Irenaeus opposes the god of the Gnostics, who cannot make himself known since he is a prisoner of his transcendence, to the true God, who not only could but in fact has made himself known through the agency of his Word.

3. Cf. Rom 1:20.

4. Cf. Matt 11:27; Luke 10:22, but Irenaeus inverted the first two phrases. For a thorough analysis of Irenaeus's method of quoting this text, see R. Luckhart, "Matthew 11, 27 in the 'Contra Haereses' of St. Irenaeus," *Revue de l'Université d'Ottawa* 23 (1953): 65*–79*. The passage is quoted nine times by Irenaeus: twice as used by the Gnostics, and seven times as his own. The major difference is that the Gnostics changed the present tense (*cognoscit*) to the perfect (*cognovit*) in order to bolster their error (see A.H. 2.14.7). In his own citations, Irenaeus at times inverts the first two phrases, which does not affect the essential meaning. See also Rousseau's remarks on this in SC 293.266 (SC 294.293 n. 3) and SC 100*.207–8 (SC 100**.435 n. 1). Rousseau

(SC 293.219 [SC 294.61 n. 2]) notes that even though the Gospel text does
not make clear the object of this revelation, according to Irenaeus, the Son
reveals both himself and the Father.

    5. Lat. Iren. has *ratio*, which supposes *logos*. A. Orbe ("San Ireneo y el
conocimiento natural de Dios," *Gregorianum* 47 [1966]: 712–13) also punctu-
ates this sentence in this way, namely, with the *quando ratio...revelet eis* clause as
a temporal parenthetical remark, so that *quoniam est unus Deus*, etc., is the
object not of *revelet* but of *cognoscunt*. This paragraph recalls Rom 1:19–20. It
is a classic passage in Irenaeus for our knowledge of God through the light of
reason. Th.-A. Audet ("Orientations théologiques chez Saint Irénée: Le
Contexte mental d'une Γνῶσις Ἀληθής," *Traditio* 1 [1943]: 33–39) denies that
Irenaeus held that we can have a natural knowledge of God. He claims that
such a clear distinction between the natural and supernatural order is premature in Irenaeus. Was it, perhaps, premature also in the book of Wisdom,
and in Romans, to which Irenaeus is alluding? The reality is clearly in
Irenaeus, as in the Bible, though the more modern terms of natural and
supernatural are not used. Orbe ("San Ireneo," 441–71, 710–47) stresses the
need of being aware that the Gnostics admitted that one could know the
Creator-Demiurge *ex creatis*, and that Irenaeus was fully aware of their tenet,
which he did not reject, but accepted. He did, however, insist that the Creator
God is the same as the supreme God. In the passage under consideration, it
is true, Irenaeus speaks not of human but of angelic knowledge of God
through his providence. Still, it has rightly been applied as a parallel case to
humankind, because if the Angels should come to a knowledge of God
through his care of them, then other intelligent beings should too. And,
indeed, as Irenaeus proceeds, he speaks of the knowledge of God by all creatures. At the end of the paragraph he quotes Luke 10:22 about the Son's
revealing the Father. In other words, for a knowledge of the Trinity a revelation is needed. But Irenaeus immediately speaks of our natural knowledge of
God as ruler of all things. Moreover, from the second paragraph, as well as
from the beginning of this first paragraph, it is clear that he means natural
knowledge, because he tells us that God is known as the Ruler and Creator of
the world. The example about the emperor removes all doubt. As Orbe ("San
Ireneo," 467 nn. 45, 46) notes, this illustration was classic in Hellenism. It is
knowledge gotten by reason from the dominion of God, not by faith in a statement of God; and infused knowledge is altogether out of the question. In
A.H. 2.7.5 Irenaeus speaks of God as the architect of this world—again, a
proof that he is speaking of natural knowledge. In A.H. 2.1.3–4, when arguing against the Gnostics as never coming to a full stop in God unless they
admit that he is the Fullness, containing absolutely all things (cf. also 2.7.5;
2.16.1–3), the bishop really uses the rational argument from the absolute and
infinite perfection of being. Besides, in other passages he expressly and
clearly speaks of our natural knowledge of God. In A.H. 2.9.1 he distinguishes

four sources of our knowledge of God: tradition from Adam on, the preaching of the prophets, the preaching of the apostles, and the knowledge derived by the heathens from a contemplation of creation: "...whereas the heathens learned it from creation itself. Really, creation itself manifests him who created it, and the work itself suggests him who made it; and world manifests him who put order into it." The first three of these sources are based on supernatural revelation, but the fourth, being that of the heathen, without Scripture, is reason. In A.H. 2.27.2 he gives two sources, Scripture and creation. Having spoken of the Prophets and the Gospels as clear voices of God, he says: "Furthermore, since the very creation in which we are testifies, by the things that come under our eyes, to this same thing, namely, that there is one who made it and governs it, those persons will seem very dull who blind their eyes in the face of such clear manifestations and refuse to see the light of the preaching." In A.H. 2.25.1 it is evident also that creatures can know their director through providence; and some heathens, as a matter of fact, did come to a knowledge of him. See also A.H. 4.20.7, where he distinguishes natural knowledge from the supernatural. In our present passage, Irenaeus says that God might have been invisible because of his eminence, but he could not have been unknown because of his providence. In A.H. 4.20.1 he claims that God is invisible and unknowable by reason of his greatness, but knowable and known by reason of his love. Some scholars claim, therefore, that Irenaeus holds that God can be known only through supernatural revelation, which he grants out of love. That conclusion is unwarranted. The bishop means that God out of love granted to us to know him even through providence, namely, from creation. "Because of his providence" in 2.6.1 is the same as "by reason of his love" in A.H. 4.20.4. But Irenaeus, some will say, insists that we cannot know God without God, that is, according to them, without the revelation through the Son of God, as he says in A.H. 4.6.6; 4.20.6. However, to understand him it is necessary to note that he holds that the eternal Word began to reveal God through creation already; the works of creation are his and are made according to his image. So through them the Word reveals God to us in the light of our reason. This he teaches openly in A.H. 4.20.7: "To be sure, if the revelation of God through the creation bestows life on all who live on earth," which he contrasts with "much more does the manifestation of the Father through the Word bestow life on those who see God." In other words, if the lowest form of knowing God, through creation, gives life, much more so does the highest form, seeing God, bestow life. So Audet's statement ("Orientations théologiques," 36, 37 n. 115, 50–51) that the revelation through the Word is all in the supernatural order is not correct at all. The same objection must made against L. Escuola, "Saint Irénée et la connaisance naturelle de Dieu," *RSR* 20 (1940): 252–70, who claims that a critical study led him to hold a different view from J. Lebreton, who defended the natural knowledge of God in *Histoire du Dogme de la Trinité des Origines au Concile du*

Nicée, vol 2: *De Saint Clement à Saint Irénée,* 8th ed. (Paris: Beauchesne, 1927), 529, 590–601; idem, "La connaisance de Dieu chez S. Irénée," *RecSR* 16 (1926): 385–406. In conclusion, we would note that, according to the bishop of Lyons, all the Word's revelation, even through creation, tends to the supernatural order in the present economy, but that does not mean that all is of the supernatural order. Irenaeus does not speak about special help from God— we would call it actual grace—to be able to see that "revelation" of God in creation. But even if he had such grace or help in mind, this knowledge of God would still be by reason, not by faith.

    6. Cf. Rom 9:5.

    7. Cf. Jas 2:19.

    8. Cf. Phil 2:10; 1 Cor 15:27.

    9. Cf. Hermas, *Mand.* 1.

    10. Cf. Rom 9:5.

    11. Savior was the cause of the fructification of Achamoth, and from her came Demiurge and the entire material creation. Demiurge was unaware that he was merely the instrument of Savior. See A.H. 1.4.5.

CHAPTER 7

    1. See A.H. 1.5.1, 5.

    2. The editors (Grabe 125; Massuet MG 7.726–27 n. 17; Stieren 1.294 n. 10; Harvey 1.265 n. 4) all read a genitive absolute in the Latin (which would be a Greek construction) without saying what the MSS had. This is the sentence: *Quid autem si non...aporiata esset Mater ipsorum, non habuisset Saluator per quae honoraret plenitudinem, extremae confusionis non habentis propriam substantiam, per quam honoraret Propatorem?* In A.H. 1.4.1 Achamoth is said to have been perplexed because she had no proper substance, only matter, until Christ came to give her form. With the genitive absolute she, as the "extreme confusion," is said to have had no proper substance, and that is why her son, Savior, did not have wherewithal to honor the Fullness, or the First-Father. And so this construction can pass, though it is awkward to have Achamoth mentioned as Mother and subject of the dependent clause and then introduced as the "extreme confusion" in a genitive absolute sandwiched into the independent clause. As the sentence stands, Savior must be the subject of the second *honoraret Propatorem,* as he is of the first *honoraret plenitudinem.* And yet one would almost expect the last part to read: "just as she because of the extreme confusion did not have the proper substance whereby she might honor the First-Father." Be that as it may, Lundström (Lundström *Studien* 46–47) came up with a different reading. He found *habemus* in the Clermont MS, but could not make any sense out of it. But he thinks that the participle should be *habens,*

namely, Savior did not have the proper substance of the extreme confusion. Yet that would be a rather elliptical manner of stating that Savior did not have this because of the extreme confusion of the Mother. So I hesitatingly stay with the customary reading. Rousseau (SC 293.221-22 [SC 294.67 n. 1]) also follows Grabe and Massuet in taking *extremae confessionis non habentis* as a genitive absolute in a causal sense. He notes that in A.H. 1.4.1 Irenaeus describes the passions of Achamoth: grief, fear, perplexity, and ignorance. Irenaeus returns here to perplexity, which, when solidified and crystallized, becomes the material substance out of which the world was made (cf. A.H. 1.4.2, 1.4.5, 1.5.4). The thought of Irenaeus here becomes clear when one recalls this background information.

3. Following Klebba, BKV 3.110, I have taken aeon in its original meaning of perpetual time, as *tunc* in the next phrase seems to demand. ANF (1.366 n. 3), following Massuet (MG 7.727 n. 18), and Rousseau and Doutreleau (SC 294.67) understand it of an Aeon who is without honor because the things Savior had made to honor it have been destroyed.

4. *Indissimilis* occurs only here in A.H.; see B. Reynders, *Lexique comparé du texte grec et des versions latine, arménienne, et syriaque de l' "Adversus haereses" de saint Irénée*, vol. 2: *Index des mots latins*, CSCO 142 Subsidia Tome 6 (Louvain: L. Durbecq, 1954), 157. *In-* simply emphasizes the negation. *Dissimilis*, in the same meaning, occurs a few lines later in the paragraph. On *indissimilis* in this sense, see TLL 7.1, s.v. "*indissimilis.*"

5. Rousseau (SC 293.222 [SC 294.69 n. 1]) notes that "Maker of the world" refers to Savior and "image of Only-begotten" is the Demiurge. For more on this passage, see Sagnard *Gnose* 407–8.

6. See chapter 6, n. 11.

7. "Varied" is according to the editors' guess. Though all the MSS have *vacua*, this does not fit with *multa* as its pair, while *varia* does. The contrast is to the small number of thirty Aeons, for which *vacua* does not fit. In the next sentence there is talk of variety of creation.

8. Rousseau (SC 293.223 [SC 294.71 n. 1]) would prefer to read *in Pleromate* for *Pleroma* and *adnumerari possunt* for *esse adnumerant eos* (var. *adnumerantes*) *ostendere*.

9. Cf. Matt 25:41.

10. Cf. Dan 7:10, but the phrases are in inverse order.

11. As Harvey (1.268-69 n. 5) notes, Irenaeus seems to reason thus: In the Gnostic system, the Aeons and the Angels of the Fullness are homogeneous, while things created here below are heterogeneous. Yet the former are said to be the archetypes of these latter. So either those Aeons must be heterogeneous, which is contrary to their theory, or created things are homogeneous, which is contrary to fact.

12. The translation is here is influenced by Rousseau's remark (SC 293.224 [SC 294.77 n. 3]) that *effusa et locupletia* may be a doublet.

CHAPTER 8

1. Rousseau (SC 293.225 [SC 294.79 n. 1]) agrees with Grabe that in *ut...esse* the Latin translator has brought over a construction that is normal in Greek but harsh in Latin.

2. *Unum* is not determined further, but from what had been said earlier, it is clear that Irenaeus means that the things in the Fullness are of like nature, and so they are one.

3. "Shadow of the void" sounds first like an error for "shadow or void," but that is the Latin: *umbra cenomatis.* That *cenomatis* should be in the genitive is confirmed by the translator's explanatory word *uacui.* Void existed first, and from that came shadow; and so shadow is said to be that of void.

4. This is a play on the name of Profundity, the supreme god of the Gnostics.

CHAPTER 9

1. Cf. Matt 5:16, 45; 6:1, 9.

2. Cf. n. 5 of chapter 6 on the natural knowledge of God. Rousseau (SC 293.226 [SC 294.85 n. 1]) compares this material to A.H. 4.6.6.

3. Cf. A.H. 1.10.1 and ACW 55.48–49, 184.

4. Cf. A.H. 1. 23.1–2.

5. Rom 1:25.

6. Gal 4:8.

7. Isa 46:9.

8. Cf. Exod 3:14. We accept Rousseau and Doutreleau's reading (SC 294.87) of *super hunc qui sit fingentes.*

CHAPTER 10

1. Rousseau (SC 293.226–27 [SC 294.87 n. 2]) notes that *parabolas* is not referring to parables as we commonly understand them (e.g., the Parable of the Prodigal Son) but rather refers to any fact or event in the Scripture that can make known beyond its immediate content a more profound reality that it represents or claims to represent. Rousseau also remarks that in parables in this sense the heretics imagine that they have discovered symbols that disclose realities that are superior to our world and its Maker. See A.H. 2.20.1 for other examples of parables in this sense.

2. A.H. 1.3.6.

3. Cf. A.H. 1.8.1.

4. The construction of this sentence is a puzzle to scholars. The beginning, *ut enim sciant*, sounds at first like a wish: *utinam sciant*. But there is a second *ut* clause later, which is paired with the first one by *et*. This second one is obviously a final *ut* dependent on *uanos sermones collegerunt* toward the end of the sentence. It seems certain to me that the first *ut* is also dependent on *collegerunt*, as I have translated. Massuet (MG 7.735 n. 77) missed the point of the first phrase by explaining it as *ut sciant se hoc ipsum scire*. *Se* has no business in the clause. The *hoc* before *non discentes* I referred to *baptismum*, that is, though they concocted stories and referred to the baptism, they did not really grasp its meaning. Of course, it is possible for this *hoc* to refer to *hoc ipsum*; namely, though they knew this fact of the baptism, they really did not grasp it. The baptism is called "of the Truth" because it pertains to the Catholic system of the Truth, and these heretics really were not initiated into this Truth through baptism. I do not think that it merely stresses the reality of the baptism, namely, the "baptism in Truth," as authors usually think. Rousseau (SC 293.227 [SC 294.89 n. 1]) feels that *ut enim sciant hoc ipsum scire* is unacceptable. He suggests that *sciant* is a corruption of another verb and proposes to substitute either *uideantur* or *putentur* for *sciant*.

5. Cf. Wis 1:14; 2 Macc 7:28. Another echo by Irenaeus of a phrase from Hermas, *Mand.* 1.1. For more on this, see SC 293.227–28 (SC 294.89 n. 2); ACW 55.80, 226; and SC 263.276–78 (SC 264.309 n. 1).

6. Cf. A.H. 1.5.4.

7. Cf. A.H. 1.30.3.

8. Cf. Luke 18:27. Theophilus of Antioch, *Auto.* 2.13, has the same combination of ideas about God's making things out of nothing and his power to do everything as worded by Jesus in Luke 18:27. See R. M. Grant, *Theophilus of Antioch Ad Autolycum: Text and Translation*, Oxford Early Christian Texts (Oxford: Clarendon Press, 1970), 47; see also Theophilus of Antioch, *Auto.* 1.5 (Grant, *Theophilus of Antioch*, 7) about knowing God through his providence.

9. The translation is influenced by Rousseau's remark (SC 294.91 n. 2 [SC 293.228–29]) that the words *quidem eius* of all the Latin MSS do not seem appropriate for the situation. He thinks that the Latin should be something like *extra ipsam factam*.

CHAPTER 11

1. Rousseau (SC 293.229 [SC 294.93 n. 1]) notes that "wise" here means the Architect's "skill" or his technical "talent" and that this expression has a polemical intent: the "skill" of God the Creator is opposed to the ignorance of the Demiurge of the heretics. Irenaeus has returned repeatedly to this theme in the course of the preceding chapters.

2. That the world was created by Angels was a favorite Gnostic opinion: see Simon Magus, A.H. 1.23.3; Menander, 1.23.5; Saturninus, 1.24.1; Basilides, 1.24.4; Carpocrates, 1.25.1.

3. *Three Hundred Aesop's Fables*, trans. G. F. Townsend (London and New York: Routledge, n.d.), 11.

4. Cf. Matt 11:25.

5. Cf. John 17:2–3.

6. Rousseau (SC 293.229–30 [SC 294.93 n. 2]) thinks that *haec* of the Latin is out of place here and should really be *habere*. He also remarks that this passage refutes the theory of those who do not see continuity in the plan of Irenaeus through all five books of the *Adversus haereses*. For more information about the continuity in Irenaeus's plan for the whole work, see P. Bacq, *De l'ancienne à la nouvelle Alliance selon S. Irénée: Unité du Livre IV de l' Adversus haereses* (Paris: Lethielleux, 1978), 22–29.

CHAPTER 12

1. Cf. Luke 3:23.

2. The translation is based on Rousseau and Doutreleau's reading *hac...decidente*. For their rationale for this emendation, see SC 293.230 (SC 294.97 n. 1).

3. His discussion of their system by reason of "defect" runs on through paragraph 6. Paragraph 7 begins the discussion by reason of "excess." For more on this, see SC 293.139–40.

4. We have not translated the phrase *et propter hoc incapabilis* because we were influenced by Rousseau's opinion (SC 293.231 [SC 294.97 n. 2]) that those words seem to be nothing more than a gloss repeating *quem nemo capit.*

5. Only the Ptolemaeans included Profundity in their count of the Triacontad. See A.H. 1.8.5.

6. Our translation of "Thought or Silence" is influenced by Rousseau's remark (SC 293.231 [SC 294.99 n. 1]) that for this phrase to make sense, the Latin should be emended to *primam emissionem Ennoiam* uel *Sigen uocantes.*

7. See A.H. 1.30.3.

8. Material creation with all its evils sprang from Wisdom's degeneracy.

9. "For these are destructive of each other...no darkness." These two sentences are found in Armenian translation in *The Seal of the Faith of the Holy Catholic Church.* For more on this Armenian fragment, see SC 293.108–10.

10. We note here that the Gnostics used a term for the Word that was used also by Origen and Nemesius Emesenus in a correct sense, namely, ἐνδιάθετος. This is contrasted with the Word that was emitted and called *Verbum*

emissionis (A.H. 2.28.6) and *emissibilis* (A.H. 2.13.2), or *prolatiuus* (A.H. 2.13.8). The Greek for this was προφορικός.

11. Rousseau (SC 293.232 [SC 294.107 n. 1]) remarks that the Latin text is manifestly incoherent. We base our translation on Rousseau's and Doutreleau's reconstruction of the Greek text: Ἔτι τε προβολὴν λέγουσι γεγονέναι ὑπὸ του Μονογενοῦς Χριστοῦ καὶ Πνεύματος ἁγίου. Rousseau thinks that Χριστοῦ and Πνεύματος ἁγίου can only be connected to προβολήν.

12. "All." Harvey (1.279 n. 2) suggested that perhaps the author had written ὄρον (Limit), which was misread as ὅλον and translated as *Totum*. Klebba, BKV 3.122 accepted that. Yet Savior was known as the "All" (cf. A.H. 2.5.2). Below, "Limit" is distinguished from "Savior."

13. "Stake." We followed Grabe's suggestion (134 n. 6) that *Sotera* (Lat. Iren. here uses this Greek transcription) should be *Stauron* ("stake"); actually Savior (now given with the Latin *Saluatorem*) is spoken of immediately after as distinct from "Limit" (*Horos*), which would be an awkward sentence if *Sotera* were correct. Rousseau (SC 293.232 [SC 294.107 n. 2]) agrees with Grabe's suggestion here.

14. As we translated, Irenaeus is saying that these "emissions" would not be worthy of the name of the Aeons or of being classed in their number. Lat. Iren. has *appellatione et numero* in the ablative. Lundström (Lundström *Studien* 52) thinks it certain that *numeri* (genitive singular), which is in the Clermont and Voss MSS and was written by Erasmus, is correct. He remarks that we have here a pair of genitives depending on *indignos*. But he does not say what the other genitive is. It could not be *Aeonum*, but *appellatione*.

15. "Weaker...weak." Lat. Iren. has *infirmiores* according to the Arundel and Voss MSS. The Clermont MS has the odd superlative *infimus* made comparative *infimiores*, for which, as Harvey (1.279 n. 4) notes, there would be no thinkable Greek equivalent. And so *infimi* (lowest) in the next sentence should read *infirmi*, as giving better sense.

16. Translators stumble on the Latin construction here. Harvey's suggestion (1.280 n. 1) that Pleroma be implied as object of *auferri* seems improbable. The translation seems, as often elsewhere, very literally Greek, and so *illorum Aeonum* is a genitive of separation governed by *auferri*. Rousseau (SC 293.232–33 [SC 294.107 n. 3]) reconstructs the Greek original as ἐκείνων τῶν Αἰώνων...ἀφαιρεῖσθαι and remarks that the Greek should have been translated into Latin by *ab illis Aeonibus...auferri*. Thus, Irenaeus is placing a dilemma: either class the four Aeons with the other Aeons of the Fullness, or deprive also the Aeons of the Fullness of the honor of belonging to the Fullness.

17. Our translation is based on Rousseau's (SC 293.233 [SC 294.109 n. 1]) tentative restitution of the Greek: ἐπὶ γὰρ τοιούτῳ ἀριθμῷ εἰ τὸ πλεῖον ἥ τὸ ἔλαττον ἀδόκιμον ποιήσει τὸν ἀριθμόν, πόσῳ μᾶλλον τὰ ἀμφότερα.

18. Irenaeus touched on this in A.H. 1.3.3.

19. "Babble nonsense" is *delirant*.

CHAPTER 13

1. This translation is based on Rousseau's remark (SC 293.234 [SC 294.111 n. 1]) that the Latin *ipsum quod est principale et summum* is a doublet for the Greek τὸ ἡγεμονικόν, a Stoic term that indicated the principal part of the soul or intellect.

2. This translation is based on Rousseau's remark (SC 293.234 [SC 294.111 n. 1]) that the relative clause *quae ab hoc est* should be linked not to ἔννοια (thought) but to *motio* (activity). He also compares the definition of ἔννοια provided by Irenaeus to a definition of βούλησις (will, purpose) given by Maximus Confessor and notes that they are more or less stereotypical formulae that quite likely originated in the philosophical schools.

3. "It would have been more plausible...body and soul." There is an Armenian fragment of the text beginning here and continuing through the first sentence of 2.13.3. Rousseau and Doutreleau have designated this fragment as Fr. arm. 1. It has been preserved among the ancient Armenian translations of the works of Evagrius Ponticus. For more information on this fragment, see SC 293.102–7, 366–70.

4. This translation is based on Rousseau's (SC 293.235 [SC 294.111 n. 2]) remark that *principalem et primum locum* is a doublet translating τὸ ἡγεμονικόν.

5. This translation is based on Rousseau's (SC 293.235–36 [SC 294.111 n. 2]) remark that *in cogitatu dispositae* is clearly a translation of the Greek ἐνδιάθετοι.

6. This sentence is rather obscure in its conciseness. It seems he is saying that the activities of the same mind have different names because there are both a continuance and a development in the acts, but not because there is a complete change. These words are not capitalized here because they refer not to the Aeons but to acts of the mind in general.

7. We follow Rousseau's suggestion (SC 293.236 [SC294.111 n. 2]) that the reading *in cogitationem* (the reading of S) is to be preferred to *in cognitionem* (the reading of all the other MSS and Erasmus).

8. We accept Rousseau's (SC 293.236 [SC 294.111 n. 2]) reconstruction of the Greek original: κτίζοντος καὶ διέποντος αὐτεξουσίως and accept his argument that *administrante et gubernante* are a doublet translating διέποντος and the expressions *libere et ex sua potestate* are a doublet translating αὐτεξουσίως.

9. "Uttered." The Latin is *emissibilis*, evidently representing προφορικός. the opposite of ἐνδιάθετος, "immanent." Below Lat. Iren. uses *prolativum* (paragraph 8). See n. 10 in chapter 12. Rousseau (SC 293.237 [SC 294.115 n. 1]) notes that because previous editors of the Latin text have been led astray by a false symmetry, they have punctuated the text so that it would appear that "word" is a sixth and final step in the unfurling of the immanent activity in

regard to thought. He argues that διαλογισμός and ἐνδιάθετος λόγος are the fifth and final step, designated by two different expressions.

10. Rousseau (SC 293.240 [SC 294.115 n. 2]) points out that Irenaeus indicates that all men and women (the just as well as sinners) are composed of a body fashioned from the earth and a soul endowed with reason and free will. This bipartite idea, he contends, will be found also in the final chapters of Book II as well as throughout all of A.H.

11. We follow Rousseau (SC 293.240 [SC 294.115 n. 3]) as well as Grabe (136 n. 2) and Massuet (MG 7.743 n. 27), who see the Latin *ad loquendum eos* as a rather unusual translation for the Greek πρὸς τὸ λαλεῖν αὐτούς.

12. Cf. Num 23:19.

13. Cf. Isa 55:8–9.

14. We accept Rousseau's (SC 293.241 [SC294.117 n. 1]) contention that *religiosis ac piis* is a doublet translating the Greek τοῖς εὐσεβέσι. Lat. Iren. has *similimebrius*, which seems to suppose ὁμοιομερής, a term that Anaxagoras is said to have coined to express the similar nature of molecules with their substance. Cf. Harvey 1. 282 n. 2. Rousseau (SC 293.241 [SC 294.117 n. 1]), on the other hand, believes that the underlying Greek word is ὁμοιομελής. In regard to the next sentence about God's being "all hearing," and so on, and the possible use of Xenophanes, see ACW 55.54, 201 n. 4; also 2.28.4–5; 4.11.2 and Rousseau (SC 293.242–44 [SC 294.117 n. 1]).

15. "Receptacle." Harvey printed *susceptior*, following Grabe (137 note c). Massuet (MG 7.745 n. 39) has *susceptor*, which we followed. Rousseau and Doutreleau (SC 294.118) also print *susceptor*. In the next line there is obviously a parallel construction: *capabile et antiquius*, a positive and a comparative. So in the first case it should not be two comparatives.

16. We accept Rousseau's (SC 293.246 [SC 294.121 n. 1]) reconstruction of the Greek for this sentence and his suggestions for making this sentence more coherent.

17. We follow Rousseau's (SC 293.247 [SC 294.123 n. 1]) emended text: *Vbi enim ignorantia, Patre adimplente? Si enim adimpleuit, illic ignorantia non erit.*

18. Rousseau (SC 293.247–48 [SC 294.123 n. 2]) notes that in this context Irenaeus means a well-determined group of heretics whom he discussed in A.H. 1.11.1 and whose teachings he described in A.H. 1.29–30 and that the presence of the adjective *reliquos* (which would translate the Greek λοιπούς) in no way invalidates that interpretation.

19. Lat. Iren. has the strange expression *addivinantes adversum Deum*, which Massuet (MG 7.747 n. 48) interprets with *temere de Deo conjicientes*. The Greek might have been παραμαντευόμενοι (Harvey 1.285 n. 2), or καταμαντευόμενοι (Grabe 138 n. 6), or simply μαντευόμενοι as in 1.16.1.

20. Lat. Iren. has an awkward double ablative absolute for a causal clause that begins with *in eo (Deo)* and, after some parenthetical remarks, has the verbs *habente* and *perseverante*. We broke this down into shorter sentences.

The phrase *aut (nec) alterius habente in se* has stumped some translators. *Alterius*, first introduced by Grabe (138 note k) is now certain from the Clermont MS, in place of *anterius*. Irenaeus here expresses a usual thought that all things belong to God and so it is impossible for him to have anything foreign in himself, something that is also excluded by his simplicity. Rousseau, on the other hand, feels that instead of *alterius* the primitive text would have had something like *aliud posterius*. For his reasons, see SC 293.249–50 (SC 294.125 n. 1).

21. On the "uttered" word, see n. 10 in chapter 12.

22. Irenaeus clearly teaches the eternity and divinity of God's Word, thereby definitely anticipating the refutation of the Arian heresy, as Grabe (138 n. 8) already noted. See also *Proof* 3. On the Trinity in Irenaeus, see the very fine article by J. Lebreton, "La théologie de la Trinité chez saint Irénée," *Analecta sacra Tarraconensia* 2 (1926): 89–148. For a detailed treatment and bibliography on the Son, especially his eternal pre-existence, see D. J. Unger, "The Divine and Eternal Sonship of the Word According to St. Irenaeus of Lyons," *Laurentianum* 14 (1973): 357–408; and A. Rousseau, "La doctrine de S. Irénée sur la préexistence du Fils de Dieu dans *Dém.* 43," *Museon* 84 (1971): 5–42. See also Rousseau's remarks in SC 293.250–51 (SC 294.125 n. 2).

23. "God is Life...that is God, should at any time be without life." An Armenian fragment designated by Rousseau and Doutreleau as Fr. arm. 2 begins here and continues to the penultimate sentence of this paragraph. For more information on this fragment from the Galata 54 MS, see SC 293.101–2.

24. Our translation here is influenced by Rousseau's statement (SC 293.251–52 [SC 294.127 n. 1]) that the Armenian version helps establish that the underlying Greek prepositional phrase would have been κατ᾽ ἐπιγονήν, and in an abstract sense ἐπιγονή means development or growth.

25. Irenaeus concretely presents the absolute simplicity of God. "With God's name" is the same as "with God himself." "Heard together with" is the translation for the Latin *coobaudientur*, which occurs only here in Irenaeus and, as it seems, nowhere else in Latin literature. On this, see B. Reynders, *Lexique comparé du Texte et des Versions Latine, Arménienne, et Syriaque*, vol. 2: *Index des Mots Latins*, CSCO 142 Subsidia Tome 6 (Louvain: L. Durbecq, 1954), 71. The context indicates that the sense should be of harmonizing, and so Harvey (2.285 n. 7) suggests that it stands for συμφωνήσουσι. But the Latin translator was used to that Greek word and would scarcely have rendered it by such a unique Latin verb, which seems to copy a Greek word slavishly. The context rather calls for the sense of being identical with. Above he said that God is all Mind, and so on, and for what follows it is certain that here the identity is precisely in this that God and his perfections are all equally eternal. Elsewhere Lat. Iren. used *obaudire* for listening to and obeying. Here he prefixed the *co-* to the verb to indicate that all their perfections are listened to or heard at one and the same time with the Name of God, which is the same as saying that they are identical with it. The Greek verb must have been a similarly coined

word. Massuet (MG 7.747–48 n. 54) rightly interprets it with *simul intelligun-tur...et intelligenda*; but he incorrectly thinks that the ablative should be read in *appellatione*. But the dative is correct. We do not understand them at the same time "by the Name of God"; but they correspond to God's name; that is, they are identical with it. So when we hear the one, we also hear the other.

26. Rousseau (SC 293.252 [SC 294.129 n. 1]) feels that the *ex his secunda* is a Latin translation of the Greek ἑξῆς. Hence our translation of "the follow-ing" for *ex his secunda*. See SC 263.313–15 for Rousseau's discussion about the Gnostics being the immediate forebears of the Valentinians. The translation "fight them...accusing them" is based on Rousseau's contention (SC 293.252 [SC 294.129 n. 1]) that in writing *aduersus invicem* the Latin translator ought to have read πρὸς αὐτούς or ἑαυτύς and in writing *semetipsos* the Latin transla-tor misread αὐτούς or ἑαυτούς for αὐτούς.

27. Rousseau (SC 293.253 [SC 294.129 n. 2]) notes that here and in A.H. 2.14.8 Irenaeus sets forth a two-step process by which the heretics propagate their ideas. First, they make speeches offering a semblance of truth in order to soften up the simple. Second, when they feel their position has been accepted, they pour out the worst nonsense without the slightest regard for plausibility.

28. Matt 7:7.

29. We accept Rousseau's contention (SC 293.254 [SC 294.131 n. 1]) that the likely underlying Greek word ἔπειτα is distorted by the Latin *si sunt*: more likely the Latin should be *deinde* or *postea*.

CHAPTER 14

1. The Latin text actually has Antiphanes. Although there is a middle comic poet named Antiphanes (ca. 388–ca. 311 BC), and some even contend that there may have been two such comic poets named Antiphanes—cf. "Antiphanes," by William G. Waddell, *OCD*, 61—this poet is never accredited with a work entitled *Theogonia*. However, as Harvey (1.287 n. 1) notes, Aristo-phanes gives a description of the heathen cosmogony in his work the *Birds*, which has much in common with the statements Irenaeus ascribes to Antiphanes. For this reason, we accept the rationale presented by Rousseau (SC 293.254 [SC 294.131 n. 2]) for the translation "Aristophanes...in a theogony." Rousseau agrees with R. M. Grant, "Early Christianity and Greek Comic Poetry," *CPh* 60 (1965): 157–59, who believes that Antiphanes is a mistake in the Latin text, which should contain instead the name of Aristophanes.

2. Throughout this chapter we follow the example of Rousseau, who introduces the term *Valentinians* where the Latin text is not so specific.

3. Our translation of this sentence is based on Rousseau's suggestion (SC 293.255 [SC 294.131 n. 3]) that the Latin translation *quasi naturali dispu-*

tatione commenti sunt would have been a paraphrase of the Greek ἐφυσιολόγησαν. He also notes that since φυσιολογέω means "to speak on the matters of nature," Irenaeus is making a very biting criticism of the Valentinians. Even though they believe that they are speaking about matters divine, in taking the fable of Aristophanes as their own they are doing nothing more than what Aristophanes had done—that is, speaking about the matters of nature.

4. Aristophanes, *Av.* 700.

5. "Fictitious cloak" is *finctum superficium,* which some scholars think means the outer garment, arguing that Tertullian, *Cult. fem.* 2.13 (CCL 1.369) uses *superficies* in that sense. But Tertullian's meaning is doubtful, and *superficium* supposes ἐπιπολήν ("surface"), which means a building above the ground. As Harvey (1.289 n. 2) observes, more likely ἐπιβολήν ("cloak") was original and was misread as ἐπιπολήν. The context speaks of sewing, patches, or rags.

6. On Thales, see Hippolytus, *Haer.* 1.1 (GCS 26.4) and *OCD*² 1050.

7. Cicero, *De nat. deor.* 1.10: *Aquam dixit esse initium rerum, Deum autem eam mentem, quae ex aqua cuncta fingeret.* Thus, his god would be superior to water. Cf. also Diogenes Laertius 1.27; Ps.-Plutarch, *De placit. philos.* 1.2–3; Aristotle, *Metaph.* 1.3.

8. Homer, *Il.* 14.201. See also Hippolytus, *Haer.* 10.7 (GCS 26.266).

9. On the relevant fragments from Anaximander, see H. Diels-W. Kranz, *Die Fragmente der Vorsokratiker,* 8th ed. ([Berlin]: Weidmann, 1956), 1.81–90.

10. Immensity is a boundless expanse that, according to Anaximander, was the first principle of all things. See Hippolytus, *Haer.* 1.6 (GCS 26.10–11) and 10.6 (GCS 26. 266).

11. On the relevant fragments from Anaxagoras, see Diels-Kranz, *Die Fragmente der Vorsokratiker,* 8th ed. ([Berlin]: Weidmann, 1956), 2.5–44.

12. Cf. what Hippolytus said in *Haer.* 1.8 (GCS 26.14).

13. Cf. Ibid. 1.13 (GCS 26.16–17).

14. Cf. Ibid. 1.22 (GCS 26.26–27).

15. According to Hippolytus, *Haer.* 6.22 (GCS 26.149), Plato's *Timaeus* was a kind of textbook for Valentinus.

16. Democritus was an atheist, making atoms the first principle of all being. Cf. Diogenes Laertius 9.44; Cicero (*De nat. deor.* 2.30) writes: *Primum igitur aut negandum est esse deos, quod et Democritus simulacra et Epicurus imagines inducens quodam pacto negat.* The forms, according to Democritus, were expressed from the universe, the PAN. These forms were of a divine character, existing in space, visible only to favored individuals. See Sextus Empiricus, *Adversus Mathematicos* 9 (*Adversus Dogmaticos* 3), *Adversus Physicos* 1.19, 42 (Sexti Empirici, *Opera,* ed. H. Mutschmann [Leipzig: Teubner, 1912–14], 2.217, 222).

17. Cf. Ps.-Justin, *Coh. Gr.* 6 (MG 6.253). Hippolytus, *Haer.* 1.19; 10.7 (GCS 26.19, 268), gives the same information. Pseudo-Plutarch agrees that

Plato ascribed the origin of things to three principles (*De placit. philos.* 1.10). But Diogenes Laertius 3.69 says that Plato's system was dualistic: "He set forth two universal principles, God and matter, and he calls God mind and cause" (Diogenes Laertius, *Lives of Eminent Philosophers*, trans. R. D. Hicks, 2 vols., Loeb Classical Library, 1 [Cambridge, MA: Harvard University Press, 1980], 1.337). Ideas put form into matter; matter is recipient of form. It seems that the ideas, coming from the divine mind, were the one principle, almost identical with God; and matter was the other principle. According to Plato, the prototypal ideas existed eternally in the divine nature and were the origin of form and order. Cf. Plato, *Ti.* 28–29). See also Diogenes Laertius 3.13. Democritus, too, speaks of ideas, but in quite a different sense. For Plato they were the ideal world that was the archetype of present realities; for Democritus they were this world in which there was nothing real. See Sextus Empiricus, *Adversus Mathematicos* 7 (*Adversus Dogmaticos* 1) 135, 138 (Sexti Empirici, *Opera*, 2.33, 34). On this see also Harvey 1.293 n. 1 and Rousseau SC 293.257 (SC 294.137 n. 1).

18. We accept Rousseau's proposed emendation (SC 293.258 [SC 294.137 n. 1]) of *illas* in place of *illius*.

19. Hippolytus, *Haer.* 6.22 (GCS 26.149) refers to Plato's *Timaeus* for these Valentinian notions. See also Harvey 1.293 n. 2.

20. "Existent" stands for *subjecta*, which is here just a variant for *subjacentia*. Aristotle is witness that Anaxagoras taught creation from pre-existing matter, as noted by Harvey 1.294 n. 1. See Aristotle, *Ph.* 1.4.

21. Cf. Hippolytus, *Haer.* 7.29 (GCS 26.210–15).

22. Ibid. 1.19 (GCS 26.19).

23. The Valentinians claimed that they are the authors of the doctrine and were inspired by their mother Achamoth. So if the philosophers taught it, they must have been inspired by her too.

24. Homer claimed that Jupiter was subject to fate. The entire system of the Stoics was built up on this principle, as Eusebius testifies in *De Theophania* 2.21 (GCS 11, 2.90*). Seneca, *Prov.* 5.7 similarly held that principle. Cicero rejected it in *De nat. deor.* 2.30.

25. Cf. Hesiod, *Theogony* 561–612 and *Op.* 60–105. See also M. Hofinger, "L'Ève grecque et le mythe de Pandore," in *Mélanges de linguistique, de philologie et de mythologie et de méthodologie de l'enseignement des langues anciennes offerts à René Fohalle à l'occasion de son soixante-dixième anniversaire* (Gembloux: J. Duculot, 1969), 205–17.

26. Cf. A.H. 1.2.6.

27. This translation is based on Rousseau's conjecture (SC 293.259 [SC 294.139 n. 2]) that the Latin translator had a Greek text in which the preposition περί had accidentally been omitted.

28. "Noble lineage" is *generositatem*, which supposes εὐγένειαν. The Valentinians held that Achamoth was their mother, and since she had a spark

of Wisdom of the Fullness in herself, they considered themselves spiritual. Tertullian used the word in the same sense in *Adv. Marc.* 4.5.2 (CCL 1.551), and in *Carn.* 9.8 (CCL 2.893). Irenaeus has in mind particularly the Marcosians; cf. A.H. 1.12–22.

29. "Company." *Testamentum* in Latin supposes διαθήκη, which should have been translated by "company" since it can have that meaning. See LSJ, *s.v.* For a different viewpoint on translating and interpreting *testamentum*, see Rousseau's remarks in SC 293.259–60 (SC 294.139 n. 2).

30. Tertullian, too, marks the trait as Aristotelian in *Anim.* 6.7 (CCL 2.789). Rousseau (SC 293.260 [SC 294.139 n. 3]) notes that *multiloquium... subtilitatem* is a doublet translating the Greek λεπτολογίαν.

31. Cf. Hippolytus, *Haer.* 6.28, 34 (GCS 26.154–55, 162–64). Of all things numbers are the most abstract and capable of indefinite evolution. So they were thought apt symbols of the Divinity.

32. For the Pythagoreans "one," an uneven number, was the male and was the cause of dyad. It symbolized the Supreme Intellect. Dyad, susceptible of indefinite development as it was, symbolized the indefinite series of beings generated and created by the gods. Cf. Hippolytus, *Haer.* 6.23 (GCS 26.149–50).

33. Our translation is based on suggestions made by Rousseau (SC 293.260–61 [SC 294.139 n. 4]) to shed light on these obscure sentences.

34. Rousseau (SC 293.262 [SC 294.139 n. 6]) rightly notes that one gropes to understand the Latin translation of this sentence owing to a hopelessly corrupt phrase.

35. 1 Tim 6:20. "Novelties," as in the Vulgate and in a few Greek MSS (καινοφωνίας). The better MSS of the Bible have "vain talking" (κενοφωνίας).

36. Their mother, Achamoth, brought them the offspring of Father by means of Wisdom from on high; cf. A.H. 1.5.6. "Or" was inserted because a few lines down this disjunctive is used twice, and the "seed" is the mother's. It is therefore in apposition to "her," the mother. Rousseau (SC 293.262 [SC 294.141 n. 1]) also supports the adoption of this reading.

37. Matt 11:27.

38. Our translation has been influenced by Rousseau's (SC 293.263 [SC 294.143 n. 1]) contention that the Greek text should be restored to αὐτοῦ since Father is the center of interest for the whole paragraph.

39. Rousseau (SC 293.263 [SC 294.143 n. 2]) remarks that this is yet another instance of Gnostic writers using either the expression τὰ ὅλα or τὰ πάντα to designate the Aeons of their Pleroma.

40. We accept Rousseau's (SC 293.263 [SC 294.145 n. 1]) proposal to read *adsuetis suadentes* in place of *mansueti dissuadentes* and agree that the logic of the thought here requires that the Latin read *praedictas emissiones* in place of *praedictam emissionem*.

41. We accept Rousseau's contention (SC 293.263 [SC 294.145 n. 1]) that the Latin should read *congruentes*. "Plausible" is *opinatas*, which in postclassical

Latin means famous, reputable, plausible. However, Grabe (143 n. 9) and Harvey (1.301 n. 4) conjecture that the Greek was προσδοκήτους, which would mean "expected." This does not seem acceptable. Below Irenaeus says that their system does not have proof or witness or plausible argument (*verisimilitudinem*). That favors "plausible" in the sense of not having solid proof. Klebba, BKV 3.134 translates it with *unwahrscheinlich*, that is, improbable.

    42. Cf. A.H. 1.1.2 and ACW 55.24, 134–35 n. 12.

    43. Cf. A.H. 1.2.2.

    44. Cf. A.H. 1.5.

    45. Cf. A.H. 1.12.4; 2.14.9; 2.19.9.

    46. Lat. Iren. has *in labe facti*; but Savior was made in the Fullness out of all the other Aeons, not out of degeneracy, and the context demands this. Hence the Greek original πληρώματι (Fullness) must have been misread as ὑστερήματι (*labes*), or perhaps as ἐκτρώματι, which also means *labes*.

CHAPTER 15

    1. We follow Rousseau and Doutreleau (SC 293.265 [SC 294.149 n. 2]) in doubting the authenticity of the words *consentientes ad consonantionem* and have thus omitted them in this translation.

    2. This translation is based on Rousseau's translation (SC 294.151) of *octiforme et deciforme et duodeciforme* as *en groupes de huit, dix, et douze Éons*.

    3. We accept Rousseau and Douteleau's (SC 294.150) textual emendation of *rhythmizata ipsa esset*.

CHAPTER 16

    1. We accept Rousseau's suggestion (SC 293.266 [SC 294.151 n. 1]) that it would be better to read here *cogebuntur confiteri*.

    2. Cf. A.H. 1.24.3.

CHAPTER 17

    1. Cf. 1 Tim 2:4. We accept Rousseau's suggestion (SC 293.266 [294.157 n. 1]) that it would be better to read here *nobis...qui et uelimus*.

    2. Rousseau (SC 293.267 [SC 294.159 n. 1]) believes *efficabiliter* translates the Greek ἀποτελεστιως. The context here is whether Aeons are pro-

duced in the way that human beings are produced by other human beings as well as whether they are constituted in a distinct existence that is appropriate to them and that enables them to act in an autonomous manner.

3. Accepting Rousseau's (SC 293.268 [SC 294.161 n. 1]) emendation of the text: ...*sed [in] figuratione discret(us) et circumscriptione definit(us)*.

4. 1 Cor 15:41.

5. Father spoken of here is not Profundity, but Mind. Profundity is First-Father.

6. We accept Rousseau's hesitant emendation (SC 293.268 [SC 294.169 n. 1]): *sed ne ipsi quidem alteram quondam* speciem emissionis *reddentes aliquando cogniti sunt nobis....*

7. "Blind" is *caecutientes*. Some MSS have *circumeuntes*, which Massuet (MG 7.765, n. 61) approves. But that would be an awkward construction and would make poor sense: *a recta ratione circumeuntes circa veritatem!* Blindness is in this entire context, and so *caecutientes* fits well. Irenaeus's subtle irony shines in this section. The Valentinians, who present God's word as blind to the Father, are themselves blinded to the truth. Rousseau also prefers *caecutientes*, which appears in A (Arundel manuscript), Q (Vatican manuscript 187), S (Salamanca manuscript), and e (first edition by Erasmus in 1526), over *circumeuntes*, which appears in C (Clermont manuscript) and V (Voss manuscript). For more on A, Q, S, C, and V, see ACW 55.12–13. For more on e, see ACW 55.13, 120 n. 65. Rousseau makes some good observations on Irenaeus's use of irony here and in the next paragraph. We also accept Rousseau's suggestion that it is likely that the Latin originally would have been *elongantur et a recta ratione* or *elongant se a recta ratione*. On all this, see Rousseau (SC 293.268–69 [SC 294.169 n. 2]).

8. Harvey (1.311 n. 2) notes that Lat. Iren. has *deminoratio*, which elsewhere stands for ὑστέρημα, "degeneracy." But here there is question of the Aeon on high, Word, as being produced in a lower state, but not in degeneracy. So here the Greek was most likely κατ' ἐλάττωσιν. Yet I think Grabe (149 note o), Massuet (MG 7.766 n. 63), and Stieren (1.337 n. 10) are correct in thinking *deminoratio* here translates ὑστέρημα, and really means that Word was emitted in degeneracy, which ignorance is. The next sentence makes this clear.

9. Cf. John 9:1–41.

10. The Latin sequence of words is somewhat obscure. The rest of the paragraph and also paragraph 10 are a big help. The bracketed insertions should help the reader. See also Rousseau (SC 293.269 [SC 294.171 n. 1]).

11. 1 Pet 1:12.

12. Word, according to the Valentinians, is the firstborn of Only-begotten, who is the same as Mind. Harvey (1.312 n. 2) is wrong in noting that *primogenitus* is *Nous*.

13. Rousseau (SC 293.269 [SC 294.175 n. 1]) notes that we find here

two traits that mark the true God according to Irenaeus: greatness and superabundant love.

CHAPTER 18

1. Rousseau and Doutreleau (SC 293.269 [SC 294.175 n. 1]) also observe that we find here two traits that mark the true God in the eyes of Irenaeus: his greatness and his superabundance.

2. Matt 7:7.

3. The two verbs used here allude to the nouns in the title *Exposé and Refutation.* Rousseau and Doutreleau (SC 293.270 [SC 294.179 n. 1]) also observe that the parallelism with God invites us to see here the "Word of the Father." On the one hand, God (= the Father) is light. On the other hand, the "Word" of the Father is present, conferring his help. That is the sense of συμπάρειμι—to unmask and refute heresies.

4. This father of the Valentinians is Wisdom, who, though feminine, was said to be the father (parent without consort) of Intention; see A.H. 2.18.7; 1.4.1; 1.5.1.

5. Menander wrote a play titled *Misoumenos* (The Hated One), in which a jealous soldier, Thrasonides, falls in love with his captive maid, Crateia. Because of his boasting about his deeds, he makes himself hateful to her. He quarrels with her but then ardently desires reconciliation. (See *Menander: The Principal Fragments*, trans. F. G. Allinson, Loeb Classical Library (New York: G. P. Putnam's Sons, 1921), 408–12. See also Theodor Kock, *Comicorum Atticorum Fragmenta* 3 (Leipzig: Teubner, 1888; repr., Utrecht: HES, 1976), 97–101.

6. *In passione consternationis.* When Achamoth experienced passion it was that of consternation. So this is a genitive of explanation.

7. Matt 7:7.

8. Cf. A.H. 1.2.2. *Exterminatus* is to be taken very literally, "brought to an end, to nought," that is, annihilated, rather than destroyed in its usual sense.

9. The Aeon here is Wisdom, but she is presented as father because she alone emitted Achamoth, their mother.

10. Cf. Matt 15:14. It is difficult to decide what the intended meaning is here of *subiacentem* modifying *profundum. Subiacere* can mean to underlie, to be present, to be existent, actual, real; also to be supposed, or assumed, to be ready at hand. Klebba, BKV 3.149 uses a phrase: "*der vor ihren Füssen sich auftut,*" that is, which is ready at hand. Irenaeus is obviously playing on the name of their God, Profundity. The word could have its normal meaning of a profundity that is supposed or assumed in their system.

CHAPTER 19

1. Irenaeus has already made use of some of these expressions in A.H. 1.4.5 and 1.5.6.

2. "Certain nature" is *qualitas* in Latin, which supposes ποιότης, a certain type of nature, or a nature with a certain quality.

3. We accept Rousseau's suggestion (SC 293.275 [SC 294. 187 n. 2]) that the Latin text should be restored to *cum sint tantum homines* or, more simply, *cum sint homines*.

4. Matt 12:36.

5. Cf. A.H. 1.6.1.

6. "The perfect Word" is *perfectae rationis*, and below *perfecti sermonis*, but in 2.19.6 *perfectum Verbum*. Lat. Iren. was here indulging in his elegant variation. Λόγος must have been the Greek in all cases. I translated it as Word, because there seems to be a reference to their receiving, ultimately, the knowledge of Word, through Wisdom. Massuet (MG 7.773 n. 23) and others think the translation should be *ratio*, supposedly with its reference to the knowledge received, or the power of reasoning.

7. We follow Rousseau (SC 293.276–77 [SC 294.191 n. 1]), who believes that (*apt)abilior et utilior* is a doublet translating the Greek χρησιμωτέρα.

8. Cf. A.H. 1.2.2.

9. "Contrary." These things are opposites in their nature and so incapable of receiving the same things.

10. "Ensouled being" is *psychicam* also in Lat. Iren. instead of the normal *animalem*, being endowed with a soul; not "animal" in character.

11. Cf. 1 Cor 15:54; 2 Cor 5:4.

12. Rousseau (SC 293.277–78 [SC 294.195 n. 1]) remarks that the force of this passage is only clearly revealed when one compares it to the pages of Book V, where Irenaeus will reestablish, contrary to the Gnostic misrepresentations, the true nature of the Spirit.

13. Lat. Iren. has *in eam cognationem concurrentes*. The *cognation* is kinship established by the "seed" common to all. See the end of the paragraph. Since those mentioned were rulers, kings, and priests, they had, according to the Valentinians, the "seed" and belonged to that kinship. There is no question of a kinship established with Christ through faith as ANF (1.387 n. 2) suggests by way of opinion; nor is the meaning *und ihn erkannt*, as in Klebba, BKV 3.153, seemingly changing *cognatio* to *cognitio*.

14. 1 Cor 1:26, 28. But his citation differs from the Vulgate and the Greek text.

15. Grabe (155 n. 10) cites Athenagoras, *Legatio pro Christianis* 12 (Athenagoras, *Legatio and De Resurrectione*, ed. and trans. William R. Schoedel, Oxford Early Christian Texts [Oxford: Clarendon Press, 1972], 26) as a parallel. Athenagoras says that he has a few things out of the many, because who-

ever wishes to taste honey and wine judges from a small amount whether the whole is good.

16. Our translation is based on the following suggestions of Rousseau (SC 293.279 [SC 294.197, n. 1]): first, *ea quae sunt maxime continentia* clearly seems to be a translation of τὰ συνεκτικώτατα... κεφάλαια (already suggested by Billius). Second, it would be seem more suitable to read *scienter* rather than *scientes* at line 152. Third, at lines 155–56, the words *Demiurgum, id est Fabricatorem* seem to be a doublet translating τὸν Δημιουργόν.

17. Rousseau (SC 293.279 [SC 294.199 n. 1]) notes that the Latin *collatum et congestum* is a doublet translating συνηρανίσθαι.

18. Rousseau (SC 293.279 [SC 294.199 n. 2]) notes that the Latin *deserta ac destituta* is a doublet translating ἔρημα.

19. The Valentinians claimed that Christ and Jesus were made only after and because of the defection of Wisdom. St. Irenaeus severely criticizes them for this view and insists that the Word was eternal and did not begin either after and because of the fall of Adam and Eve or at the incarnation. So from this passage it is certain that the Word as God was not made after the fall and because of the defection of Wisdom. Franciscans claim that if Christ had been willed primarily for the redemption of the human race and only after the foreknowledge of Adam's fall, then he would be merely an occasional good. That would be unworthy of God and of Christ's dignity. For this, Irenaeus's reasoning is at least a parallel case. But it seems that it is more than that. Irenaeus objects so strongly to the idea that Christ and Savior were made on account of remedying a defection in Wisdom that we have to understand this in a sense that, not only the Word as such, but also the Word Incarnate, Christ Jesus, was not willed primarily because of the defection of the human race. Certainly this interpretation fits with the entire doctrine of Irenaeus about Christ's role in the universe. See Dominic J. Unger, "Christ's Rôle in the Universe according to St. Irenaeus," *Franciscan Studies* 5 (1945): 3–20, 114–37, but particularly 134–37.

CHAPTER 20

1. Rousseau (SC 293.279 [SC 294.201 n. 1]) remarks that the expression "parables and deeds of the Lord" is really a hendiadys, since it is really an issue of deeds of the Lord having an equivalence of parables. Such deeds of the Lord are capable of making known through and beyond their visible appearance an invisible reality that somehow they represent.

2. Cf. A.H. 1.3.3.

3. Lat. Iren. has *quam praeesse dicunt*. This cannot mean "which…had a previous existence" as in ANF 1.388. *Praeesse* in Lat. Iren. means to have authority or power. Klebba, BKV 3.154 translates *von jener vorzüglichen Kraft*.

4. Cf. A.H. 1.3.3.

5. Acts 1:20 and Ps 108 (109):8.

6. Our translation here is based on Rousseau's (SC 293.281 [SC 294.203 n. 3]) suggestion that the Latin text ought to be read *quoniam enim Christus uenit ad passionem…, et ipsi confitentur.*"

7. "Would not fail." Lat. Iren. has *quae non accederet*, according to the Clermont and Voss MSS, but the Arundel MS and Rousseau (SC 294.202) have *cederet*. Harvey (1.323 n. 1) thinks that *accederet* suggests *accideret* as the correct reading, supposing καὶ οὐ τυχόν. It seems, however, that *cederet* confirms this root, and even *accederet* has the root of *cederet*—namely, that it would not yield, that is, would not be conquered or fail. Klebba, BKV 3.155, skipped the phrase!

8. Our translation is influenced by Rousseau's remark (SC 293.282 [SC 294.205 n. 2]) that the Latin *inualidum et infirmum* is a doublet.

9. Eph 4:8; Ps 67 (68):19.

10. Luke 10:19.

11. "Was the cause of ignorance." The Latin is *substituit* for the verb. That supposes ὑπέστησε. This was accepted by Massuet (MG 7.777 n. 48), ANF (1.388 n. 7), and Klebba, BKV 3.156, and also in my translation. According to A.H. 1.3.3 this Aeon *separated* ignorance for herself after having suffered passion and produced it as a formless offspring. Harvey (1.323 n. 2) thinks that the reading in our passage should be *separated*, that is, ἀπέστησε, which was misread as ὑπέσθησε. In either case the meaning would be the same: Wisdom was responsible for the existence of ignorance.

12. A.H. 1.2.5–6. Rousseau (SC 293.282 [SC 294.207 n. 1]) notes that the expression κατὰ συζυγίαν was current in Gnostic language to express the manner in which a male Aeon and the corresponding female Aeon were united to each other.

13. Matt 26:24; Mark 14:21.

14. John 17:12.

15. We accept Rousseau's suggestion (SC 293.283 [SC 294.209 n. 1]) that, even though every MS has the reading *duodecim*, the coherence of the passage clearly dictates that the underlying Greek word would have been δύο.

CHAPTER 21

1. We accept the emendation proposed by Rousseau (SC 293.283 [SC 294.209 n. 2]):…*cum possit Saluator…et alios decem eligere, (ut) ostend(at) secunda(m) Decade(m), et ante hos quoque alios octo, ut illam principalem et primam ostendat Ogdoadem per apostolorum numerum typum factum.*

2. Cf. Luke 10:1, 17.

3. Cf. A.H. 2.14.15; 1.2.6.

4. Lat. Iren. has the Greek for the quotation and then the Latin translation. Hesiod, *Op.* 77–82, which Irenaeus cites loosely, has: "Also the Guide, the Slayer of Argus, contrived within her lies and crafty words and a deceitful nature at the will of loud thundering Zeus, and the Herald of the gods put speech in her. And he called this woman Pandora, because all who dwelled in Olympus gave each a gift, a plague to men who eat bread" (Hesiod, *Homeric Hymns, Epic Cycle, Homerica*, trans. Hugh G. Evelyn-White, 2nd ed., Loeb Classical Library 57 [Cambridge, MA: Harvard University Press, 1936], 6–9). I omitted the Latin translator's explanation that she was called Leto in the Greek because she secretly stirred them up.

5. Cf. 2 Tim 4:3.

6. Our translation is based on Rousseau's recommendation (SC 293.284–85 [SC 294.213 n. 2] to accept the proposal of Einar Löfstedt, which was later repeated in Lundström *Studien* 52, to adopt the reading of A but with a slight correction: *sed et* in *Pindari* lyricis.

7. Cf. Pindar, *Olympian Odes.* 1.38–51.

8. Rousseau (SC 293.285 [SC 294.213 n. 2]) notes that Lundström argued that *qua* should refer to *Mater* and not to *Pandora*. Lundström's view was that because the heretics were aroused or inspired by Mother they repeated the history of Pandora as they were following in the footsteps of the two poets who had already spoken under the influence of that same Mother.

CHAPTER 22

1. "Silent" is in the accusative in Lat. Iren., modifying Aeons. There is no authority or need for changing it to the nominative singular, referring to Savior, as Harvey (1.326 n. 6) prefers. Savior did no public work for thirty years, thus indicating the thirty Aeons (1.3.1), who are considered silent because they sprang from Silence, according to Massuet (MG 7.781 n. 71).

2. Isa 61:2; Luke 4:19.

3. Lat. Iren. is literally "according to the sound of the very words."

4. Cf. Rom 2:6; Matt 16:27.

5. Matt 5:45.

6. Isa 5:12.

7. Rom 8:36; Ps43 (44):23.

8. Cf. 1 Cor 2:10.

9. Cf. John 2:1–11.

10. John 2:23, with "in him" instead of "in his name."

11. Cf. John 4:1–42.

12. John 4:50.

13. Cf. John 5:1. Irenaeus interpreted this unidentified feast as another Passover, as has been done recently. See Franz Schubert, "Das Zeugnis des Irenäus über die öffentliche Tätigkeit Jesu," *Biblische Zeitschrift* 4 (1904): 39–48. See also A. Orbe, "San Ireneo y la primera Pascua del Salvador (Io 2, 13—3, 21), *Estudios Eclesiásticos* 44 (1969): 297–344.

14. Cf. John 5.2–15.

15. Cf. John 6:1–13.

16. Cf. John 11:1–44.

17. Cf. John 11:47–54.

18. John 12:1.

19. Cf. John 12:12.

20. These "three times" of the Passover are the three periods of his public life separated by the four Passovers; or they are the three Passovers after his public life had begun. That makes his public life definitely three years. It is interesting that so early in Christianity these paschs of John were used to calculate the length of Christ's public ministry. It is also noteworthy that already in Irenaeus's time the order of the chapters in John was the same as the order in our critical text, namely, 4, 5, and 6. On this problem, see U. Holzmeister, *Chronologia Vitae Christi* (Rome: Sumptibus Pontificii Instituti Biblici, 1933), 150–53.

21. Cf. Exod 12:2, 17–18; Lev 23:5; Num 9:5.

22. Irenaeus divides human life into five periods here and in 2.24.4. The stages are: *infantes*, that is, infants, newly born babies until perhaps weaning time. The *parvuli* (children) are possibly from two to twelve. The *pueri* (youths) are the adolescents, from twelve to about thirty. There may be an allusion here to Luke 2:42–43, where Jesus is called a *puer* when he was twelve. The *iuvenes* (young adults) were those from thirty to forty, as he explains in our present passage (2.22.5). The *seniores* (elderly) were from forty and up (2.22.5). This passage is a precious testimony to infant baptism in those days. Irenaeus says that Christ came to save all humankind, "all who would again be born to God." Among these he lists infants first, and they are on a par with the others. And so to be saved by Christ they had to be reborn to God; but rebirth to God was not possible in Irenaeus's thought, except through baptism. In fact, the two ideas are presented as synonymous: see 3.17.2; 3.22.4; 4.15.3. See also W. R. Powers, "St Irenaeus and Infant Baptism," *American Presbyterian and Theological Review* n.s. 5, no.18 (April 1867): 239–67, who ably defends this view against the Antipedobaptists. Rousseau (SC 293.287 [SC 294.221 n. 3]) notes that it would not be wrong to consider Irenaeus as a witness of the practice of infant baptism in the church of his time.

23. Cf. Col 1:18.

24. Cf. Acts 3:15.

25. Luke 3:23.

26. Rousseau (SC 293.287–88 [SC 294.225 n. 1]) suggests that either a scribe has inadvertently substituted *et* for *si* or the translator had accidentally substituted καί for εἰ.

27. *Indoles* occurs only one other place (3.23.5), where it means nature or quality. Here it obviously means a sign or an indication. Rousseau (SC 293.288 [SC 294.225 n. 2]), on the other hand, notes that he knows neither what acceptable sense to give to *prima indoles* nor how to correct this expression in a way that is truly plausible.

28. Cf. 3.3.4. This is a valuable note in regard to St. John. "Witnesses...Trajan" is the first Greek fragment of Book II still extant. It can be found in Eusebius, *H.e.* 3.23.3 with some slight adaptations. For more information about this fragment, see SC 293.86–87. Our translation has been influenced by the three remarks that Rousseau makes in SC 293.288 (SC 294.225 n. 3).

29. John 8:56–57.

30. Irenaeus's statements here and in the following paragraphs about the length of Christ's public ministry and of his age are quite confusing. The Gnostics maintained that Christ's public ministry lasted only one year (cf. 1.3.3; 2.20.1). This Irenaeus refutes emphatically. He calls attention to the four paschs reported in John's Gospel, supposing at least three years of ministry. He claims, too, that Christ, according to the Scriptures, was about thirty years old when he was baptized (cf. Luke 2:23; A.H. 2.22.4; 3.10.4). One would be inclined to conclude from this that Jesus was, according to Irenaeus, about thirty-three years old when he died. In subsequent paragraphs, however, he argues that Jesus was in his forties when he was preaching. He uses two arguments. First, Christ came to save all men and women, in all age brackets, including the elderly (2.22.5). And so Christ also reached the age of the elderly, and that, in reality, not merely in appearance (2.22.3–4). Second, the Gospel itself (John 8:56–57) confirms this. The Jews who wanted to show the disparity between Abraham's age and Jesus' would have guessed his age in the thirties if that is what he was. For these reasons Irenaeus thinks that we must hold that he was in his forties. To make the confusion worse, Irenaeus claims that this is the tradition of the presbyters of Asia who got their information from John (2.22.5). But their tradition was wrong in regard to millenarianism; it could have been wrong on this date also. Did he accept it without questions? Let us note some facts. Irenaeus knows that it was under Tiberius Caesar that Jesus was baptized (3.14.3) and then preached (4.22.2; also 4.6.2, which is not about his birth, but about his public revelation, according to the context). Irenaeus knows, too, that Jesus was crucified under Tiberius Caesar (1.27.2). He notes frequently that Pontius Pilate was then procurator of Judea (1.25.6; 27.2; 2.32.4; 3.4.2; 5.12.5). Must we accept that he knew nothing about the end of Tiberius's or Pontius Pilate's regime? Or that if he held Jesus to be in his forties when he preached and died, he did not advert to the fact that it would no longer have been under Tiberius or Pilate, but under Claudius? But he knew

that Simon Magus already performed under Claudius Caesar (1.23.1), and so
Jesus could hardly have been living under Claudius. True, in *Proof* (n. 74) he
had Pilate procurator under Claudius! Did he contradict himself? Or did a
scribe substitute the wrong Caesar? Since Irenaeus has everything in order
here (four paschs and three years of ministry, beginning at about thirty years
of age, all under Pontius Pilate and Tiberius Caesar), I am inclined to think
that he himself stresses his two arguments (Christ's being among the elderly
and John 8:56) as weapons against the Gnostics. They argue literally from
Scripture and its numbers. Irenaeus would say, Good, I too can choose that
type of weapon and refute you by your own methods. He uses parables in that
way, I believe. So why not about this? And yet he seems so sincere in arguing
about the reality of what he says. F. Vernet ("Irénée [Saint]," DTC
7.2.2463–64) thinks that the three years of public ministry established by the
Passovers preceded the death of Jesus, but there were many years in between
the baptism and the beginning of his ministry. But that is not according to
Scripture, nor according to Irenaeus. In 2.22.4, his statement about Jesus'
ministry following the baptism is grammatically so presented that it is difficult
to admit any long gap between the baptism and the ministry. J. E.
Steinmueller (*A Companion to Scripture Studies*, rev. ed., 3 vols. [New York:
Joseph F. Wagner, 1969], 3:184–85) thinks that Irenaeus agrees with the facts,
in that Jesus was about forty-one years old when he died and about thirty-
seven or thirty-eight when he was baptized, because the Lucan term "about
thirty" is to be taken in a broader sense of the liturgical age for public ministry. But he overlooks the fact that Irenaeus himself tells us expressly that
Jesus had not completed his thirtieth year when he was baptized (2.22.5).
Either Irenaeus misunderstood the presbyters (so J. Hoh, *Die Lehre des hl.
Irenäus über das Neue Testament*, NTAbhand. 7, pts. 4/5 [Münster: Aschendorff,
1919], 160–62), or the presbyters already misunderstood John, and Irenaeus
followed them blindly, as he did in the millenarist theory. Cf. U. Holzmeister,
Chronologia Vitae Christi, 99–100. J. Chapman ("Papias on the Age of Our
Lord," *JThS* 9, no. 33 [1908]: 42–61) holds that both Irenaeus and later
Victorinus (*De fabrica mundi*) quote from a common source, which is undoubtedly Papias's work. Irenaeus thought that, because of Papias's remark in the
prologue, all this rested on apostolic tradition. See also J. Chapman, "On an
Apostolic Tradition that Christ Was Baptized in 46 and Crucified under
Nero," *JThS* 8, no. 32 (1907): 590–606. More recently, H. A. Blair ("The Age
of Jesus Christ and the Ephesian Tradition," *Patristic Studies* 7, TU 92 [1966]:
427–33) made an attempt to justify Irenaeus's older age for Jesus for postu-
lating a longer period of discipleship for Jesus under John the Baptist, so that
he would have been born between 20 and 12 BC, and yet died about AD
30/33. But even as the author admits, though this solves some problems, it
creates others. G. Ogg ("The Age of Jesus When He Taught," *New Testament
Studies* 5 [1958–59]: 291–98) comes to a similar conclusion, but by a different

method, about an earlier date for Christ's birth, as a justification of Irenaeus's opinion.

    31. Homer, *Il.* 4.1.

CHAPTER 23

    1. Cf. Matt 9:20–23.

    2. Cf. A.H. 1.3.3.

    3. Rousseau and Doutreleau (SC 293.289 [SC 294.231 n. 1]) remark that the expressions *secundum materiam et secundum substantiam* and *habitum et lineamenta* are doublets.

    4. Luke 13:16.

    5. Cf. John 5:5.

    6. Irenaeus ends by saying that there is no similarity between the type that the woman is and the *negotium Aeonum*. *Aeonum* is witnessed by the Clermont MS and is demanded by the context, in which there is question of a similarity that must exist between a type and the Aeons. It is not the arrangement of the Gnostics, with *eorum* in place of *Aeonum*. And what is *negotium*? At the end of 2.24.1 Lat. Iren. has *negotiatio* in the same sense, and both words suppose the same Greek word πραγματεία, as Harvey (1.334 n. 3) notes for 2.24.1. It is either the arrangement or the affairs, that is, of the emissions, of the Aeons. Harvey (1.333 n. 1) incorrectly thinks that the reading should be *negatio eorum*. As noted above, *eorum* is not correct. And *negatio* would have to be subject of the passive *ostenditur*, which would leave *typus* unaccounted for. Besides, *negotiatio* in 2.24.1 confirms *negotium* here.

CHAPTER 24

    1. Cf. A.H. 1.14ff.

    2. Cf. A.H. 1.14.4.

    3. The numeric value of Σωτήρ is 1408; namely, 200 for σ, 800 for ω, 300 for τ, 8 for η, and 100 for ρ.

    4. How did Irenaeus count the half letter? In Hebrew, the word is *Yeshu*. Harvey (1.334 n. 4) correctly, I believe, surmises that a letter was a consonant plus a vowel, and a half letter was a consonant without a vowel. So *wāw*, without the vowel, would be the half letter. Others explain this by taking *yōd* as the half letter, because at times it is a vowel.

    5. The Latin is confusing and incomplete. It is not probable that Irenaeus gave an explanation for earth but not for heaven. Yet, as the Latin

stands, that would be the case, since the words I have put in an angular bracket are missing. Really there must be an explanation in Hebrew for heaven as well, since Irenaeus says afterward that Jesus contains heaven and earth. Moreover, grammatically *autem* connects the *terra* phrase; but in Irenaean style, this presupposed a *quidem* and its phrase, which are missing. By haplography a scribe jumped from the first "and earth" to the second. With Harvey (1.334–35 n. 5) we have restored the words skipped. The Latin scribe's attempt to transliterate (from Gen 1:1) *ueres* with *suru usser* is quite faulty. The name Jesus means heaven and earth in the sense that the initial letters of the Hebrew words, namely, *Yahweh, shamim, ueres*, spell the consonants for *Yeshu*, as Stieren (1.367) had already suggested. Cf. Th. Schneider, "Die Amwâs-Inschrift und Irenaeus Elenchos IV 23, 3," *ZNTW* 29 (1930): 155–58. So, the name of Jesus would mean "the Lord of heaven and earth." Rousseau (SC 293. 290 [SC 294. 235 n. 2]) suggests a slightly different reconstruction of the Latin text: "...*significans Dominum eum qui continent caelum et terram, quia 'Dominus' Iah secundum antiquam hebraicam linguam, 'caelum' et 'terra' autem iterum samaim uaarets dicitur*." Rousseau also notes that the word *sura* of the Latin MSS would be a corruption of *sma* (= *samaim*) and the word *use* would be a corruption of *uers* (= *uaarets*).

6. These last two sentences are quite obscure in Latin. "Common" is for *sacerdotales*. It is not apparent why these letters should be called priestly. Massuet (MG 7.789 n. 15) does not give a satisfactory explanation by saying that they are old Hebrew letters that the priests continued to use after the introduction of the square script. Harvey (1.335–36 n. 4) says that they were the first ten, which were used in common computation. *Sacerdotales* represents λειτουργικά, which here represents common and should not have been given by *sacerdotales*. I find it difficult to admit that a scribe would have made that switch. Lat. Iren. uses *sacerdotalis* a number of times in reference to priestly vestments or functions. Where the Greek exists it is ἱερατικός. Several times it is paired with *ministerialis*, ἱερουργικός; see especially A.H. 3.8.11. So if "priestly" does not yield a good answer, maybe "ministerial" does, and if so, it is possible that the scribe misread ἱερατικά for ἱερουργικά. The two words are rather similar. Ἱερουργικά would have fit into Harvey's explanation about common computation. In puzzling over these phrases Rousseau (SC 293.290–91 [SC 294.235 n. 3]) comments that they can be neglected without anything being taken away from the development of the thought. He also wonders if the real problem here was a marginal gloss that was unduly brought into the text itself by a careless scribe or translator.

7. Lat. Iren. reads: *Decem quidem sunt numero; scribuntur autem quaedam* (litterae) *per quindecim, novissima littera copulate primae.* That is puzzling. The first of the ten letters is *'ālep*, with the numeric value of one; the last is *yōd*, with the value of ten. *Yōd* put beside *'ālep* should, as Irenaeus says, give fifteen. But in Hebrew fifteen is really *yōd* (10) plus *hē* (5), which were, however, not used,

because they were the abbreviations of Yahweh. Instead, *wāw* (6) and *tēt* (9) were used. Still *quidem* and *autem* present a contrast that demands fifteen. Harvey (1.335–36 n. 4) suggests that the Greek scribe had written IE, as a transcription for *yōd* and *'ālep*, and that Irenaeus was thereby saying that *yōd* and *'ālep* were *matres lectionis*. The Latin scribe then misread IE as fifteen. But what sense would *novissima littera copulate primae* then have? In the *matres lectionis* it is not a question of joining these two together, but of joining each to other consonants. Klebba, BKV 3.166 has *reichen aber bis fünfzehn*, but *'ālep* and *yōd* make only eleven. We must continue to wait for a satisfactory solution.

8. This last sentence is equally obscure. Irenaeus evidently wishes to say that sometimes the letters of the Hebrew language are written in sequence as in Greek. At other times the sequence is reversed so that the writing of the letters will begin at the right and the letters will then, in relation to each other, have changed position from left to right. Harvey (1.335–36 n. 4) claims that this may be done in Hebrew without changing the numeric value of a word; for example, the consonants for Yeshu when written either YSHU or USHY have the same value in Roman numerals, that is, the value of 216. That is not true in Roman numbers; for example, IV and VI. But it seems certain that Irenaeus is not contrasting the Hebrew system with the Roman or Greek, but one Hebrew method with the other Hebrew method.

9. Cf. Rom 9:5; Mark 14:61. How does Baruch have two and a half letters? Again, Harvey's suggestion (1.336 n. 3) makes sense. *Bêt* with its vowel and *rēš* with its vowel make two full letters; final *kap* without a vowel is the half letter. But Baruch is actually not the name referred to here, as Schneider ("Die Amwâs-Inschrift und Irenaeus Elenchos IV 23, 3") points out.

10. Cf. Exod 25:10.

11. Cf. Exod 25:17.

12. Cf. Exod 25:23.

13. We accept Rousseau's position (SC 293.291 [SC 294. 239 n. 2]) that the phrase *haec autem sancta sanctorum* is a marginal gloss unduly introduced into the text.

14. Cf. Exod 25:31. The Bible has only six branches. Massuet (MG 7.792 n. 25) solved the problem by saying that Irenaeus counted the center point as a branch.

15. Cf. Exod 26:1. "Curtains" is correct according to Lat. Iren.

16. Cf. Exod 26:7.

17. Cf. Exod 26:2.

18. Cf. Exod 26:16. The *columnae* were actually upright planks.

19. Cf. Exod 26:26.

20. Cf. Exod 30:23–25.

21. Cf. Exod 30:34.

22. Cf. Matt 14:15–21.

23. Cf. Matt 25:1–13.

24. Cf. Matt 17:1–8; Mark 9:2–8.

25. Luke 8:51. John is omitted—by Irenaeus or a scribe?

26. Cf. Luke 16:19–31.

27. Cf. John 5:2–15.

28. We follow Rousseau (SC 293.293 [SC 294.243 n. 2]), who argues that the words *fines et summitates* are a doublet translating the Greek noun ἄκρα. That middle piece was a prop used as a saddle to carry the weight of the body. See Justin, *Dial.* 91 (Goodspeed 205–6), which could have been the source for Irenaeus. See also Tertullian, *Apol.* 16.6 (CCL 1.115). For other ancient testimonies, see U. Holzmeister, "Crux Domini eiusque Crucifixio ex Archaeologia Romana illustrantur," *Verbum Domini* 14 (1934): 149–55, 216–20, 241–49, 257–63. See also A.H. 5.17.4. In *Proof* 34, having stated that God's word pervades the whole world, Irenaeus adds that he encompasses its length, height, and depth, and that the Son of God was also crucified in these dimensions, "imprinted in the form of a cross on the universe."

29. Cf. A.H. 2.22.4 and chapter 22, n. 22.

30. That was the old Jewish idea; see Josephus, *Antiquities* 3.6.

31. Cf. Exod 26:37. By mistake Irenaeus gives the number of pillars for the veil at the entrance of the tabernacle instead of those for the veil at the entrance of the Holy of Holies, as in Exod. 26.32.

32. Exod 27:1 and 38:1. "Wide" is correct instead of "height," as in Lat.Iren.

33. Cf. Exod 28:1.

34. Cf. Exod 28:5.

35. Cf. Josh 10:16–27.

36. Note the allusions to the title of this work.

37. Cf. A.H. 1.24.3–5.

38. Namely, five more days are added to twelve times thirty or to 360.

39. "Days" here is the hours of light, which are shortest in winter and longest in summer. The variation is from nine to fifteen hours, and in reverse fifteen to nine.

40. Lat. Iren. reads: *sinistrae manus existentes levamen, non esse salutis consentire eos necesse est.* This is the punctuation of Massuet (MG 7.797), which I followed. Harvey (1.342) puts the comma before *levamen* and then one after *salutis*. But that does not catch the correct meaning: since they are on the left hand, they would have to agree that the raising is not of salvation! Also in the next sentence *levamen* governs *sinistrae manus*. This refers to the custom of raising the left hand to count all things up to ninety-nine inclusive, but the right hand for things above one hundred. That the Gnostics used this system is witnessed by *Evangelium veritatis*; see H. I. Marrou, "L'evangile de verité et la diffusion du comput digital dans l'antiquité," *VC* 12 (1958): 98–103. According to Scripture, the ninety-nine sheep that had not been lost were in safety, as Irenaeus admits. But according to the Gnostics and this ancient

method of counting, they would be on the left side, and so not in safety. Rousseau (SC 293.293–94 [SC294.249]) notes that no author has satisfactorily explained the precise function of the word *leuamen*. But the enigma that it poses does not prevent the global sense of the passage from emerging in all certitude.

    41. A.H. 1.5.1; 1.6.1; 1.16.2.

CHAPTER 25

    1. Rousseau (SC 293.295–96 [SC 294.253 n. 2. 1]) notes that the expressions "giving of names," "choice of apostles," "Lord's activity," and "arrangement of created things" recall the indications of a divine Pleroma superior to the Author of our world that Valentinians and Marcosians have maintained that they have discovered in the Scriptures and in the makeup of the world. Irenaeus has refuted these pretensions in the previous four chapters.

    2. Toward the end of this paragraph we have the similar expression "existing system of truth." Rousseau (SC 293.296–97 [SC 294.253 n. 1]) believes the words *siue rationi* are a corruption of the original reading *ueritatis*. It is a question of the first article of the Rule of Truth: there is only one God, the all-powerful Father, who has created all things by his Word. Irenaeus recalls this fundamental doctrine throughout the whole of the *Adversus haereses*.

    3. This and the preceding paragraph indirectly testify to Irenaeus's love for the beauty and harmony in all of God's work. Rousseau (SC 293.300 [SC294.253]) notes that Irenaeus will take up again the comparison of melody to the development of the history of salvation in A.H. 4.20.7.

    4. These expressions seem parallel to the preceding triplet and so indicate a difference of pitch and not of volume, as Klebba, BKV 3.172 would want. The *extensio* comes from the idea of tightening the strings, the *laxatio* from loosening them, thus giving higher and lower notes.

    5. "Change" is *transferentes*. Harvey (1.343 n. 6) incorrectly thinks that this word means to "apply" and supposes παραφέροντες. Not here. He would not tell them never to apply the rule, but never to adapt it or change it. Rousseau (SC 293.300–301 [SC 294.255 n. 1]) believes that *transferentes* is translating παραφέροντες. But he contends that the underlying meaning of the participle is "to turn away from," "to interpret falsely," or "to distort." If one compares the end of this paragraph with the first few lines of 1.10.3, clarity will result. The movement of the thought is identical from one part to the other. Not only does Irenaeus evoke the fact of alteration of "doctrine" by the heretics; he also states concisely of what this alteration consists. The heretics

distort the fact that there is only one God who created all things and who is continually present to his creation.

6. The goodness of God in creating is a capital idea of Irenaeus, against Marcion's bad god—as is also the idea of learning gradually and achieving perfection. See especially 4.38.

CHAPTER 26

1. With the aid of the Greek fragment and Harvey's suggestion, we were able to punctuate the Latin text better. "To come near God" is a very prominent idea of Irenaeus's Book IV. It means to be like God and to be united with Him. "Sovereign" is *Deum* in Lat. Iren., for which Harvey (1.345) suggests reading *Dominum*. But the Greek is not κύριος but δεσπότης. For more on this second Greek fragment, which is excerpted from John Damascene's *Sacra Parallela*, see SC 293.89.

2. 1 Cor 8:1. This marks the end of the third Armenian fragment, which starts at the beginning of this paragraph. For more on this fragment, which can be found in the Galata 54 MS, see SC 293.101.

3. Cf. Ps 118 (119):73; Job 10:8.

4. Cf. Gen 2:7.

5. Cf. John 15:9–10.

6. "Love (for God)...gives life to man" is a beautiful and pregnant phrase.

7. Cf. 1 Cor 2:2.

8. Matt 10:30.

9. Matt 10:29.

10. Cf. A.H. 1.13.1; 1.28.1.

11. Our translation is based on Rousseau's contention (SC 293.306 [SC 294.263 n. 1]) that *consentientibus et confitentibus* is clearly a doublet.

12. "Harmony...insight" is *aptatio...conscientia. Aptatio* occurs only once more in Irenaeus, a little later; but its meaning is clear. For the occurrences of *aptatio*, see B. Reynders, *Lexique compare du texte grec et des versions latine, arménienne, et syriaque de l' "Adversus Haereses" de Saint Irénée*, vol. 2: *Index des mots latins*, CSCO 142 Subsidia Tome 6 (Louvain: L. Durbecq, 1954), 33. *Conscientia* occurs more often, but mostly in the sense of conscience for *synderesis*. Here it cannot have that meaning. The context calls for knowledge. "Sublime" points to knowledge. The Greek could have been ἐπίγνωσις. These nouns seem to indicate a result that is just the opposite of what would be if the Creation had acted *vane et ut provenit* (uselessly and aimlessly), adverbs that occur just above.

13. "Reason" is *ratio*, which could represent λόγος, but also αἰτία. We have here a graphic picture of God's unlimited knowledge. Rousseau (SC

293.307 [SC 294.263 n. 3]) believes that the underlying Greek would have been θαυμαστὸν Λόγον καὶ ὄντως θεῖον. He argues that here Irenaeus is visualizing the Word as the sovereign Reason through which, at the same time, the Father has conceived the infinite diversity of creatures and the harmonious order thanks to which they were uniquely made.

CHAPTER 27

1. "For itself" was added from the Greek fragment. "Exercise" is in Greek the word from which we get our English word "ascetics."

2. This marks the end of the third Greek fragment, which began at the beginning of this chapter. For more on this fragment, which is excerpted from John Damascene's *Sacra Parallela*, see SC 293.89. Rousseau (SC 293.307–8 [SC 294.265 n. 1]) observes that Irenaeus defines with clarity what might be called the twofold book of divine revelation: on the one hand, knowledge of the world that surrounds us and, on the other hand, the Holy Scriptures. Irenaeus takes up this distinction twice in this chapter.

3. "Body of the Truth"; cf. A.H. 1.14.9; 1.9.4, and n. 24 to chap. 9 (ACW 55.182–83). We agree with Rousseau (SC 293.308–9 [SC 294.265 n. 2]) that the Latin should read *ueritatis corpus* instead of *a ueritate corpus*.

4. Rousseau (SC 293.308 [SC 294.265 n. 2]) remarks that Irenaeus categorically rejects an interpretation of the parables that would deny that there is only one God who is the Creator of all things. Both the Scriptures and the universe itself give testimony to this fundamental truth. Any parable has to be interpreted in light of it.

5. The phrase in brackets is not in Lat. Iren. The construction requires it, or a similar idea. We also accept Rousseau's suggestion (SC 293.309 [SC 294.267 n. 1]) of adding *(irrationabile est)* to complete the thought of this phrase.

6. Cf. Matt 25:1–12.

7. Note that Gospels are put on an equal footing with the Prophets as Scripture.

8. This is a clear indication of two sources of our knowledge of God: Scripture and creation. See A.H. 2.6.1 and chapter 6, n. 5.

9. Cf. Matt 19:12.

10. Our translation is based on Rousseau's remarks (SC 293.312–13 [SC 294.269 n. 1]) that in the phrase *per argumenta et aenigmata et parabolas* the word *argumenta* makes little sense and is probably the result of a dittography. We also accept his contention that it would be better to read *et alium qui per parabolas et aenigmata significatur Pater* rather than "*Patrem...Pater.*"

11. Cf. Matt 7:24–27.

CHAPTER 28

1. Our translation is influenced by Rousseau's suggestion (SC 293.314 [SC 294.271 n. 1]) that the expression "*regulam ... ueritat(is)* "is more comprehensible in this context than "*regulam... ueritatem.*"

2. The antecedents of the pronouns in this sentence must seem ambiguous. But *apud ipsum* must refer to God, in whom human beings will find their highest stages of development. The minor stages are also God's, since he is the Creator of all things, as Irenaeus stresses in this context. He opposes the Gnostic system, in which the creator of the lesser things outside the Fullness is not the god of the greater things in the Fullness. We should note the concise creedal statement about God as Creator. Rousseau (SC 293.315 [SC 294.217 n. 1]) notes that this entire paragraph is important for a correct understanding of the theology of Irenaeus.

3. Cf. Matt 3:12.

4. Cf. Gen 1:28.

5. This is an explicit, though casual, expression of the Trinity of Persons in God and of their unity. It is also a concise, but exact, expression of the inspiration of the Scriptures. Though we cannot understand all things in them, we must accept them, because they are the word of God, and so they are "perfect." They are God's word because they are somehow spoken by God's Word together with the Spirit. And since they are God's word, they cannot contain error. See ACW 55.8. "Given by God's Word and Spirit" is based on Rousseau's contention (SC 293.315 [SC 294.271 n. 2]) that *dictae* is a corruption of *datae*.

6. Irenaeus denied the γνῶσις of the Gnostics, but he postulates a true γνῶσις, knowledge, of God's mysteries. He treats of this at length in this chapter 28, which is consequently at the very heart of a refutation of the "falsely so-called *gnōsis*." Irenaeus's teaching is quite refreshing. We are given a special grace from God to know much about him and his creation, but we can never know everything. We ought humbly to keep our place. Our translation "inferior to" is based on Rousseau's remark (SC 293.315 [SC 294.271 n. 2]) that *minores sumus et novissimi* is a doublet.

7. This section reminds one strongly of Job 38–39. Other church writers expressed humankind's inability to know what lies beyond the ocean. See Clement of Rome, *1 Clem.* 20.5–8 (ACW 1.22); Augustine, *Civ.* 16.9 (CCL 48.510).

8. Cf. Job 38:22.

9. The fundamental distinction between Creator and creature involves this, too, that the Creator is all-knowing and must teach the creature, who must always learn from God. This marks the end of the fourth Greek fragment, which starts at the beginning of this paragraph. For more on this fragment, which is excerpted from John Damascene's *Sacra Parallela*, see SC 293.90.

10. Cf. 1 Cor 13:9–13.

11. How well the bishop of Lyons grasped the role of the three theological virtues in the spiritual life of every Christian. See Rousseau's reflections (SC 293.318 [SC 294. 277 n. 1]) on the rich thought of Irenaeus concerning a certain permanence of faith and hope in the heavenly life.

12. In Latin this clause reads: *et per dictionum multas voces unam consonatam melodiam in nobis sentient.* For this we have a Greek fragment. This is the fifth Greek fragment, which began several lines back with these words: "So if, according to the method stated, we leave some of the questions in God's hands." For more on this fragment, which is excerpted from John Damascene's *Sacra Parallela,* see SC 293.90. The variety of meanings in Scripture constitutes a polyphony, which is the Greek word for *multas voces.* What is the subject of *sentiet* or αἰσθήσεται? In Greek "one harmonious moment" is neuter and can be subject of "be heard." But αἰσθήσεται, which is normally a deponent verb, would have to have a passive meaning here. This is nothing unusual in Irenaeus, as Grabe (174 note m) observed; and so he adjusted the Latin to the Greek, reading *sentietur.* This is the simplest and best solution in Latin. Grammatically, in the Latin, it would be possible for *Scriptura,* which is the subject of *invenietur* a little earlier, to be subject of *sentiet.* But *sentiet* would not readily lend itself to mean that Scripture causes this one melody to be heard. And it would still be necessary to read the passive *sentietur.* But "among us" calls for the one melody to be heard, and not the Scriptures. And so the Greek runs more smoothly. Stieren (1.383–84 n. 8), Harvey (1.352 n. 3), and Rousseau (SC 293.318 [SC 294.277 n. 2]) think that the verb should be ἀσθήσεται, which the Latin misread. This would mean: "will be sung."

13. Cf. Gen 1:1—2:4. "Complete" translates *apotelestikos,* a transcription in Latin of the identical Greek word ἀποτελεστικῶς, which ordinarily has a causative meaning, as if God put active energy into the created world to work out its end and keep on reproducing itself. Ἀποτέλεσμα seems to have that active meaning in Hippolytus, *Haer.* 7.24; 10.12 (GCS 26.201, 273). However, in A.H. 2.33.5 the past participle ἀποτελεσθείς has a passive meaning; and since there is an allusion here to Gen 2:4, where God is said to have completed creation, it seems that the passive is correct.

14. Cf. 2 Tim 2:23.

15. The Latin has *velle* govern two other infinitives, but has itself no finite verb to govern it. Grabe (175 note b) supplied *decet.* Harvey (1.353 n. 2) rejects that and thinks the Greek for *velle* (τὸ θελεῖν), is the subject and, as it seems, goes back to *subjacet.* But I fail to catch the sense of this. The answer to these things of which we are ignorant is left to, reserved to, or known to God. Our not willing is another matter. That is not left to or reserved to God. I think we have here a normal Greek use (though rare) of a negated infinitive for expressing a prohibition. No need of another verb to govern *velle.*

16. Cf. Matt 11:25; Luke 20:21.

17. Our translation is influenced by Rousseau's observation (SC 293.319 [SC 294.279 n. 2]) that the Latin adverbs *grauiter...et honeste* constitute a doublet translating the Greek σεμνῶς.

18. Cf. A.H. 2.13.

19. Our translation here is based on Rousseau's observation (SC 293.320 [SC 294.281 n. 1]) that the Latin logos *quod est principale, quod excogitat* seems incoherent and that it would be better to emend the text in this way: *aliud enim est...quod est principale* (τὸ ἡγεμονικόν)..., *aliud organum per quod emittitur verbum.* Other ancient Christian writers were aware of the varied functions of the λόγος. Consult Lactantius, *Inst.* 4.9. (CSEL 19.300–301) and Tertullian, *Or.* 3 (CCL 1.258–59).

20. For a possible use of Xenophanes, see A.H. 1.12.2 (cf. ACW 55.54, 201 n. 4); also 2.13.3 above; and 4.11.2.

21. Lat. Iren. has simply *principalis mens. Principalis* must be "chief," and not "powerful," in connection with emissions, which are in the context. Mind was the first emission of Profundity. But in the thought of the Gnostics "chief or first Mind" is not used. So I think this is either an elliptical phrase, implying the word "emission," or this dropped out. I inserted it in brackets.

22. Cf. Isa 53:8. Also in *Proof* 70 Irenaeus speaks of the inexpressible nature of the generation of the Son, and he quotes this same Isaian passage. See D. J. Unger, "The Divine and Eternal Sonship of the Word According to St. Irenaeus of Lyons," *Laurentianum* 14 (1973): 357–408.

23. Matt 24:36; Mark 13:32. On the Son's not knowing the time of the last day, see below 2.28.6, 8.

24. Cf. Matt 10:24.

25. Cf. Isa 53:8.

26. These two pairs of angelic powers remind one of the construction in Rom 8.38, where *potestates* is not in the critical text, but it is found in some MSS. Nor is *Archangeli* there, but this must have been used as a pair with Angels in Irenaeus's time; he does this for the Catholic system and for the Gnostics; see 1.5.1; 1.23.2; 1.24.1; 1.30.5; 2.30.3, 4, 6, 9; 3.8.3.

27. Rousseau (SC 293.323 [SC 294.285 n. 2]) notes that here it is a matter of the emission and "primordial" generation of the Logos that is anterior to all other emissions and generations and the source of them as well.

28. That the majority of God's creatures were fulfilling his plan is a very optimistic note in Irenaeus's thought.

29. Ps 109 (110):1.

30. Cf. Rev 3:21.

31. 1 Cor 2:10.

32. 1 Cor 12:4–6.

33. 1 Cor 13:9.

34. Cf. Matt 25:41.

35. Cf. Matt 24:36.

36. Lundström (Lundström *Studien* 62), like Massuet (MG 7.810 n. 47) already, accepts *nunc* in place of *nec*, according to the Clermont and Voss MSS. But *nec* makes good sense, and it makes this clause parallel to the preceding in construction, which is in keeping with the consistent style of Irenaeus to write in contrasts. Actually it implies the idea of *nunc*.

37. Rousseau (SC 293.323–36 [SC 294. 289 n. 1]) remarks that the numerous blunders and inaccuracies of the Latin translation make the text nearly incomprehensible if one relies on the rules of Latin syntax. But the structure and sense become clear when one reestablishes the Greek forms. Rousseau also outlines the thought of Irenaeus here in this way: First, one must reserve to God the knowledge of things that are beyond us. Second, one must not run the extreme risk of reserving nothing to God and from there coming to an extreme audacity of dissecting the divinity. Such a risk occurs when one makes God the Creator a product of degeneration and ignorance in pretending to reach a superior God without a connection to our material world. This risk happens as well when, after having formed all the pieces of this theory, one tries to prop it up by all sorts of fanciful speculations about numbers in the Scriptures or by parables interpreted in an arbitrary manner.

38. Cf. Matt 24:36.

39. John 14:28.

40. Cf. 1 Cor 7:31. In 2.28.6, Irenaeus quoted Matt 24:36; Mark 13:32 about the Father alone knowing the hour of the judgment, and he refers to that again and definitely ascribes some superiority of knowledge to the Father. And this superiority consists in the fact that the Father is greater in his divine nature than the Son in his human nature, since he quotes John 14:28. It might mean that the Father did not grant this knowledge to the Son for revealing it to others. Irenaeus's words do not mean that Christ as man simply did not have this knowledge. In no way do they mean that the Son as God did not have it. For Irenaeus, the Son has everything in common with the Father.

41. Cf. Rom 11:33.

42. 1 Cor 13:9.

43. Cf. 1 Cor 2:10.

CHAPTER 29

1. The Latin *discessio* should be *descensio*. The change might have been made already in the Greek from καταλλαγή to ἀπαλλαγή. Rousseau and Doutreleau (SC 294.296) also prefer *descensio* here.

2. The Latin is corrupt: *Si autem animae quae periturae essent inciperent.* As Grabe (179 note 3) followed by Massuet (7.813 n. 64) noted, the simple con-

struction should have been *Si autem animae perire inciperent*, and he thinks a marginal notation explained this Greek construction by *periturae essent*; later this was introduced into the text. Harvey (1.359 n. 4) judges this attempt ingenious but not necessary, if one considers the Greek construction that underlines the Latin. Then *quae* is superfluous and *essent* should be *esse*. But in the next sentence we have a parallel construction with the simple infinitive: *cedere incipient*. This simple construction, not the periphrastic participle, is constant in Irenaeus with *incipere*. I retained this view. Massuet (MG 7.813 n. 64) would also allow this reading: *Si autem animas, quae perire inciperent, nisi iustae fuissent; iustitia potens est salvare: et corpora, quid utique non salvabit, quae et ipsa participaverunt?* Lundström (Lundström *Studien* 114–16) approved of that. But that calls for too many unnecessary changes.

3. Harvey (1.359 n. 5) says that *corruptela* should be changed to *incorruptela*, but that would not be in keeping with the context. Irenaeus wishes to say that if men and women are saved by the very fact that they have souls, then all men and women alike must be saved; but if salvation depends on virtuous living, then even the bodies will share in the merit of the souls, since the bodies, just like the souls, would go into corruption if not saved. Rousseau (SC 293.326 [SC 294.297 n. 1]) observes that when Irenaeus speaks here of bodies, which, just like the souls, would go into corruption, he is presenting the views of an adversary who maintains this belief. Elsewhere in A.H. we can find the views of Irenaeus himself on the immortality of the soul.

4. Cf. Rom 8:11.

5. The last sentence is an excellent expression of God's ability to work miracles, even of the resurrection. "The reason is…rich and perfect" is the sixth Greek fragment in Book II. For more on this fragment, which is taken from John Damascene's *Sacra Parallela*, see SC 293.90.

6. "Impulse." Harvey (1.360 n. 2) and ANF (1.403 n. 1) identify this with "impulse" in A.H. 1.4.1. Grabe (180 note 4) thinks that the reference is to 1.5.1 about Achamoth turning back to the light.

7. Cf. A.H. 1.4 and 5.

8. The Latin is obscure: *Si igitur illa quod enixa est, omni modo… ingrediuntur, quod autem…residet.* Harvey (1.360 n. 3) would change *quod* to *quidem*, but that would not be satisfactory: *illa* needs a correlative. *Quod autem* indicates a contrast. *Quidem* is not expressed in the first clause, because, as usual, it is included in *igitur*. In the preceding sentence *quod* is collective, referring to the entire offspring. So here, though *illa* is plural, *quod* is singular, unless it was originally written *quae*. But there is still a careless confusion of numbers. *Illa* is plural and is subject of *ingrediuntur*; but as the offspring it is considered collective and its relative pronoun is singular, *quod*, and also takes a singular predicate adjective, *spiritale*, and verb, *est*.

CHAPTER 30

1. Cf. Exod 20:11; Ps 145 (146):6; Acts 4:24; 14:15.

2. The Latin in all the MSS is *inhonorate cum sint carnes propter tantam suam impietatem.* Some scholars (Harvey [1.361 n. 4], Lundström [Lundström *Studien* 119–21]) would change to *inhonoratae cum sint carnis:* "though they belong to the dishonored flesh." But a simpler change was from *carnales* to *carnes. Carnales* fits in well. It balances with *spiritales:* they wish to be spiritual, though they are carnal. Then the *propter* clause would be a reason for being carnal: they are shamefully carnal because of their great impiety. It makes less sense to say that they belonged to the dishonored flesh because of their great impiety.

3. Cf. Ps 103 (104):4.

4. Cf. Ps 103 (104):2.

5. Cf. Isa 40:22.

6. Rousseau (SC 293.328 [SC 294.303 n. 1]) remarks that the Latin *uelut* is an inexact translation of the Greek ὡς. Here the adverb ὡς does not have a comparative value but serves to reinforce the intensity of the underlying Greek adverb ἀληθῶς.

7. The hellebore is an herb with short poisonous roots. Cf. Horace, *Ars poetica* 300. Irenaeus seems to have known Horace well.

8. Irenaeus borrows this phrase from Justin, *1 Apol.* 22.4, quoting it here, in 2.30.5, and also in 3.12.11. See SC 210.301 (SC 211.229 n. 2).

9. For the sake of clearer sequence I have rearranged the phrases of this long period and its parenthesis. "Expose and refute" again allude to the title.

10. Matt 7:7.

11. "Certainly...by what it is." This is the seventh Greek fragment in Book II. For more on this fragment, which is taken from John Damascene's *Sacra Parallela,* see SC 293.90.

12. Our translation here is influenced by Rousseau's remark (SC 293.329 [SC 294.305 n. 1]) that the Latin *rationabilius* is a translation of the underlying Greek ἀξιολογώτερον, which means "more remarkable" or "more memorable" rather than "more intellectual."

13. Cf. Ps 32 (33):6.

14. Cf. Job 38, to which Irenaeus is obviously alluding.

15. Cf. Sir 1:3. These are fine words in praise of the Creator's wisdom and power. Irenaeus must have taken great delight in the marvels of creation.

16. Grabe (181 note u) and Harvey (1.363 n. 3) would change *quanta* to *qualia,* but *quanta* makes good sense. Klebba, BKV 3.188 retains it. For the names of the angelic powers in the following sentences, see Col 1:16; Eph 1:21.

17. Literally, "and of the entire contemplation, which she saw." Cf. A.H. 1.4.5; 5.5, where the Greek θεωρία (*contemplatio*) was given by *visio* in the first case, and by *inspectio* in the second.

18. For more on this ironic designation of "Pandora" for Savior, see SC 293.259 [SC 294.139 n. 1]).

19. We follow Rousseau's (SC 293.329–30 [SC 294.307 n. 2]) suggestion that the Latin text ought to read *perficiente Matre uel* Saluatore. This recalls what Irenaeus wrote in the previous paragraph: "For whether Savior or their Mother...used this Being [Demiurge]...for making the image of the beings that are one in the Fullness."

20. Literally, "the images of all things." Rousseau (SC 293.330 [SC 294.309 n. 1]) remarks that this is an expression familiar to the Gnostics to designate their Aeons.

21. Cf. Col 1:16; Eph 1:21.

22. The Latin is cryptic: *ad nullum opus facti Matri.*

23. A phrase found in Justin, *1 Apol.* 22.4. Irenaeus quoted this at the beginning of 2.30.2. For more on this phrase, see SC 210.301 (SC 211.229 n. 2).

24. Cf. Col 1:16.

25. Cf. 2 Cor 12:2–4. Rousseau (SC 293.330 [SC 294.313 n. 1]) remarks that Paul did not undergo two distinct "abductions" and that "paradise" mentioned here is nothing other than the third heaven.

26. Literally, *intus homo.* Later *homo* by itself and *interior homo* have the same meaning. This expression comes from Paul in Rom 7:22; 2 Cor 4:16; Eph 3:16. For more on how the Marcosians understand this Pauline expression, see SC 293.275–76 [SC 294.189 n. 1]).

27. 2 Cor 12:2–3.

28. Cf. Gen 1:1.

29. Cf. Gen 2:7.

30. Cf. Gen 2:15.

31. Cf. 2 Cor 12:2.

32. Cf. 2 Cor 12:4.

33. Cf. John 4:24. Rousseau (SC 293.332 [SC 294.317 n. 2]) remarks that the sense of the phrase is clear: the God who created spiritual beings cannot be of an "ensouled" nature. He can only be spiritual. On the sense of πνεῦμα, see SC 152.202 [SC 153.23 n. 1].

34. Lat. Iren. has merely *substantia,* which could be correct in the sense that God's will is the basis for creation, implying, of course, that this is because he is the cause. But then perhaps, as Harvey (1.368 n. 1) notes, the Latin translator read οὐσία where actually αἰτία was written. Our translation "made and ordered" indicates that we accept Rousseau's suggestion (SC 293.333–34 [SC 294.321 n. 1]) that *disposuit et perfecit* is a doublet that seems to translate the Greek κατήρτισε.

35. Heb 1:3 (?). Although the editors are unanimous in seeing in the Latin *uerbo uirtutis* an implicit citation of Heb 1:3, Rousseau (SC 293.334 [SC 294.321 n. 1]) contends that it is doubtful, not to say impossible, that this is indeed the case.

36. Cf. Prov 8:1; Ps 103 (104):4; Jer 51:15. Our translation is based on Rousseau's contention (SC 293.333 [SC 294.321 n. 1]) that *aptauit et disposuit* is almost certainly a doublet translating καταρτίσας. The phrases about God's creating and harmonizing things alone are an implicit citation from Hermas, *Mand.* 1.1. See B. Hemmerdinger, "Observations critiques sur Irénée, IV (*Sources Chrétiennes* 100) ou les mésaventures d'un philologue," *JThS* 17 n.s. (1966): 308–9.

37. Cf. A.H. 1.29.2.

38. Cf. Eph 1:21.

39. Wisdom is the Holy Spirit; cf. 2.30.9; 4.8.4; 20.1, 3; *Proof* 10.

40. Cf. Exod 20:11; Ps 145 (146):6; Acts 4:24; 14:15.

41. There are not two gods, one just and one good, as Marcion taught, but only one God who is both just and good.

42. Cf. Gen 2:7.

43. Cf. Gen 2:8.

44. Cf. Matt 22:32.

45. See ACW 55.10–11, 119–20 on tradition.

46. Cf. 2 Cor 1:3; 11:31; Eph 1:3; 3:14; Col 1:3; 1 Pet 1:3.

47. Cf. Matt 11:27. The Son, not merely the Word, is clearly eternal and is the revealer of God to humankind. See D. J. Unger, "The Divine and Eternal Sonship of the Word according to St. Irenaeus of Lyons," *Laurentianum* 14 (1973): 357–408. To reveal God to humanity was an important reason for Word's becoming man, according to the bishop. See D. J. Unger, "Christ's Role in the Universe according to St. Irenaeus," *Franciscan Studies* 5 (1945): 14–18.

48. Cf. 1 Pet 3:22.

CHAPTER 31

1. The long periods of this and the next paragraph were broken down. Cf. A.H. 1.27.2–4; 23.1–5.

2. Our translation is influenced by Rousseau's remark (SC 293.334 [SC 294.327 n. 1]) that it would be more appropriate to read *circumscriptam* and not *circumscriptum* and to link *circumscriptam* with *conditionem.*

3. Cf. A.H. 1.24–25. Rousseau (SC 293.334–35 [SC 294.327 n. 2]) makes the observation that the Latin translator interpreted *Gnosticorum* as a generic term encompassing Saturninus, Basilides, and Carpocrates, who were treated previously. But in fact the matter under discussion here is a particular sect whom Irenaeus termed "Gnostics." Irenaeus presented their teachings at length in A.H. 1.29–30. The underlying Greek expression τοὺς λοιποὺς Γνωστικούς should be understood here, as in A.H. 2.13.8, to mean "all the other (heretics who are the) Gnostics."

4. Underlying his statement is the fact that the Valentinians used the Scriptures but distorted them, while the Basilidians borrowed from the pagans and used their imagination. The Latin clause: *magis quam hi qui ea quae sunt extra veritatem transferentes* has made scholars stumble. Massuet (MG 7.823–24 n. 25) and Stieren (1.402 n. 5) cancelled *qui,* though it is in all the MSS. Lundström (Lundström *Studien* 121) changed *hi* to *hic,* referring to Basilides. Yet *hi* must be plural governing *transferentes,* and the reference is certainly to the large group referred to, namely, "those" Valentinians. The *qui* clause cannot refer to the same people as *hi;* they are the Basilidians and others who bring pagan ideas into their doctrinal system. Irenaeus has a contrast here between the two participial clauses: *dicentes....transferentes.* This is indicated by *autem,* though for some reason no *quidem* was placed in the first clause. The contrast is between the fact that, on the one hand, Basilidians say things similar to the Valentinians and, on the other hand, the Basilidians drag in extraneous matter from the pagans more than other groups, notably the Valentinians. *Qui* need not be dropped. It represents, as so often, the definite article in a Greek participial construction. Of course, in Latin it is not proper with a participle. ANF (1.407 n. 1) accepted this reading. Klebba, BKV 3.194–95 got something quite different: *und nur die Zahl der Irrtümer in ihrer Lehre noch vermehrt haben.* With no explanation given, it is not possible to know how he arrived at this.

5. Though Irenaeus says harsh things about the obstinate heretics, he is always solicitous about their repenting and returning to God.

6. The very fact that they possessed the *gnōsis* was for them resurrection. See Tertullian, *De carnis resurrectione* 19.6 (CCL 2.945). See 2 Tim 2:17–18.

7. Luke 8:55.

8. It is worth noting the expression "the whole church in every place." The Greek fragment does not have "every," just "in a place." Klebba, BKV 3.195 dropped the adverbial phrase completely. The cryptic clause *donatus est homo orationibus sanctorum* (the Greek fragment has the same) bears two interpretations, I believe. Either "the man was given (back) to the prayers of the saintly people" or "the man was endowed (with life) because of the prayers of the saintly people," with, namely, an ablative of cause in Latin, or a dative of cause in Greek. "They are so far...entreaties of saintly people" is the eighth Greek fragment in this book. For more on this fragment, which is taken from Eusebius, *H.e.* 5.7.2, see SC 293.87.

9. Cf. Zech 7:9.

10. This is certainly a fine example of Christian charity and true community in the church of the second century. Christians functioned as a community in these charities, which is expressed in the preceding paragraph by "the whole church in every place."

11. Literally, "phantasm of idolatry." The idea is that they will pretend to

be God and deceive people into worshiping them, which will in reality be idolatry. Compare 2 Thess 2:4.

12. Cf. Rev 12:4. The dragon is the Antichrist.

13. Cf. Eph 6:12. Rousseau (SC 293.336 [SC 294.331 n. 1]) comments that for Irenaeus human beings are composed of body and soul. At death there occurs the separation of the body from the soul. We can understand the use of word "soul" here if we recall an expression used by Irenaeus in the raising of the daughter of Jairus in Luke 8:55. In Irenaean thought it is simply the matter of the soul of someone who is deceased. If Irenaeus had used the word πνεῦμα, it would have been in imitation of the word used by the evangelist in the narrative.

14. The Clermont MS, Massuet (7.826 n. 40), and Harvey (1.371 n. 5) read *Quam prophetiam si observaverit quis, eorum diurnam conversationis operationem.... Prophetia* would be the prophetic spirit according to which they did magical deeds, about which he spoke above. It would call for *et* before the second phrase, because it would seem to be awkward to take that daily conduct in apposition to this prophetic spirit. But the other MSS have *Quapropter etiam* in place of *Quam prophetiam.* This seems much more likely. Besides, *prophetia* was not in the previous context. *Phantasia* definitely was; another reason why *prophetia* is suspect. I do not think it necessary to add *et*, with some scholars, in the reading I followed. Rousseau (SC 293.336 [SC 294.333 n. 1]) remarks that Irenaeus has just said that the heretics have received a portion of a "spirit of iniquity." So, according to Irenaeus, it is justly for that reason (*Quapropter etiam*) that if only we observe their conduct, we would not see their behavior differ from that of the demons themselves.

CHAPTER 32

1. Cf. A.H. 1.25.4.
2. Cf. Matt 5:27–28.
3. Cf. Matt 5:21–22.
4. Cf. Matt 5:43–44.
5. Cf. Matt 5:33–34.
6. Cf. Matt 5:22.
7. Cf. Matt 5:39.
8. Cf. Matt 5:40.
9. Cf. Matt 5:44.

10. This paragraph is a summary of part of the Sermon on the Mount; cf. Matt 5:21–48.

11. Matt 13:43. These heretics had no objective standards for morality.

12. Cf. Matt 25:41.

13. Mark 9:48; Isa 66:24.

14. Cf. A.H. 1.25.4.

15. The ancients divided the arts and sciences into the intellectual and the practical. For more on this topic, see H.-I. Marrou, "Les arts libéraux dans l'antiquité classique," in *Patristique et Humanisme: Melanges par Henri-Irénée Marrou*, Patristica Sorbonensia 9 (Paris: Éditions du Seuil, 1976) 37–63.

16. The Latin is *meditationem*. Cf. 1.6.4 and ACW 55.38, 167 n. 21.

17. We accept the emendation of Rousseau and Doutreleau in SC 294.336.

18. Cf. Titus 3:11.

19. "Little boys" are *pueri investes*. An *investis* was still not "clothed" with puberty, and so the term became a male correlative of virgin. See Tertullian, *De virginibus velandis* 8.3 (CCL 2.1218): *Si virgo mulier non est, nec vir investis.*

20. If, however, they claim...renders service gratuitously" marks the ninth Greek fragment in Book II. For more on this fragment, which is recorded in Eusebius, *H.e.* 5.7.3–5, see SC 293.87.

21. Cf. Eph 4:7. "Perform"—*percipere* does not have an expressed accusative, but it is obviously *gratiam*, from the preceding phrase. This is confirmed toward the end of the paragraph where the same verb is used with *numerum gratiarum* as the object.

22. Simon wanted to bribe the apostles; see Acts 8:9–25; 1 Tim 3:8.

23. Cf. Matt 10:8.

24. Because of this sentence Grabe (189 note 2) and J. Turmel ("Histoire de l'angélologie des temps apostoliques à la fin du Vᵉ siècle," *Revue d'histoire et de literatures religieuses* 3 [1898]: 289–308, 407–34, 533–52) denied that a cult directed toward the Angels existed in the early church. But in the context it is plain that Irenaeus merely states that the church does not invoke the Angels for working wonders, even magically, as do the Gnostics. See G. Bareille, "Angélologie d'après les Pères," DTC 1.1.1219–20.

25. We accept Rousseau's proposed emendation (SC 293.337 [SC 294.343 n. 1]) of reading *ad* Deum *qui omnia fecit* in place of *ad* Dominum *qui omnia fecit.*

26. Cf. Bar. 3:38.

27. Cf. Eph 1:9.

CHAPTER 33

1. Cf. Clement of Alexandria, *Ecl.* 17 (GCS 172.141 Stählin): "For it would be necessary that we know where we had been if we pre-existed." "[Their opinion] about the transmigration...forgetfulness skillfully compounded," which encompasses the first two paragraphs of this chapter, is also

the extent of the tenth Greek fragment. For more on this fragment, located in Florilège antiorigéniste, Vatopédi 236 (= V), fol. 116v (A. de Santos Otero, *Emerita* 41 [1973]: 486–88), see SC 293.93–100.

2. This last sentence is in its proper place; there is no need of transposing with Harvey (1.378 n. 1).

3. Rousseau (SC 293.338–39 [SC 294.345 n. 3]) notes that, for Irenaeus, Tertullian, and Clement of Alexandria, a dream is peculiar to the body since the soul cannot sleep. A dream is comparable to death—the soul retreats in a certain manner from the body to be alone in itself. All this comes from Stoicism. For more information on this, see M. Spanneut, *Le stoïcisme des Pères de l'Église de Clément de Rome à Clément d'Alexandrie* (Paris: Éditions du Seuil, 1957) 217–18, 229.

4. The transmigration of souls was an early belief in Egypt (cf. Herodotus, 2.123 [Loeb 424]). According to H. J. Rose and H. W. Parke, "Transmigration," OCD2.1089, Pherecydes of Syros (fl. ca. 550 BC) is the earliest person to whom this theory is attributed. So Plato, who remarks about it in *Timaeus*, was not the first to teach it.

5. Other churchmen denounced this Platonic dream. See Tertullian, *Anim.* 24 (CCL 2.816–18); Augustine, *De Genesi ad litteram* 7.9, 10, 11; 10.4 (CSEL 28, 1.207–11, 300–301); Lactantius, *Inst.* 7.22 (CSEL 19.654).

6. Rousseau (SC 293.339 [SC 294.349 n. 1]) comments that the Latin has nothing corresponding to the Greek λοιπή, which may have been accidentally dropped in the Greek text available to the translator. Furthermore, the Latin *artificiose compositum* does not correspond well to the Greek τεχνολογία. We agree that the reading of the Greek *florilegium* does seem more natural in this instance.

7. We accept Rousseau's contention (SC 293.339 [SC 294.349 n. 2]) that the phrases *cogitationem* and *mentis intentionem* constitute a doublet translating ἔννοιαν.

8. "Return to themselves" is literally, *in hominem conversi*, which Massuet (MG 7.832 n. 85) already explained with: *Ad seipsos ex exstasi reversi.*

9. Cf. Rev 21:27.

10. Irenaeus clearly teaches resurrection of the identical body. In this sentence he does not speak of trichotomy, that is, three parts to man. Men and women are made of body and soul; but when spiritualized through grace, they also have the Spirit. Rousseau (SC 293.339–42 [SC 294.353 n. 1]) makes some useful remarks on this topic in anticipation of the careful treatment Irenaeus gives to it in the first part of A.H. 5. The use of the plural here (Spirits) can be accounted for if one admits with Irenaeus that the Holy Spirit truly can be given to each just person as if the Spirit was a third component (i.e., in addition to body and soul). This is thanks to the fact that women and men are constituted children of the Father and participate in the very life of God.

11. Cf. Matt 22:30.

12. "On the contrary...harmony of the Father" is the eleventh Greek fragment in Book II. For more on this fragment, see SC 293.90–91. My translation follows the Greek fragment, where only one change was necessary; namely, the masculine ἀποτελεσθεὶς was made neuter to modify "crowd." The Latin cannot be translated as it stands. Both nominatives (*multitudo* and *compago*) cannot be correct. According to the Greek, *compago* should be accusative. *Perfectorum* could, grammatically, go with *compaginem*, but both the construction and the sense would be awkward. So, even that should be *perfecta*, modifying *multitudo*.

CHAPTER 34

1. The same idea is found in Tertullian, *Anim.* 7 (CCL 2.790). "That the souls...Abraham's bosom" encompasses the second Syriac fragment. For more on this fragment, which is attested in four MSS, see SC 293.113–15.

2. Cf. Luke 16:19–31. Our translation is influenced by Rousseau's remarks (SC 293.342 [SC 204.355 n. 23]) that the words ἐν τῇ ἱστοριογραφίᾳ are likely the words that lie beneath the Latin *in ea relatione quae scribitur.*

3. I translated "prophetic spirit," not because I agree with Grabe (192 note g) that a word like "spirit" fell out, but because the Greek τὸ προφητικού has that meaning here.

4. We accept Rousseau's assertion (SC 293.342 [SC 294.357 n. 1]) that it is not likely that the Latin *unamquamque gentem* would reflect the original Irenaean thought. *Unamquamque animam* or *unumquemque hominem* are much more likely candidates to reflect the thought of Irenaeus.

5. Our translation here is influenced by Rousseau's remarks (SC 293.343 [SC 294.357 n. 2]) that the underlying Greek comparative πλεῖον should be given full value. In that case, the sense of ἐπὶ πλεῖον ἐπιμένοντα is "to exist (always) for a longer time," or "to exist indefinitely."

6. Cf. Wis 7:5. "Through being made" is *initium generationis*. But the context is not about generation but about creation, or being made. In 2.34.3 we read the *initium...facturae*, which is obviously the same idea as in our present passage. So the Greek must have been γενέσεως, which can have the meaning of generation, but not here.

7. What a grand expression of God's eternity and unchangeableness.

8. Cf. Ps 20 (21):5.

9. Irenaeus's statements in this section do not imply that the soul is not naturally immortal. Irenaeus merely insists that the immortality of the soul, which is a created being, is not the same as the immortality of God, who is ingenerate. The soul is immortal because God willed to create it so, not because it has that of its own power. God willed that it be immortal naturally, but this is God's gift. See 4.38.3; 5.4.1.

10. Our translation is based on Rousseau's remarks (SC 293.345 [SC 294.357 n. 3] as well as SC 293.248–49 [SC 294.123 n. 2]) on the enlarged significance of the adjective λοιπός.

11. Cf. Gen 2:1.

12. Cf. Ps 32 (33):9; Ps 148:5–6.

13. Ps 20 (21):5.

14. Cf. 1 Cor 3:10. Evidently this is not a denial of the immortality of the soul. Irenaeus stresses the gratuity of God's grace.

15. Irenaeus rightly insists that hell is in a true sense self-inflicted. Cf. also 4.39.4; 5.27.2.

16. Irenaeus has here a combination of Luke 16:10–11 with "great" instead of "greater" from somewhere else. It is found in the same way in *2 Clem.* 8 (*The Apostolic Fathers: Clement, Ignatius, and Polycarp*, ed. and trans. J. B. Lightfoot, vol. 2, part 1, *Clement* [London and New York: Macmillan, 1889–90; repr., Peabody, MA: Hendrickson, 1989], 226–28).

17. Rousseau (SC 293.346 [SC 294.359 n. 1]) also comments on the connection between this paragraph and 4.37.1. In both cases Irenaeus mentions a gift God presents to humanity. In this instance it is "life" (ἡ ζωή). In that instance it is the "good" (τὸ ἀγαθόν).

18. Many commentators have noted that this seems to be from Justin, *Dial.* 6 (Goodspeed 98). Rousseau (SC 293.348 [SC 294.361 n. 1]) notes that the old man in *Dial.* and Irenaeus mean very different things by the world "life." For the old man, life is simple existence. But for Irenaeus, life is the life of the Spirit that is the privilege of the just. It would be a serious methodological error, then, to pull the present passage out of context and to claim that the two passages are strictly parallel based on their similar verbiage.

19. Cf. Gen 2:7. In Irenaeus's thought, soul and life are not identical absolutely, as they are in God. The God who created the soul also gave it life.

CHAPTER 35

1. Cf. A.H. 1.24.3–7; 2.1.3.

2. Cf. A.H. 1.30.10–11; cf. also 1.23.3; 24.2, 5.

3. *Eloae* seems to be the biblical *Elohim*, the usual name for God. *Elloeuth* is not in the Bible. It might mean Godhead, as does the Rabbinic Aramaic *elahuth*, which is found in the Targum of Cant 8:1, 6.

4. *Yahweh* was the unnameable Jewish name for God. In its place in the Bible *Adonai* was read. Hence, it would correct to call *Adonai* the nameable name, as Irenaeus does. But perhaps as Harvey (1.385 n. 2) observes, Irenaeus had actually written "unnameable," because that would pair with "admirable,"

the second characteristic given for this name. Rousseau and Doutreleau (SC 294.364) read *innominabile* here, following Massuet and Stieren.

5. *Addonai* causes difficulty. Massuet (MG 7.839 n. 2) incorrectly thought that Irenaeus wanted the word written *Adthonai*. *Adonai* has as its root *din*, but in no word of that root is the *daleth* ever duplicated. So Harvey (1.385 n. 3) suspects that a different root was used, namely, *adan*, of where there exists a noun meaning foundation. With that lead he looked for a Scripture text in which this word occurs in a context where God separates the land from the water and makes boundaries. This he found in Job 38:4–11. Whatever value there is to this explanation, it does not satisfy completely. A. Mormorstein ("Zur Erklärung des Gottesnamen bei Irenäus," *ZNTW* 25 [1926]: 253–58) seems to have hit upon a better solution. The name of God with the double *daleth* is not *Addonai*, but *Shaddai*, the Almighty. He claims that this same explanation is found among the rabbis. So Irenaeus must have obtained his information from reliable Jewish traditions. But that still leaves unanswered the change from *Shaddai* to *Addonai* in the MSS, and Irenaeus's method of pairing the other names supposes a closer similarity to *Adonai*.

6. *Sabaōth* he says means "Voluntary." That gives us a clue. The Hebrew word *saba'* means "he willed." From that is formed the noun *sabhūth* ("will"), which is not found in the Bible but in the Targum of Jonah 31.16. *Sabaoth* is used often in Scripture in God's title "Lord of Hosts" (*Sabaoth*). Perhaps one could say that it means first heaven because the firmament contained the stars, which were the heavenly hosts. And so there may be a reference to Gen 2:1, "and all their hosts."

7. *Yaōth* must be related to the biblical Yahweh. The different spelling might be accounted for by the fact that originally it was written *Yaō* in Greek, which gradually became *yaōth*, by analogy with *Sabaoth* and *Eloeuth*, as Harvey (1.386 n. 4) observes. The Gnostics held that this meant "a predetermined measure," which would be a short way of saying that God's will predetermines all things. And the rabbis saw this attribute implied in the name Yahweh. *Yaoth* seems to be the biblical *Yah* (cf. Ps 78 [79]:4). It was written *Yao* by Irenaeus. When *yaō* became *yaōth*, *yao* became *yaoth*, as Harvey (1.386–87 n. 5) suggests. The interpretation "He who puts evils to flight" is not the meaning from the etymology of the word. It must have been derived from some passage where that action was ascribed to Yaoth.

8. Since the preaching of the apostles has been mentioned already, this *dictatio* of the apostles could be their letters. Klebba, BKV 3.206 translates "die Predigt der Missionäre." Rousseau (SC 293.355 [SC 294.367 n. 1]) thinks that *apostolorum dictatio* is a redoubling of the words *praedicatio apostolorum*. For that reason he believes that this phrase should be suppressed.

9. Irenaeus lists as his final source *legislationis ministerium*. Grabe (195 note l) and others who follow him think that this is the Mosaic Law, which was given through the ministry of the Angels (cf. Heb 2:2). But the word *minis-*

terium does not seem to refer to the manner by which the law was brought to the people. *Ministerium* elsewhere (or *ministeriale*) refers to the ministerial service, the liturgy. I think that is what is meant here. The law as such was already included under "Prophets."

10. The translation is based on Rousseau's suggestion (SC 293.355 [SC 294.367 n. 1]) that *dispositionem* be considered a direct object of *aptat* and that *et* be given the value of an adverb.

11. Cf. John 1:3.

OLD AND NEW TESTAMENTS

AUTHORS

GENERAL INDEX

green press
INITIATIVE